Critical Ethnography in Educational Research

Critical Social Thought

Series Editor: Michael W. Apple

John Bascom Professor of Curriculum and Instruction and Educational Policy Studies, University of Wisconsin-Madison

Critical Ethnography in Educational Research

A Theoretical and Practical Guide

Phil Francis Carspecken

ROUTLEDGE *New York and London*

Published in 1996 by
Routledge
29 West 35th Street
New York, NY 10001

Published in Great Britain by
Routledge
11 New Fetter Lane
London EC4P 4EE

Copyright © 1996 by Routledge
Printed in the United States of America on acid-free paper.
Book design by Charles B. Hames

Library of Congress Cataloging-in Publication-Data

Carspecken, Phil Francis. 1951–
Critical ethnography in educational research:
a theoretical and practical guide/by Phil Francis Carspecken.
p. cm.—(Critical social thought)
Includes bibliographical references and index.
ISBN 0–415–90492–7. ISBN—0–415–90493–5 (pbk.)
1. Education—Research—Methodology. 2. Ethnology—Research—Methodology.
3. Social Sciences—Research—Methodology.
I. Title II. Series.
LB1028.C289 1995
370'.78—dc20   95–30106
          CIP

Contents

Figures

This book is dedicated to

Lucinda Mary Carspecken,

my dearest, longest friend.

Series Editor's Introduction

This society is riven by social antagonisms and inequalities. The effects of poverty, greed, exploitation, and domination are massively present. They are visible all around us. They are not somewhere "out there" in an abstract realm, but are "right here" in all of our institutions—in our paid and unpaid work places, schools, hospitals, government offices, corporate boardrooms; in our homes; and on the streets where we walk. Dominant relations are contested, of course, sometimes consciously and sometimes less consciously, as in popular culture (Willis et al. 1990). However, it should be clear that this is a society that is characterized by increasing cultural, political, and economic struggles and dislocations.

These conditions are best seen through a process of "repositioning" ourselves, that is, by seeing the world from below, from the perspectives of those who are not dominant. This is a complicated issue. There are multiple axes of power and multiple relations of domination and subordination in which all of us participate. For the socially committed researcher, this becomes an ever more complex issue, since not only does it involve understanding both how power circulates and is used and who benefits from the ways this society is organized, but it also requires some serious reflection on the role of the researcher in all of this (Roman and Apple 1990).

The creative tension caused by dealing with these issues has generated an array of strikingly interesting work on the methods, concepts, and politics of being a critical researcher (see, e.g., Gitlin 1994). This has led to more than a few differences within the multiple orientations that might be labeled "critical." But one thing binds these diverse communities together: a deep and abiding concern with all too painful realities experienced by identifiable people in this society.

In this book, Phil Francis Carspecken describes the value orientation that underpins critical research in the following way. "We are all concerned about social inequalities and direct our work toward positive social change. We also share a concern with social [and cultural] theory and some of the basic issues it has struggled with since the nineteenth century. These include the nature of social structure, power, culture, and human agency."

Stereotypes of critical qualitative research abound. One of the most widely circulated and most pernicious is the implication that—unlike "normal" forms of social and cultural research—critically oriented research is too value laden. A binary opposition is constructed: neutrality vs. values. Even though binary logics are undergoing severe criticism currently, a more dangerous issue arises here. This stereotype is naive, both in its construction of "normal" models of research and in its understanding of the conceptual and methodological richness of critical qualitative research.

Michelle Fine (1994) argues that all researchers are agents, "in the flesh and collective." Whether wittingly or not, they make choices among sets of political and epistemological stances that are both constraining and subject to intense debate and controversy. She distinguishes between three stances that researchers can take: ventriloquy; voices; and activism.

The first—ventriloquy—denies that there are choices among political and epistemological positions. It covers itself in a veil of "neutrality" by describing the actions of "Others" in such a way that these descriptions seem static and immutable. The Others are "out there" and are unconnected to "self" or to political context. Texts such as these "refuse to ask why one research question or interpretation has prevailed over others or why this researcher selected this set of questions over others" (Fine 1994). In this process, this stance makes the way in which researchers construct their narratives and analyses opaque. Such a stance leaves little room for any role for the researcher except that of a "vehicle for transmission."

The second—voices—involves the researcher in importing into her or his text the "voices of Discarded Others who offer daily or local meanings, which seemingly contrast with or interrupt hegemonic discourses and practices." With the voices and experiences of the other now given center stage as the vehicle for social representation, here too the researcher as "self" often remains unarticulated (Fine 1994, 17).

The last stance—activism—works to "unearth, disrupt, and transform existing ideological and/or institutional arrangements" (Fine 1994). In this case, the researcher's epistemological and political stance explicitly frames the texts that are produced in such a way that it "carves out the space in which intellectual surprises surface". Thus, the writers position themselves as political and interrogative beings, "fully explicit about their original positions", about changes in these positions, and about where their research actually took them as investigators and as political actors (17) (See also Roman and Apple 1990).

This latter stance has not gone uncriticized. For instance, Daphni Patai has raised a number of questions about what she sees as the dangers inherent in a position that "effaces any distinction between political agendas and the protocols of research" (Patai 1994, 62). While my own sympathies lie with those scholar activists characterized by Fine's third stance, it is clear from Patai's and others' comments that the entire area of critical research—what it is, how it does and does not differ from other from other forms of inquiry, what its strengths and silences are—is subject to intense debate. This is a sign of a very real vitality as researchers attempt to come to grips with what and for whom "our" research is for.

This is why Carspecken's volume is so important right now. It provides an exceptionally clear guide to the conceptual and methodological foundations of one of the most crucial forms of critical qualitative research. In many ways, the book is a unique contribution. It is both a rigorous analysis of what such critical research stands for and what it stands upon, and a step-by-step presentation of the process involved in doing this kind of critical qualitative research in disciplined and caring ways.

This in and of itself is quite an achievement, but Carspecken does a number of other things as well. He examines many of the standard discussions of qualitative research and finds them wanting. He examines many of the criticisms of critically oriented research and finds their claims to be weak and filled with misunderstandings. He portrays a kind of research orientation that is methodologically rigorous and nuanced, one that does not fall into the solipsistic and relativist traps so common among some postmodern methodological commentators.

Finally, Carspecken does all this with an engaging style. Like all forms of research, critical qualitative work has developed its own vocabulary and perspectives. This is neither new nor particularly problematic. However, some members of the critical research communities seem to delight in writing in such a way that their insights are nearly lost in a barrage of neologisms and nearly unreadable prose (for further discussion of this problem, see Apple 1993 and Apple in press). Yet Carspecken has evidently taken the time to struggle with his own voice, to find a way to communicate some very complex political, theoretical, and empirical points in a refreshing manner. *Critical Ethnography in Educational Research* is all the better for his efforts in this regard.

Carspecken has taken a position here that may not fully please everyone who calls herself or himself "critical." He has not abandoned totally the call for methodological rigor or the need for a coherent social theory to guide our activities as researchers. He has not abandoned the "global" for the "local," nor has he allowed rhetorical strategies (which are important at times, of course) to substitute for empirical substantiation. Yet he is in no way a supporter of the kinds of dust-bowl empiricism that still characterize so much social research today or the vulgar objectivism that fails to recognize the role of the researcher and the society in which she or he lives both in constructing the lenses through which research is accomplished and the social role of the researcher in accomplishing it.

Critical Ethnography in Educational Research seeks to show how a critical stance on the nature of the power in this society can be wedded to a process of inquiry that wants to ask how power circulates in our daily realities. In doing so, this book provides important assistance in generating ways of uncovering such relations of power.

Michael W. Apple
University of Wisconsin-Madison

References

Apple, Michael W. (1993). *Official Knowledge: Democratic Education in a Conservative Age.* New York: Routledge.

Apple, Michael W. (in press) *Cultural Politics and Education.* New York: Teachers College Press.

Fine, Michelle (1994). "Dis-tance and Other Stances: Negotiations of Power Inside Feminist Research." In *Power and Method,* edited by Andrew Gitlin. New York: Routledge.

Gitlin, Andrew (ed) (1994). *Power and Method.* New York: Routledge.

Patai, Daphne (1994). "When Method Becomes Power." In *Power and Method,* edited by Andrew Gitlin. New York: Routledge.

Roman, Leslie, and Michael W. Apple (1990). "Is Naturalism a Move Away From Positivism?" In *Qualitative Inquiry in Education,* edited by Elliot Eisner and Alan Peshkin. New York: Teachers College Press.

Willis, Paul, et al. (1990). *Common Culture.* Boulder, CO: Westview.

Acknowledgments

In 1985 I flew from England, where I was doing my graduate work, to Wisconsin, where my parents live. I had been living outside the United States for four years and this was one of my rare visits home. En route to Wausau, I stopped off in Madison. On a sort of whim, I dialed Michael Apple's campus number from a phone booth in the student union. I was well acquainted with Apple's work, which is as widely known and influential in Britain as it is in the United States and, in fact, in many other nations of the world.

To my surprise, Michael was in. And to my further surprise, Michael warmly inv̈
me to come over immediately and to introduce myself to him. No need
appointment! I found this famous man to be warm, generous, acc⸍
supportive. He asked to read some of my papers, so I left one with hı⸍
Apple never forgot our acquaintance. He has provided invaluᷱ'
usually unrequested, at key moments in my career.

Michael Apple inadvertently started me writing this bᷧ
me to coauthor a chapter on critical qualitative
Qualitative Research in Education (LeCompte, Millroy, ⸽
for that invitation, I might never have oriented my wͺ

theory. Because he invited me, methodological theory became my major academic interest for several years. Working on that chapter gave birth to many of the ideas I develop further in this book, and it led to two other books I have nearly completed and may one day see published.

Michael Apple has been a model for many of us, as a socially engaged academic who is as committed to "real" social change as he is to ideas and open debate. He helped specifically with this book by being enormously patient as I produced version after version, going well over the deadline I contracted for. I will always appreciate his generosity.

This book is dedicated to my wife, Lucinda Mary Carspecken. She has been my best friend for fourteen years. Writing books obviously affects those closest to you, particularly family members. It robs them of your time. Lucinda is a poet, writer, and student of music who made many sacrifices while I worked on this volume.

Another person I would like to thank is Peter McLaren. Peter's own work in the field of qualitative research is highly original and inspiring. He is a unique thinker who displays insights in surprising and refreshing ways. Peter's work has drawn my attention to the embodied nature of meaning, a theme I have addressed in other works much more than it is addressed in this one. During the past four years, Peter has read and supportively commented on many of my papers and articles. I am very grateful for Peter McLaren's support and friendship.

Meeting Henry Miller of Aston University, England, was a transforming event many years ago. Henry got me started in the career I love and played a large role in making my first book possible, *Community Schooling and the Nature of Power*. I shall always remember Henry Miller as a benefactor and friend.

Thanks go as well to the CUSTodians at the University of Houston. The CUSTodians are advanced doctoral students working in cultural studies. Our weekly seminars have stimulated and refined my thinking in many ways. Past and current CUSTodians include Lauri MacGillovray (now assistant professor at the University of Southern California), Martha Campos, Bill Hord, Doris Georgiou, Lauri Weaver, Barbara Korth, Barbara Peterman, Dennis Tangeman, Khadija Janna, Linda Traxlor, and Patti Sparks. Students more loosely associated with the CUSTodians who have been supportive and stimulating include Myrna Cohen (now professor at the University of Houston), Liz Stephens, Judy Rubovitz, Liz Deikman (the master of us all, when it comes to field skills), Carolyn DeLeon, and Gaye Lang (watch for this woman in politics and social movements: she is destined to aid the disadvantaged in marked ways). Many of these talented people ought to have publications of their own out soon: look for them!

For my wonderful parents, Margaret and Phil, my gratitude and love are boundless. Gillian Williams has been an admired friend, an inspiration, and an unfailing support since I married her daughter thirteen years ago. Lastly, my two shining boys, Sunil (Briel) and Roland, have been bright lights in my life since they first appeared my watching eyes. I cannot do anything, anywhere, without feeling my love for

1

What is Critical Qualitative Research?

Items covered in Chapter 1:

- Universal applications of critical methodological theory

- Distinguishing between critical value orientation and critical epistemology

- The value orientation of criticalists

- Intuiting critical epistemology: core imagery

These days, trying to learn about social research is rather like walking into a room of noisy people. The room is full of cliques, each displaying a distinctive jargon and cultural style. There is, of course, a large group talking quantitative research much as it has been talked for decades. But there are new, flashy groups heatedly discussing "constructivist," "postmodern," "post-positivist," and "critical" research. Most of these people are talking about qualitative social research, but they disagree with each other on such basic issues as the nature of reality, the nature of knowledge, and the concept of truth. You cannot get more basic than that!

At the center of the qualitative groups are a number of people who have attracted the most attention. They not only advocate one type of research practice, they also claim to have categorized and explained all the rest of us. In their hands are typological charts listing the principal schools of contemporary research methodology along with some definitive statements for each. Some have us sorted out according to the purposes for which we conduct research (Lather 1991). Some compare us according to our ontological and epistemological assumptions (Guba 1990a; Guba and Lincoln 1994).

The noise in the room is intimidating enough for anyone wishing to become a new voice on research methodology. But it is the typological schemes that give me the most angst. The problem they present for a new book on qualitative social research is that a new voice will tend to get placed before it is understood.

I have set myself up for this sort of trouble with the title of my book, *Critical Ethnography in Educational Research*. Many of you will have preconceptions of what critical social research is because many of you will have read some of the popular methodological typologies. "Critical" always gets a place within them, but rarely is it well described.

So, I must begin this book with a request to my readers: put away, as best you can, all your preconceptions of what "critical" means. Wait to see what sense I give this term before trying to position me in relation to other methodological theories. Forget about the methodological charts and schemes you have seen in other research books: their descriptions of critical research are usually far removed from my own practice and conception of it. Wait until the book's end before trying to compare me with other methodological theories. For my part, I will pretty much ignore the noise surrounding us as I present my critical methodological theory. I will not construct typologies of my own, will not diverge into discussions of other methodologies or even other works on critical methodology. I will aim for a fresh start; taking basic issues in all forms of inquiry and showing how they may be treated from a critical perspective.

UNIVERSAL APPLICATIONS OF CRITICAL SOCIAL RESEARCH

This book is intended to be useful for all people wishing to either conduct their own qualitative projects or to simply learn more about qualitative research. The fact that the methodology is critical does not rule out the book for people who wish to study features of human life and human experience that are not overtly political. Sociologists, anthropologists, educational researchers, and psychologists could all use this methodological framework.

Doctoral students at the University of Houston have used the methodology presented here to study a wide variety of phenomena. Houston dissertations using this framework include the following:

- "The Hidden Curriculum of a Bilingual Education Classroom"
- "Case Studies in Religious Experience"
- "Perceptions of Afro-Centric Pedagogy by African-Americans"
- "Therapist Reactions to Client Suicides"
- "Site-Based Management: The Creation of a New Bureaucratic Tier"
- "The Culture of Resisting High-School Males"
- "Male Perceptions of Intimacy"

- "Male Perceptions of Masculinity"
- "Case Studies of High-Achieving Hispanic Female Migrants"
- "Fathers of Terminally Ill Children"
- "World System Theory, World Student Culture, and Asian Indian Graduate Students in the United States"

The list could go on, as I have supervised many dissertations on a wide range of topics, most of which employed this particular critical research methodology, learned by students in the courses I teach. The point I wish to make is that critical qualitative research methodology is meant to be quite universal in the topics it can investigate. This is because all acts of inquiry beg the same set of core questions, and critical theory has addressed these questions in the most promising ways. The rest of this chapter will give a basic overview of the critical perspective.

CRITICAL QUALITATIVE RESEARCH [1]

Qualitative social research investigates human phenomena that do not lend themselves, by their very nature, to quantitative methods. There are many diverse research traditions that fall under the qualitative label (Silverman 1985, 1993; Eisner and Peshkin 1990; LeCompte 1990; LeCompte, Millroy, and Preissle 1992; LeCompte and Preissle 1993, Denzin and Lincoln 1994; Miles and Huberman 1994; Vidich and Stanford 1994). "Critical" qualitative research is one of several genres of inquiry into nonquantifiable features of social life. Small numbers of social researchers have been calling themselves "critical" for about twenty years. When asked, I place my own ethnographic work within this category (Carspecken 1987, 1991, 1992).

Those of us who openly call ourselves "criticalists" definitely share a value orientation. We are all concerned about social inequalities, and we direct our work toward positive social change. We also share a concern with social theory and some of the basic issues it has struggled with since the nineteenth century. These include the nature of social structure, power, culture, and human agency. We use our research, in fact, to refine social theory rather than merely to describe social life. Together, we have begun to develop critical social research.

Up to the present, however, criticalists have not really shared a methodological theory. Methodological theories provide the principles by which to design a research project, develop field techniques, and interpret data. Only quite recently have efforts been made to describe critical methodology, and the authors of these efforts do not completely agree with each other (Anderson 1989; Lather 1991; Carspecken and Apple 1992; Quantz 1992; Kinchloe and McLaren 1994).

Thus, critical social research (which is usually also qualitative) has up to this time been an orientation rather than a tight methodological school. This book differs from other articles and texts on critical research because it attempts to construct a tight methodological theory by making use of various insights from critical social theory. The methodology presented here, moreover, is intended to apply to all forms of social research, not just to social research motivated by the typical concerns of criticalists. Critical theory has enormous implications for all the basic concepts employed in social research: concepts like "validity," "reliability," and "objectivity," among others.

You will find a number of articles and some books on the market today that attempt to review the field of critical social research (Anderson 1989; Lather 1991; Carspecken and Apple 1992; Quantz 1992; Kinchloe and McLaren 1994). Each such publication provides one or more statements attempting to characterize the critical orientation. They are not identical characterizations, but they are all within the same ball park. Here is one I pretty much agree with; it can be found in a recent publication by Joe Kinchloe and Peter McLaren (1994). Be warned; it is dense and will not be fully intelligible to all readers. I will clarify its main points in a discussion following:

> We are defining a criticalist as a researcher or theorist who attempts to use her or his work as a form of social or cultural criticism and who accepts certain basic assumptions: that all thought is fundamentally mediated by power relations which are socially and historically constituted; that facts can never be isolated from the domain of values or removed from some form of ideological inscription; that the relationship between concept and object and signifier and signified is never stable or fixed and is often mediated by the social relations of capitalist production and consumption; that language is central to the formation of subjectivity (conscious and unconscious awareness); that certain groups in any society are privileged over others and, although the reasons for this privileging may vary widely, the oppression which characterizes contemporary societies is most forcefully reproduced when subordinates accept their social status as natural, necessary or inevitable; that oppression has many faces and that focusing on only one at the expense of others (e.g. class oppression versus racism) often elides the interconnections among them; and finally, that mainstream research practices are generally, although most often unwittingly, implicated in the reproduction of systems of class, race and gender oppression. (139–140)

That, readers, was a single sentence! It is, probably unfortunately, very typical in style to what you will find in the critical and postmodern research literature. I say "probably unfortunately" because Kinchloe and McLaren's article is actually an important contribution to the field. The dense writing style they use works well with readers like myself, who have already read many works in the critical and postmodern traditions. Some things are best said through a style like theirs. What is unfortunate is not that some writings on critical methodology are densely composed, but rather that virtually all writings in the field are composed in this way. This has made work in the critical tradition basically inaccessible to a large number of people. Hence, I will make every effort in this book to write clearly and accessibly, inviting a wide range of students and practitioners to my ideas.

Let us now concentrate on the content of Kinchloe and McLaren's dense passage, rather than the style in which it is written. I can clarify the gist of this quotation by grouping the points it makes into two distinctive categories: (1) the value orientation of critical researchers and (2) the principles of critical epistemology. By elaborating on Kinchloe and McLaren's list of points within these two categories, I should be able to give a clear, introductory understanding of what the critical orientation is all about.

Facts and Values

But wait a minute, does not the distinction I make here between value orientation and epistemology contradict one of the points in the quoted passage: that "facts can never be isolated from the domain of values or removed from some form of ideological inscription"? The value orientation of critical social researchers obviously has to do with values, and epistemology of all brands, critical or otherwise, is fundamental to any concept of "facts." It would seem that I have introduced a distinction that runs against one of the very tenets of critical social research.

Readers steeped in the critical tradition, the constructivist tradition, or the postmodern movement may have already concluded that I am unforgivably in error. Are not values and "facts" inextricably connected? Patti Lather (1986), for example, almost defines my chosen genre of work as "overtly ideological." The ideology of the researcher, including her values, is supposed to enter intrinsically and inseparably into the methods, interpretations, and epistemology of critical research.

Egon Guba, himself a social constructivist rather than a criticalist, is one of those attempting to locate all social research within a methodological typology. He also believes in the tight connection between facts and values, and he describes the "critical paradigm" with reference to this connection:

> If values do enter into every inquiry, then the question immediately arises as to what values and whose values shall govern. If the findings of studies can vary depending on the values chosen, then the choice of a particular value system tends to empower and enfranchise certain persons while disempowering and disenfranchising others. Inquiry thereby becomes a political act. (Guba 1990a:24)

So it would seem that my decision to separate the value orientation of criticalists from the principles of critical epistemology runs against the principles of critical research itself.

Well, I do not agree with those who make such sweeping claims about the fusion of facts and values. Earlier I have even stated that one does not need to share the value orientation of criticalists in order to employ critical epistemology. Frankly, I find many of the claims made for fact and value fusion to be sloppy! The relationship between research findings and values is a complex and many-layered affair. Yes, there is a connection between findings and values. No, we cannot simply claim their fusion into being without giving contexts and clarifications.

Guba's remarks, typical of many, are very much off the mark. He emphasizes value choice, and he believes that, once chosen, the values of the researcher will strongly determine the facts discovered. I totally disagree. Values are not exactly "chosen," for one thing (not usually anyway). Highly value-driven researchers like we criticalists most often feel compelled to conduct research as a way of bettering the oppressed and downtrodden. It is a personal need to do so, not exactly a choice. But that pertains to our value orientation, to the reasons why we conduct research and to our choice of subjects and sites to investigate. This orientation does not determine the "facts" we find in the field. Here, in the realm of "fact," the realm of validity claims made at the end of a study, values and facts are interlinked but not fused. And the sorts of values involved in research findings need not be the same as the values defining our orientation.

This distinction is an important one because good critical research should not be biased. Critical epistemology does not guarantee the finding of "facts" that match absolutely what one may want to find.

So research value orientations should not determine research findings. Orientations provide the reasons why people conduct their studies. They therefore have a lot to do with the choices one must make when beginning a research project: what to study and to what end. They also determine how findings will be used—what to publish and what to leave out, who to share the knowledge with and in what way. The value orientation of the researcher does not "construct" the object of study: the same "object" can be examined for a large variety of reasons, under a large variety of motivations, and yield the same findings.

Now, the term "criticalist" applies to people like me who share a distinctive, critical, value orientation. The phrase "critical methodology," however, refers to the epistemological principles we criticalists advocate: not just for people motivated in the same ways that we are, but for all researchers. This is because critical theory has provided the most convincing answers to knotty epistemological questions begged in every act of inquiry.

The essential features of critical research methodology, then, are epistemological and do not depend on the value orientation of criticalists. The value orientation of criticalists, however, is important. People operating from this value orientation have rethought traditional ideas about knowledge and reality, finding them wanting. It is therefore highly important to become familiar with the value orientation of criticalists before learning about critical epistemology.

The Value Orientation of Critical Researchers

Let us examine the value orientation shared by those of us who call ourselves "critical." Kinchloe and McLaren (1994) list a number of "assumptions" in the passage quoted above pertaining more to our shared value orientation than anything else. These are (and I will partially quote, partially paraphrase):

- that research be employed in cultural and social "criticism"
  [i.e., we find contemporary society and culture wanting in many ways and believe

that research should support efforts for change]

- that "certain groups in any society are privileged over others"
  [i.e., we are opposed to all forms of inequality]
- that "the oppression which characterizes contemporary societies is most forcefully reproduced when subordinates accept their social status as natural or inevitable"
  [i.e., reproducing inequalities over time is wrong; we should use research to uncover the subtleties of oppression so that its invisibility to those affected by it might be removed; so that oppression might become challenged, and changed]
- that "oppression has many faces"
  [i.e., researchers should not focus on one form of oppression only to ignore others; all forms of oppression should be studied and challenged]
- that "mainstream research practices are generally, although most often unwittingly," part of the oppression
  [i.e., critical researchers should practice their craft with different principles than mainstream researchers, because the mistaken principles used in mainstream research not infrequently contribute to cultural oppression. A correct epistemology would avoid oppression because its concept of truth presupposes equal power relations.]

By articulating the implicit "should" messages and the implicit references to "wrong" affairs carried by Kinchloe and McLaren's statements, we easily see what value orientation most critical researchers uphold. Criticalists find contemporary society to be unfair, unequal, and both subtly and overtly oppressive for many people. We do not like it, and we want to change it.

Moreover, we have found that much of what has passed for "neutral objective science" is in fact not neutral at all, but subtly biased in favor of privileged groups. The seedy history of intelligence testing is a good example of this. Intelligence tests have been used since the beginning of this century in studies that have "discovered" the mental inferiority of women and racial minorities. With each round of such "objective findings," loud protests have been necessary on the part of the affected groups to force the re-examination of intelligence tests and the assumptions directing our interpretations of test scores. "Objective science" has become a political battleground.

Today we still find intelligence tests widely used, despite important alterations brought about by political struggle. There are many similar kinds of research practiced today that label people "hyperactive," "behaviorally disordered," "attention deficient disabled," "special" (I like that one!), and so on. Minorities and the poor receive the negative labels much more often than do middle- and upper-class whites. Upper-middle-class whites, in fact, not infrequently pay large sums of money to private diagnosticians to have their children labeled in the way they want. Using their economic advantages in this way, middle-class whites have been able to get their children into the most advantageous schools and school tracks. Diagnosticians, both private and state-employed, unconsciously use the products of purportedly "neutral" research to support and expand a system that discriminates and oppresses. Such research is not neutral: it is part of an unfair social structure, a technology of oppression that reaches right into the personal identities of disadvantaged groups.

Part of the problem with the social science that has produced these labels and diagnostic instruments is its failure to understand the relation of power and truth. Traditional social science never regarded it as *epistemologically necessary* to allow those worst affected by such diagnostic instruments to play any role in designing them or in deciding whether the construction of such instruments was desirable.

It has been the abuse of social science that has led criticalists, given our value orientation, to interrogate closely the epistemology of mainstream inquiry. We find it seriously, and damagingly, flawed. Our new formulations, however, have universal implications. After all, the battles waged by those "scientifically" mislabeled through intelligence tests (and other diagnostic instruments) would not have had much success if their principal argument was dependent on values alone. Rather, these battles have been successful when they could point out serious contradictions in the epistemological assumptions of "neutral" research.

This is one of the ways that critical epistemology has evolved: through battles against the oppressive effects of biased research that at first appeared to be "neutral." A better epistemology has been forged in consequence. Critical epistemology does not give us recipes for helping the poor and downtrodden; it rather gives us principles for conducting valid inquiries into any area of human experience.

Now, this does not mean that common-sense understandings of "neutral research" are upheld in critical theory. As later chapters of this book will make clear, "neutral inquiry" refers to empirical studies freed from the distortion of power relationships. This implies a "limit point" belief in universal human interests (see chapter four). It does not imply that social research can, or should, be conducted without a value orientation. The act of conducting research will always be value driven, but the validity claims of the researcher must meet certain standards to avoid bias. Those standards are rooted in democratic principles that are required by a careful examination of the concept of truth. Thus, validity claims and values connect intimately through the relationship of democratic principles and truth. Truth claims presuppose the limit case of winning the consent of other people when power relations are equalized. This idea will be greatly clarified in later chapters, so do not worry if it seems unclear to you at this time.

In summary, we criticalists have both witnessed and directly experienced forms of oppression. We do not like them. We want to change them. The precise nature of oppression, however, is an empirical question and not a given belief. Much of our research attempts to clarify how and where oppression works. This is not a straightforward matter, since the identities, the forms of thinking, and the beliefs of people are all ensnared within oppressive relations. We need a rigorous epistemology to pursue our subtle investigations, one that is universal to all forms of research. It is this rigorous epistemology that is definitive for critical methodology.

Critical Epistemology

Returning now to Kinchloe and McLaren's passage we find other points that are more epistemological than value oriented in nature. These include (again, I partially quote and paraphrase):

- "all thought is fundamentally mediated by power relations which are socially and historically constituted" (p. 139)
  [i.e., thought, including the thought of researchers, involves power relations; therefore, critical epistemology must be extremely precise when it comes to the relationship of power and research claims, power and validity claims, power and culture, thus power and thought],
- "facts can never be isolated from the domain of values" (p. 139)
  [i.e., statements of "fact," which necessarily enter somehow into all research, are going to be affected by values and thus never be strictly "neutral" or "objective" in the traditional sense; therefore, critical epistemology must make the fact/value distinction very clear and must have a precise understanding of how the two interact. A precise understanding will allow us to formulate standards by which to avoid or reduce bias in our own work and by which to evaluate the work of other researchers. A careful examination of truth claims displays the necessity of democratic values: they are presupposed with every validity claim made in both everyday life and science]
- "the relationship between concept and object and signifier and signified is never stable or fixed and is often mediated by the social relations of capitalist production and consumption" (p. 139)
  [i.e., symbolic representations of events, always absolutely core to any social research project, are never just a matter of symbols corresponding to objective reality because social relations involving forms of power are always entailed in any representations; therefore, critical epistemology must include a theory of symbolic representation, its relationship to what we call "reality," and its relationship to power]

Once again I have sought to articulate issues implied by Kinchloe and McLaren's statements. This time Kinchloe and McLaren's points do not foreground value orientations but rather foreground issues central to any theory of knowledge and how it is acquired. The issues are epistemological.

Epistemology is: "The branch of philosophy concerned with the theory of knowledge. Traditionally, central issues in epistemology are the nature and derivation of knowledge, the scope of knowledge, and the reliability of claims to knowledge" (Flew 1979: 109). Critical theorists advocate an epistemology that is alternative to what one will find in traditional social science. A particular epistemological theory drawn from the critical traditions is a central part of this book. In fact, this theory owes a lot to the philosophical school of American pragmatism; to authors like John Dewey, William

James, Charles Saunders Peirce, and George Herbert Mead (good reviews of pragmatism include Bernstein 1971; Hammersley 1989). This epistemological theory is presented and concretely illustrated over and over again in chapters ahead, although, for this book, I have chosen not to present dense philosophical arguments in its favor.

To summarize the discussion so far, critical researchers share a value orientation and concern over a number of epistemological issues. We also share interest in a common set of social-theoretical concepts, like "social structure," "culture," and "social reproduction." But these concepts are subject to continuous empirical study, and the particular ways that we criticalists understand such terms are not "givens" in our research. From the Kinchloe and McLaren passage we see that critical epistemology will include an understanding of the relationship between power and thought and power and truth claims. We also see that this epistemology will provide a precise understanding of what values are, what facts are, and how they are connected. A theory of symbolic representation will also be part of the picture.

Well, it would seem that the next thing for me to do in this chapter is to provide an elaboration of critical epistemology. How is knowledge related to power? How are facts and values related? What theory of symbolic representation do we employ? But, readers, I am at a loss for a simple, readable, and short way of treating these issues. They are all explained and illustrated in the chapters to come, but not through abstract presentations. Rather, I make use of field notes, exercises, and other concrete descriptions of social phenomena to bring out portions of the epistemology, one at a time. By the end of the book, all the principles are presented, exemplified, and related to concrete methods for field work and data analysis. But I do not give them all at once alongside abstract arguments in their support.

In an earlier draft of this book I did attempt to provide an exposition of critical epistemology through abstract arguments, drawing upon the critical, pragmatist, and postmodern literature. This resulted in a two-part book: part one being abstract theory and part two deriving concrete field and analytic methods from it. It was a poor format. I found, by having friends and students read it, that only specialists in methodology wanted to read the four chapters comprising part one. Other readers, representing many people I intend for my audience, bogged down in part one.

So for this version I have done something different. I have avoided abstract arguments. Critical epistemology will become clear by learning the methods and conceptual models I provide when describing a five-stage research process, stage by stage.

Still, many readers would not be satisfied if I simply ended chapter one here without any further discussion of critical epistemology on abstract levels. So I have written a final section for chapter one that glosses over the relevant issues. It is not meant to be dense and logically tight at all. It rather aims at imagery, scenery useful for intuiting the basis of critical epistemology and contrasting it with other theories of knowledge. Readers may read through this section lightly, striving to acquire the images.

EPISTEMOLOGICAL SCENERY

Once again, the purpose of this section is to provide some basic scenery, imagery, to help in understanding critical epistemology and its difference from other theories. Readers must remember that I have abandoned, for this particular book, any effort at rigorous argumentation. Instead I have sought to paint scenes useful for gaining an intuitive understanding of the relevant issues.

Moving Away from Sense Perception as Paradigmatic Imagery

Certainty and Visual Perception

Most mainstream research epistemologies implicitly depend on our experience of sense perception to derive their definitions of validity, truth, and so on. In fact, it is visual perception especially that informs mainstream ideas about validity and truth. This is because it is a very common, compelling, experience to (1) see objects before us and (2) simultaneously feel certain that they exist much in the way we see them.

Take a moment to look at something near you. You see this object and its various qualities (its color, texture, shape and so on). You should experience, at the same time, a feeling of certainty that the object really is there: you are certain you would feel it if you touched it, you are sure it will still be there if you turn your eyes away and then look again.

This feeling of certainty, taken-for-granted certainty, is actually the basis for many theories of truth. Concepts of truth are very often based, at the end of the day, on the certainty we seem to feel when seeing something present before us. Thus, the term "observation" comes up repeatedly in methodological works. We learn about the world by observing it. Specific forms of validity have been worked out to ensure unbiased and repeatable observations.

The sort of dense and philosophical argumentation that I have had to leave out of this book would include the critique of sense perception made by phenomenologists and Jacques Derrida's poststructuralism. I think it is important to understand the gist of these critiques, so I will give glosses of them.

The Objection from Classical Phenomenology

First, the critique made by phenomenologists. By "phenomenologists" I do not mean Alfred Schutz and those influenced by his more sociological version of phenomenology (1967). This quasi-phenomenology is almost always what other methodologists are referring to when they refer to "phenomenological research." I am not thinking of them. I am thinking of Alfred Schutz's teacher, Edmund Husserl, and his philosophical phenomenology (1962; 1970).

Husserl and his more orthodox students were prior, historically, to poststructuralism. In their work they criticized other schools of philosophy as well as the assumptions of natural science, partly by pointing out that we do not see objects before us in visual perception. What we really see is a perspective of the object: one of its sides, often just part of one of its sides. The object comes into experience, therefore, only through an unconscious synthetic activity of consciousness which connects perspectives together.

Again, try this out by staring at an object. If you examine your experience carefully, you will find that only a perspective is actually seen at any one moment. There should be a foreground of this perspective in your visual field as well as a background "horizon" of apperceived ("perceived with") peripherals. The "object" is "put together" by synthesizing foreground, background, and tacit anticipations of what could be seen (in general form) if we start to move about the object. If we do shift our gaze about the object through a series of moments, then the horizon comes to include retentions of immediately previous moments within its apperceived portions. The "object" is synthesized within our experience by unnoticed activity; or, as the phenomenologists put it, the object is "constituted" by synthetic, unnoticed, processes.

Thus, we cannot even be sure that a perceived object exists just by perceiving it because we do not understand the synthetic activities taking place to give us the object. Knowledge of existence is not given immediately through sense perception. All that we can be sure of is the experience of the perspective, which is not an object but rather a phenomenon.

Phenomenologists stressed the point that object existence is not given as knowledge immediately through perception, and thus attacked the core assumptions of natural science. They put the question of existence "into brackets," postponing it until a full theory of object constitution could be developed through phenomenological methods.

What were these phenomenological methods? All I want to say about them is that they were driven by the desire to find a certain ground of truth from which theories of object constitution and other such things could be derived. The "certain" ground of truth for mainstream science is rooted in the taken-for-granted certainty we commonly experience in object perception. We see an object and feel certain that it exists. Phenomenologists criticized this, as I have shown, but sought a similar sort of ground: the certain feeling we have when a phenomenon, rather than an existing object, is present before us in experience. Phenomena, by the way, include non-sensual objects like ideas and mental imagery.

Ever hear the expression, "existence before essence"? This was coined as a slogan by existentialists, like Sartre, who were influenced by Husserl's phenomenology but critical of some core phenomenological tenets (Sartre 1956; Husserl 1962, 1970). Knowledge of existence is one of these. "Existence before essence" refers both to Husserl's bracketing of existence and Hegel's objective idealism (which made the "category" of existence secondary to the "category" of essence). Sartre's existentialism, Heidegger's ontology of being, and other twentieth-century philosophical movements owed much to Edmund Husserl: they were enormously in debt to Husserl's insights, but they departed from some of his fundamental beliefs, like the bracketing of existence.

The Objection from Poststructuralism and Postmodernism

Jacques Derrida is one of those who owes much to Edmund Husserl. He began his spectacular career with two famous works on Husserl's phenomenology: Edmund Husserl's "Origin of Geometry": An Introduction (1962) and *Speech and Phenomena: And Other Essays on Husserl's Theory of Signs* (1973). These works played a major role in launching what are now called "poststructuralism" and "postmodernism."

Among many other things, Derrida shows in *Speech and Phenomena* that truth cannot be ensured from the feeling of certainty that perceived phenomena bring. He does this through a careful, rigorous, discussion of Husserl's writings: agreeing to accept Husserl's basic language, framework, and logic in order to show that Husserl's arguments, if pushed fully in the directions they themselves point, will undermine themselves and implode the whole project established by Husserl. This is the now-famous deconstructive strategy. It amounts to inhabiting the work of another author, rather in the way that a virus enters its host cell, and imploding this author's work by following her logic right to its end, rather like the way a virus employs the genetic code DNA to a cell's own demise.

In the case of Husserl's work, Derrida makes careful explorations of the phenomenological treatment of time that show, wonderfully, the impossibility of having anything present to consciousness at the same moment that we know it is present. Presence is unreachable in a knowledge-imparting way.

You can get the basic idea behind this by staring at an object yet once again. The moment your perception becomes knowledge imparting (the moment you are in a position to think or say, "this object is here before me now") is not the same moment at which you were simply aware of the object. That original moment has always already gone by by the time you feel you know the object is before you. It is as if your attention has to shift from simply being aware to being aware that you are aware. These two experiences can never be simultaneous.

You will be tempted to shift your awareness back and forth from simply being aware to being aware that you are aware. This can be done with a sort of "vibration" in attention, an oscillation between looking at (the object) and noting that (the object is there). This sort of oscillation is perfectly possible; it is the way we check some impressions to determine whether they were illusions or not, and it works in everyday life to strengthen certainty in object perception. But the logic of the situation nevertheless ruins any idea of absolute certainty through presence. At no moment can we be both simply aware of an object and aware that we are aware so that perception becomes a certain ground for knowing. At the moment of "knowledge," of being aware that we are aware, we at best have an image or trace of the object given to us presumedly just before during a moment of simple awareness. Presence cannot give us certain knowledge. Theories of truth have believed in presence, but presence is nothing other than a belief, not a certainty. And yet presence is the basis of the phenomenological theory of truth, as it is the basis of many Western theories of truth.

Derrida's later books display the dependency of a belief in presence, a "metaphysics of presence," in many diverse theories of truth (see Kamuf 1991 for representative selections). Perhaps most potently, Derrida's work displays beliefs in presence at work in common conceptions about the way symbols and signs work in language. Husserl explored quite rigorously our common-sense ideas about signs and reinforced them with his phenomenological framework. Signs, he thought, "stand for" objects given in presence. "White" stands for the color we perceive during moments in which whiteness is present to consciousness. "White," and all such signs, can be repeated an infinite number of times to stand for "the same thing" because this "same thing" is available to an experience of presence, perceptually framed.

But Derrida has undermined presence. Thus he is able to reverse the common-sense understanding of signs to say that it is infinite repetitions of signs that constitute what they stand for, not the other way around. Signs repeat infinitely, moreover, not only in the sense of the possibility of repeating words (like "white") but at the level of presymbolic experience itself. Recall the oscillation we can always produce by staring at something, noting that we have perceived it, and staring at it again. Because we never self-consciously "just see" the object, it is possible to understand this oscillation as a repetition of traces, images supposedly impressed upon our minds by the real object (or phenomenon) but traces that actually just as much "produce" the idea of the real object. In experience itself, objects present to consciousness are pointed toward, "deferred to" as the ground of the experience's validity, but never experientially reached. Thus traces, retentions, images, "stand for" unreachable objects in experience itself before we ever start assigning words. Experience has a "sign structure" because traces "stand for" moments of pure presence that are never experienced in a self-conscious way. "Standing for" is the essence of signs and symbols. It is an infinite repetition of signs ("traces") that give us the idea of permanent objects and not the other way around.

The implications of this become devastating for traditional theories of truth when applied to the idea of "identity," of something always being "the same." If sign repetitions give us the idea of objects present to consciousness rather than the other way around, then there are no standards of certainty by which to claim even that traces and signs remain "the same" from one repetition to the next. Derrida says that signs may "iterate" to change, slightly, with each repetition. Concepts of "reality" depend on some idea of identity, of things remaining "the same." Thus "reality" becomes an obsolete concept.

Postmodernism and Modern Methodological Theory

Derrida's later work, among many other things, expands the ramifications of this critique of presence into many diverse areas such as theories of the self; theories of science and logic; the traditional separation of knowledge, power, and desire; and many other things. Derrida's work has been extremely influential in some circles and now influences some works on methodological theory. All of those attracted to the idea that there is no reality and there is no truth have had a heyday with postmodernism. There are today postmodern methodologists who emphasize the limitless possibilities of interpretation, the lack of absolute standards for judging one interpretation over another. They "deconstruct" dominant ideologies, traditional methodologies, news programs, and classroom pedagogies; and they love to assault both social and natural "science."

Other methodologists have quickly noted the nihilistic effects that an uncritical appropriation of postmodern ideas produce. Pure postmodernism (or "ludic postmodernism," as Kinchloe and McLaren call it [1994]) undermines the critical value orientation discussed earlier. Why do research to help the disadvantaged if there are no grounds for claiming this sort of activity to be desirable, moral, good, and right? Why study oppression if any theory of social structure and power is deconstructable? Few critical researchers would want to claim simply that their values are arbitrary with no possible arguments to persuade others into accepting them. Few would want to say that their descriptions of society are nothing but interpretations, capable of convincing others only through the exertion of power (persuasion) rather than argument. For them, "argumentation" turns out to be nothing but "persuasion" or "rhetoric."

Therefore, many contemporary critical researchers seek to appropriate postmodern insights while retaining some notion of truth and some standards for valid argumentation. Kinchloe and McLaren are of this school. They refer to the whole project of casting postmodern insights within a non-nihilistic epistemology as "critical," or "resistance," postmodernism as opposed to "ludic" postmodernism.

Thus the point we saw Kinchloe and McLaren make about signifiers and signifieds (signs and what they stand for) is based on the work of Derrida and others in the poststructuralist and postmodern movements. But it relocates Derrida's work within a critical epistemology. Signs and signifiers do not relate to each other through universal perceptual experiences. Rather, they are "mediated" through power relations ("the relations of capitalist production"), which themselves can be explored using standards of truth. There are "good" theories of capitalist power relations, and there are "flawed" theories: critical epistemology gives us criteria for judging which are which.

Patti Lather has written an entire book, *Getting Smart* (1991), that attempts to reconcile poststructural insights with the aims of critical research. She, too, uses the expression "resistance postmodernism" and identifies her project with it. Richard Quantz (1992), like many writers seeking to characterize critical social research, also attempts to synthesize postmodern themes with critical theory. Norman Denzin has developed "interpretive interactionism," reformulating interactionist theory in light of the cultural studies movement, in a manner highly congruent with "resistance postmodernism" (Denzin 1989, 1992).

The main point for us, here, is simply that Derrida has convincingly undermined traditional appeals to presence as the basis of truth. The certainty commonly experienced with visual perception should not be a taken-for-granted basis for epistemology; yet it is such a basis in mainstream conceptions of validity, reliability, and data interpretation. Critical epistemology does not use perception as a root metaphor, and that is one of its many strengths.

Moving Away from Modified Perceptual Imagery

Some of the more popular alternative research methodologies bandied about today make vehement criticisms of traditional epistemology, particularly its naive belief that what we see is what there is; yet they then wind up using a simple modification of perceptual imagery to construct their own epistemological positions! I want it absolutely clear that critical epistemology is not guilty of this sort of error. Constructivists are prone to it, as are some self-professed (but naive) postmodernists.

Egon Guba is a good example from the constructivist camp. I think Guba is probably famous enough and wise enough not to be bothered by criticism, so I will illustrate my point by picking on him. Remember Guba's description of critical research quoted above? He claims in that passage that we criticalists assume, like himself and other constructivists, that all observations are affected by values. In other passages he explains the effects of values on observations with metaphors obviously derived from the imagery of visual perception: "value windows" and "theory windows" are inevitable in research, he claims.

The idea is that what we see is strongly influenced by what we already value and believe. Criticalists, according to Guba, accept this state of affairs and then simply "choose" the "right" values. Since all research is necessarily biased by value windows and theory windows, from the very moment we pick our objects of investigation, we criticalists just shrug our shoulders and bias our research overtly in the ways we think best. What are the ways we think best? To bias research so that the oppressed will be empowered!

Oh, how I shudder when I read descriptions of critical research like this! On the level of orienting values alone, this sort of description has led traditional researchers to call the work of criticalists flawed by bias. The dense theoretical passages on methodology you will find in most criticalist work is accused of being mere excuses for sloppy research. We simply find what we want to find and justify this phony sort of "research" with dense and impenetrable passages on methodology. If Guba's description of us were accurate, moreover, I would be the first to agree with these objections!

But let us examine Guba's ideas further. Criticalists, according to him, do believe in a single social reality. We just think that all efforts to describe and explain this reality are going to be strongly colored by value windows. Conservative researchers will interpret what is actually there in a direction that harms the already harmed: the oppressed. Criticalists will interpret what is actually there in a direction that empowers them.

Guba gives a more radical position for his favored school: the constructivists. Not only do they believe that what we see is strongly influenced by what we believe already, they also think that what we see is constructed by what we believe. Thus constructivists speak of "multiple realities": there is no single reality, only a plurality of realities "constructed" by individuals and/or cultures.

Enormous logical problems arise from the constructivist position. An immediately obvious one concerns the ambiguity over whether individuals or cultural groups are the constructing agents for any particular reality. If it is individuals, then the question of how anyone could claim to understand the world as others do is begged. It is even problematical to explain how any acts of communication between individuals ever take place.

The problem of communication and understanding arises just as much if cultural groups, rather than individuals, are taken to be reality-constructing agents. How does an outsider gain an insider's view? Would not this very process suggest transcultural principles of human understanding? If so, the constructivist view is undermined, for these transcultural principles would imply a transcultural reality having to do with human communication.

But perhaps the idea is that one never does attain an insider's view of another cultural reality. If this is the idea, then how is it that we could even know that other realities exist? Would not this very idea be the product of just one reality? If the idea is that we can gain partial understandings of other cultural realities, then some sort of transcultural standards must exist by which these partial understandings can be judged as such.

Constructivism begs important questions about human communication and human understanding. Without having space to fully argue this point and without being able to give full justice to some of the sophisticated thinking that has gone into constructivist theory, let me just point out the dependency of the core metaphors used by this school on modified perceptual imagery.

By failing to break with mainstream perceptual metaphors altogether, constructivism does not give us a viable alternative. Derrida's deconstruction of presence is profound enough to dismantle any use of this imagery, no matter how modified it becomes with value windows, theory windows, and the like. Critical epistemology does not lay much upon the idea of "windows." Visual perception is not in any way, shape, or form the basis for our theory of truth. Any theory of truth that depends on visual perception—no matter how many sophisticated modifications it introduces to this imagery—will be flawed.

Toward Predifferentiated Experience and Human Communication

Critical epistemologists say, "Forget visual perception when searching for a root metaphor upon which to base a theory of truth. Visual perception is, in fact, a secondary sort of experience rather than a primary one."

Here is some alternative imagery for you: suppose you are walking down a corridor and see me approaching. You are in a cheerful mood so you look right at my face, smile, and say: "Hello Phil! How are you today?" I look at you long enough to convince you that I heard, grunt loudly while scowling, and then look away as I pass you by. What sorts of messages have I communicated to you?

Well, to make the complexities of our communication clearer, let us imagine that you next stop and call back to me: "Phil! What is the matter?" Here are three of the many ways our communication could proceed from this point on:

A. I turn and say: "I've had a bad day! Leave me alone and I will tell you about it tomorrow. Sorry I'm so rude, but I am really fed up with this place!"
   Analysis: You took a subjective reference carried by my initial act of scowling and grunting as the foreground in your understanding by asking me what was wrong with my feelings (those portions of my experience to which you have no direct access), my *subjective state.* I confirm your suspicions that I am not feeling cheerful and explain my inner state to you. You can now understand why I acted as I did.

B. I turn and say: "Oh, sorry! I didn't see you." You answer, "Well it looked like you saw me: you looked right at me!" I say, "No, I was thinking about something some idiot said at a conference yesterday just like I was dreaming. Please forgive me."
   Analysis: First, I surprised you by challenging an *objective reference* you believed to be shared between us: that you were there in the corridor and that you had greeted me. You felt certain that these things were "true," and the basis of their truth anticipated a common set of experiences between us: perceptions of the corridor, of who is in it, and of what sense-available events took place in it.
   I now tell you that at the time of your greeting, you were basically not there for me. You were not an objective reference point during my activities because I did not notice or hear you. Now I totally accept your implicit claim that you really were there, because I believe I see and hear you now and deduce that I would have seen and heard you before had I been alert. Your not being present to me initially is interpreted to be an *illusion,* a *false appearance.*
   But you are not fully convinced by my explanation. You next question the veracity of my statement about not seeing you initially. You point out that I seemed to look right at you. You are now testing out a *subjective* claim of mine, a claim that you do not have direct access to. I claim that I am being truthful when I say I did not see you. You cannot know my present subjective state directly and thus cannot know whether I am "hiding something" from you or not. But my next response convinces you that I am, probably, telling the truth.

C. I turn and say: "What on earth do you mean? Nothing is wrong with me!" You reply, "Well then, Phil, I would say that you are very rude." I look surprised and say, "Rude? Why do you say that?" And you explain, "Well, I greeted you. You simply grunted and looked away." To which I respond with, "Yes, but what is rude about that?" Finally, you explain yourself in this way: "Well, Phil, people shouldn't grunt and look away when someone greets them! They should greet them back. You know, be friendly."
   Analysis: This time the *normative-evaluative* implications of my action come to the foreground. You castigate me for being rude. I agree with you, implicitly, that being rude is a bad thing (we agree on this *value;* if we did not I would have said, "Well what

is wrong with being rude?"). We share a value but not a *norm:* that if greeted one should return the greeting, that it is rude to not return greetings.

You first assumed that I must have known I was rude, but then explain the norm to me when you realize I am not familiar with it. Still, you imply that I *should* have been familiar with it.

This sort of common, daily experience is much closer to the root imagery employed by critical epistemologists than is visual perception. Notice that it is communicative experience, it involves the exchange of understandings. Notice also that it has holistic, undifferentiated components.

When you first notice me in the corridor, your experience is not like that of focused visual perception. It is much less focused than perception per se. You notice me *within* a cultural typification. You are simultaneously noticing me, noticing that we are in a corridor, that we are friends, that we meet accidently, and a host of other things. You do not *perceive* me so much as you *recognize the situation* in a culturally typified way. There are cultural prescriptions for how to act in situations like this one, so your recognition of the situation gives you a range of actions you could employ in responding to it. Chances are you do not even notice what specific clothing I am wearing, whether or not I have glasses on, or other specific perceptual features of the situation.

It is *holistic* experience like this that is more primordial than is sense perception. If we really focus on a visual perception, we simply foreground one part of an overall experience. We background the meaning of our activity, the reasons why we are focusing on something and noting its properties. Visual perception, and perception generally, is always caught up in projects of activity characterized by holistic, undifferentiated, modes of experience.

Communication is also important to the core imagery employed in critical epistemology. Why is this so? Because even when alone and deliberately staring at something to note its properties, we make use of communicative structures. To note the properties of some perceptual object is basically to symbolize the experience in a way that could be communicated to other people. Critical epistemologists follow George Herbert Mead's idea that self-consciousness is the result of internalizing culturally given expectations of routine social interaction (1934). This applies even on the low levels of self-consciousness involved when being aware that we are aware of something, so that we can record the experience in memory or otherwise get cognitive about it. Thus perception itself is structured communicatively.

To construct a sound critical epistemology, then, we must understand holistic modes of human experience and their relationships to communicative structures.

Multiple Ontological Categories

In the example of a corridor greeting given above, a feeling of misunderstanding was amended by making explicit certain assumptions that governed your greeting to me.

These assumptions all had to do with *shared understandings*. First, you tested your initial assumption that I was subjectively in a nontroubled state. Second, you tested your initial assumption that we both perceived the same objective conditions around us. Third, you tested your initial assumption that we both shared identical values (about rudeness) and norms (about appropriate greeting behavior). All these initial assumptions were holistically entailed at the moment you *recognized* the situation through the cultural typification.

Each test you made involved articulating *truth claims:* claims that I felt such and such a way, that such and such objects are perceivable to both of us, that such and such values/norms are correct. Notice that all these truth claims were holistically and implicitly synthesized within your original experience. You had to consciously consider them only when my response did not fit your expectations. Then you considered each assumption separately, keeping the others backgrounded and undifferentiated within the typification through which you recognized the situation. The single assumptions articulated as truth claims were differentiated away from your holistic experience but depended on many other features of the typification, left undifferentiated, to make sense.

Critical epistemology differentiates between "ontological categories" rather than between "realities." Ontologies are theories about *existence* making it possible to formulate diverse truth claims (see chapter four).

There is a subjective ontological category (existing states of mind, feelings, to which only one actor has direct access). Subjective truth claims are claims about existing subjective states (I/you are feeling such and such; I/you think such and such; I/you are being honest, etc).

There is an objective ontological category (existing objects and events to which all people have direct access). Objective truth claims are claims that certain objects and events exist (or existed) such that any observer present could notice them.

There is a normative-evaluative ontological category (existing agreements on the rightness, goodness, and appropriateness of types of activity). Normative/evaluative truth claims boil down to claims that others *should* agree to the rightness, goodness, and appropriateness of certain activities.

Different kinds of truth claims (subjective, objective, normative-evaluative) require different kinds of support to win the consent of others. Getting clear about what kinds of support are required is part of critical epistemology, our theory of knowledge and how valid knowledge may be acquired. The structures to be explored originate in everyday human communication but produce rigorous standards useful to social science.

Truth and Power Are Interconnected

It is because critical epistemology takes its core imagery from common forms of communication that power must enter centrally into the theory of truth we wish to develop. Let me illustrate this by further reference to our greeting in the corridor.

Suppose you call back to me, "Phil! You are being very rude!" Next, I turn around and say, "No I'm not! What are you talking about!?" You say, "Well Phil, it is rude not to return a greeting from a friend." I reply, "It is not! There is nothing rude about ignoring a friend in the corridor."

We disagree on normative-evaluative truth claims. We could continue to discuss the situation, trying to reach an agreement by arguing our respective views further. (The way such an argument would go is explained in chapter four.) The basic idea is, *for all kinds of truth claims it is the consent given by a group of people, potentially universal in membership, that validates the claim.* I will argue this point more extensively later on. It is a more complicated principle than it may first appear. But accepting this principle for now, that consent ultimately grounds truth claims, what do you make of the following possible scenarios?

A. I pull a gun from my pocket and point it at your head, saying: "It is not rude to ignore friends in corridors; you agree with that, don't you?" You agree quickly. You consent to my normative-evaluative truth claim.

B. You hear me claim that it is not rude to ignore friends in corridors, and you do not agree. But then you remember that I am on the tenure and promotion committee this year and that you are up for tenure. I will be reviewing your materials and you know me to take on grudges for the slightest reasons (I do not in real life, by the way!). You agree quickly. You consent to my truth claim.

C. You hear me make my claim about rudeness and do not agree. But then you start to doubt your own point of view. You remember that I am an esteemed professor, deferred to by every academic in the world: I won the Nobel Prize in critical theory last year. You also remember that I am infinitely older than you and that you grew up in a culture that esteemed the elderly, never questioning authority. Putting all this together, you decide you must be wrong. You agree quickly. You consent to my truth claim. This time you agree with entire sincerity.

In each of these scenarios we find consent to a truth claim. I asked you earlier on to accept, at least for the moment, the idea that consent is the ultimate validation of truth claims in critical epistemology. So, does your consent support my truth claim?

Of course it does not, in none of these cases. Your consent was the product of an unequal power relationship in each case. In the first two scenarios, you consented but did not have your heart in it. You were coerced. In the last case you were not coerced, and you had your heart in the consent. But you deferred to my authority at your own expense. My authority was culturally constructed, and it silenced you to the depths of your personal identity. You did not *recognize* my claim as true: you consented to my authority and doubted your own capacity for recognizing truth.

Unequal power distorts truth claims. Critical epistemology will have to be precise about the many ways, a good number of them highly subtle, in which power corrupts knowledge. This matter goes to the very heart of critical epistemology, and it allows fundamental value orientations (for democracy, equality, and human empowerment beyond the merely democratic) to fuse with epistemological imperatives.

Chapter Summary

Here, then, is an introduction to critical qualitative research. Readers should now understand what the value orientation of criticalists is, in rough terms. You should understand that one does not need this value orientation to use critical methodology. Critical methodology is based on critical epistemology, not on value orientations. You should have some basic imagery in mind to help you understand how and why critical epistemology has rejected perception models of truth and all sophisticated modifications of them. Instead, we work our theory up from holistic, predifferentiated human experience and its relationship to the structures of communication. Communication structures go to the heart of every human experience capable of becoming knowledge imparting, even solitary ones. Readers should now be on the lookout for elaborations of several issues glossed within chapter one:

- the connection of power and truth,
- the structures of communication and their universality,
- the nature of consent to truth claims and the many variations that it may take,
- the difference between subjective, objective, and normative-evaluative truth claims,
- ontological assumptions made in critical methodology.

Each of these is clarified in chapters to come, alongside explanations of field techniques, data analysis, and their validation.

Note for page 3

1. "Critical Ethnography" is a term that has historically risen as a particular form of qualitative research. The term "qualitative" is actually more appropriate to my mind than "ethnography." Hence, I will use "qualitative" much more often than "ethnography" in this book, despite its title.

2

Ontological Models and Research Design

Items covered in chapter 2:

- Social ontology and social research
- "Variables" and their ontological presuppositions
- Operational definitions, why we do not use them
- Introduction to Project TRUST, an exemplar of critical research
- Planning a research project
- Articulating initial value orientations
- Ontological models: social sites, social settings, locales, social systems, social integration, system integration, social reproduction
- Five stages for conducting critical qualitative research

Chapter one ended with a list of epistemological issues and a promise to have discussed them all by the end of this book. An "epistemology," remember, is a set of assumptions about knowledge and how it may be validly obtained. In this chapter I will be more concerned with ontology than with epistemology. Our discussion of critical epistemology will begin with chapter four.

This chapter will also introduce you to a critical qualitative study I conducted several years ago, "Project TRUST." I will be using Project TRUST to exemplify field methods and data analysis throughout the rest of the book. In this chapter, Project TRUST will be used to illustrate the initial steps to be taken when planning a research project and also to illustrate important concepts from social theory. Finally, I will present, in outline form, five recommended stages for conducting a critical qualitative research project.

SOCIAL ONTOLOGY

We came across the term "ontology" in chapter one. There we learned that ontologies are theories of existence. Here is a formal definition of ontology: "The assumptions about existence underlying any conceptual scheme or any theory or system of ideas" (Flew 1979: 256).

The core ontological theory employed in critical methodology is tightly linked to our epistemology. There are multiple ontological categories that correspond to different kinds of validity claims. Each kind of validity claim requires distinctive procedures in order to become well supported and distinctive through the nature of each ontological realm referenced. I will say more about this core ontology in chapter four, where I elaborate on critical epistemology.

In this chapter we will be concerned with a "secondary ontology," a "social ontology" giving us basic conceptual frameworks for understanding the object of social research. Social ontologies are implied each time someone thinks of a social object, issue, group, or site to study. Some conception of the social must be presupposed before any social research may begin.

All social research makes use of a social ontology, whether aware of this or not. Social ontologies are secondary to fully thought-out philosophical ontologies. Ultimately, a social ontology must be derivative from a philosophical ontology, but I will not worry about this connection: it would lead to a very dense sort of book, a book of the sort I am trying to avoid.

Variables and Ontological Presuppositions

All research designs require certain assumptions about social reality and human experience, but these are too often taken for granted. In quantitative research these core assumptions are entailed by the use of "variables." I work with many doctoral students at the University of Houston who do their dissertations by measuring such things as "job satisfaction," "attitudes," "leadership styles," and test scores. They use "instruments," like scales and surveys, to get their measurements. Then they use statistical procedures to relate variables: gender and job satisfaction, socioeconomic status and test scores, type of family and school achievement rates, etc. These sorts of studies are familiar—our social science journals are filled with them.

But what is a "variable," and what is the point of using one? Variables are abstractions from more primary assumptions about social life. In my experience, nearly all variables used in social science fall into three main categories:

1. those that abstract from human activity or performance (e.g., test scores abstracting from general problem-solving abilities; highest educational grade attained abstracting from the countless activities involved in getting an education)
2. those that abstract from human experience (e.g., satisfaction levels, loneliness scales, anxiety scales)

3. those that abstract from conditions influencing human performance and experience (e.g., age, gender, work environment, and family type as conditions *external* to actors' volitions; attitudes, beliefs, and values as conditions *internal* to actors' volitions. Volition and conditions of action will be discussed later on.)

Hence the underlying assumptions employed in variable construction hover about (1) social action, (2) human experience, and (3) their conditions. Quantitative social researchers have yet to firmly ground the abstractions they construct when producing variables. They rarely trace their assumptions back to a theory of social action, human experience, and their conditions—a social ontology.

Problems with Variables

Qualitative researchers avoid "variables." Some of us do not find the term "variable" appropriate for any form of social research. This is partly because variables seek to measure actions, conditions, and experiences that generalize across many social contexts. Yet we know that social action and human experience are always, in every instance, highly contextualized. Generalizing across contexts is dangerous.

The contexts of action and experience, moreover, are holistic: they are not in essence a set of discrete terms readily translatable into "variables." If they were, then the problem of context could be reduced to the examination of how many variables "interact" with each other. A number of statistical methods have been developed to explore variable interactions. But very often the holistic quality of action contexts simply cannot be captured through a model of interacting yet discrete factors. The factors are simply not discrete by nature, so making them discrete conceptually can greatly distort our understanding of what is taking place.

I personally believe that some actions and some conditions do lend themselves to variable constructs well enough to permit quantitative methods. Researchers have to be very careful, however, when pursuing these sorts of acts and conditions. A good theory of social action would help in identifying where variables may safely be constructed and what procedures ought to be used in constructing them. I rarely see that sort of care put into quantitative studies.

Another problem with variables in social research is that they all have to be rendered *objective* to be useful. I will give a very precise definition of objectivity in chapter four; here, just think of it in terms of "measurability" and "observability." Nothing can be quantified that is not observable. Yet all human experiences and many conditions of action are nonobjective in essence. That is why quantitative researchers use operational definitions.

Operational definitions are nothing but the construction of inference relations— "mapping rules," between objective/measurable phenomena and nonobjective social factors. An attitude survey, for example, operationalizes values and beliefs (subjective items) through a self-report instrument. The objective response of a subject to the instrument is taken to indicate nonobjective beliefs, values, and emotions. The inference relations employed in attitude scales include an assumption that people will not lie when they fill out the questionnaire. They also include the assumption that people understand themselves well enough to fill out the questionnaire accurately. These are actually very tricky assumptions! Again, a sound theory of social action would enormously help the effort to operationalize.

Qualitative Research

Qualitative research differs from quantitative by pursing the objects of social inquiry more directly. We do not use variables and we do not use operational definitions when we do qualitative inquiry. The abstractions used in qualitative studies, for the main part, come at the end of field work, not the beginning. Yet qualitative researchers are interested in the same basic things as are quantitative researchers:

- social action (and its patterns)
- subjective experiences
- conditions influencing action and experience

Because we pursue these things quite directly in qualitative research, qualitative researchers are more readily forced to examine the nature of action, experience, and their conditions as part of their methodological framework; we are forced to be more explicit about our social ontology. Quantitative researchers should do the same, but have not typically done so. This is partly why quantitative researchers are willing to use terms like "cause" and "dependent variable," while qualitative researchers avoid them. A sound theory of social action, a sound social ontology, rules out deterministic terminology. A sound social ontology conceives of action in a way that absolutely prohibits causes. Actions are conditioned by many things, but they are not determined.

ONTOLOGICAL MODELS FOR RESEARCH DESIGN

In the rest of this chapter I will present a few basic models from social theory, that specialized branch of sociology concerned with

> the construction of more or less useful conceptual tools for looking at social phenomena in a manner that fruitfully raises questions of interest and establishes methodologically proper linkages between different levels of analysis. In that sense sociological theory is not meant to produce empirically testable hypotheses, but merely to prepare the ground for an empirical investigation of social structures and actors. (Mouzelis 1991: 2)

To even formulate a question for empirical investigation is to make assumptions about basic features of social life. Social theory supplies us with a social ontology, a set of models that make research possible but that can always be refined and altered in light of empirical findings.

I have already explained that quantitative research has not, to date, made use of models like these, even though it should. I wish I could say that these models are, by contrast, employed by all qualitative researchers. I cannot. To my knowledge, social theoretical models are undertheorized in the vast majority of qualitative studies and qualitative methodology texts, outside of anthropology. In sociological and educational research, critical qualitative researchers have been by far the best at explaining their social ontologies (see, however, Silverman 1985; Hammersley 1989). In fact, good critical research results in refined ontological models. Part of the research findings are improved concepts of social structure, power, culture, subjectivity, and other matters begged at the start by every research project.

I will not discuss every relevant model here, nor will I present all there is to say about those I do discuss. We will have to learn more about critical epistemology before we can fully explore the relevant issues in social theory. But I will present a number of social-theoretical concepts crucial to research design.

I believe that the best way to introduce the models I have in mind is to make use of an example from my own empirical research. I will tell you about a study I conducted several years ago, introducing it in this chapter, and, in future chapters, sharing some of my findings with you to exemplify methodological principles.

Project TRUST

Several years ago a former student of mine, let's call him Robert (I have changed all names in this book, including names of people, schools, parks, and projects), asked me to evaluate a new school program he had designed. He was the vice principal of West Forest, an elementary school serving a low-income neighborhood in Houston. "We have a lot of trouble with discipline," he explained, "because of our high mobility rate."

The manner in which I planned and conducted an evaluation of Robert's program employs most of the principles I wish to teach in this book. From the planning stage to the final research write-up, I used principles and procedures suitable for *any* qualitative research project, including those only using interviews in explorations of subjectivity, those analyzing only media products, and those focused on social sites other than educational ones. So, regardless of your own specific research interests, the Project TRUST study will provide valuable information: it will illustrate methodological concepts appropriate for almost any study you may have in mind.

Robert's school was suffering from a high "mobility rate," which means geographic mobility in the culture of Houston school districts. Robert was referring to the movement of families from one public school catchment area to another during the course of a school year. Such movements became common in Houston from the mid-1980s on, because of a slump in oil prices that threw Texas demographics into rapid transition. Thousands of professionals and other white collar workers left Houston when they lost their jobs. Real estate values crashed, and rents dropped to record lows. Poor families, many of them African American or Hispanic, began moving into apartment complexes originally designed for the affluent, and then kept moving when unemployment made it impossible to pay even these low rents. I still remember my first visit to a Houston "slum": it was what I would have called a "luxury apartment complex" with several swimming pools, palm trees, and a microwave oven in every unit! But, closer examination showed me that everything was in bad need of new paint and repair.

Schools like West Forest, which had for years served all-white, middle-class or upper-middle-class families, suddenly found themselves with large numbers of impoverished minority students. Moreover, these new students came and went throughout the year, creating a very difficult situation for educators. As Robert explained:

> Last year we had a mobility rate of 107 percent. With students coming in and leaving all the time it has become very difficult to maintain consistent teaching or to establish control over classrooms. This idea I have will take the most disruptive students out of their regular classrooms and teach them better conflict resolution skills. It will give their regular teachers a chance to reestablish control over the remaining students, and it will return the disruptive pupils only after they have shown progress in their social skills. It will raise their self-esteem. I call it "Project TRUST."

When listening to Robert talk about Project TRUST, I recalled the literature on school extraction programs. They are notorious for singling out minority and lower-income students, who then acquire damaging labels that follow them for the rest of their educational career. Usually such programs bear attractive names and state laudatory goals. Formally, they are designed to *help* students having trouble with school. In reality, they are often desired by administrators and teachers because they *control* disruptive students. Among many other things, I wanted to find out whether this particular project would be much the same as other extraction programs; my study might help us understand more about the effects of extraction as well as refine our present understanding of power, culture, identity, and social reproduction.

Formulating Qualitative Research Questions

If you were in my shoes and if you shared my interest in Project TRUST, what would you do first? A general rule when considering any qualitative study is to become clear about what interests you; what you want to find out. You must think of some *questions*.

For qualitative research it is best not to get too precise when formulating initial research questions. This is the opposite of what you must do in a quantitative study, where questions have to be put into the form of hypotheses that are extremely specific. If you try to do something similar in a qualitative study you risk introducing biases, missing important but initially unsuspected features of the situation and closing off opportunities for developing new primary concepts from your field experience. So, definitely, do not formulate specific questions; formulate general, flexible questions.

For any qualitative study, I recommend making a list of everything that interests you about the site or problem to be investigated. Next, make a list of what you need to study in order to satisfy these interests. These are two separate lists. Understand, at the start, that these lists may well change once you are in the field. But you need something to get started, and these two lists will do that job. From them a research design can be constructed.

In the case of the TRUST study, I was interested in:

- how students were picked to be part of the program
- how teachers and administrators perceived these students
- what was taught in the TRUST classroom, intentionally and unintentionally
- what was learned in the TRUST classroom explicitly and implicitly
- what decision-making procedures had led to the implementation and funding of TRUST
- what forces were behind those decision-making procedures
- what relationships existed between TRUST and West Forest, TRUST and the immediate neighborhood, the immediate neighborhood and broader social-economic forces
- what, within the microcosm of Project TRUST, seemed ensnared within much broader social structures and institutions

Quantitative methodologists looking at a list like this would shake their heads and urge narrowing down to just one or two questions. Ignore such advice. When doing your own qualitative study begin with a list like this one. All these interests intersect, for one thing, and it may well be possible to address each and every one in a single study. On the other hand, you are free to change the list by adding and subtracting once you are in the field.

The next thing to do, I have said, is to figure out what you need to study to satisfy your interests. For most studies you will need to get information on the following:

- social routines
- the distribution of routines across related social sites
- constraints and resources affecting social routines
- cultural forms associated with social routines
- subjective experiences,
- life history narratives (total or partial)

This list is based on the three principal items investigated in all social research: social action, subjective experience, and their conditions. Different qualitative studies will prioritize items on this list in different ways, and some studies will only examine a few of the items.

With regard to the TRUST study, I decided to pursue these six items in the following specific ways:

1. Obtain a focused and dense record of social routines in the TRUST classroom

(*method:* intensive observations recorded thickly)

2. Obtain a much less focused and much less dense record of routines in the West Forest school and surrounding community (*method:* casual observations recorded journalistically and interviews)

3. Produce a detailed reconstruction of TRUST classroom culture (*method:* intensive reconstructive analysis on field notes plus in-depth qualitative interviewing with participants)

4. Look for evidence of school and community cultural themes (*method:* perform less intensive reconstructions on the journalistic field notes and interviews; use "key informants" where possible)

5. Look for evidence of social system determinants on the micro-activities in TRUST (*method:* examine all relevant policy documents; budgets; legal imperatives like standardized tests; the legal and economic constraints on parents and teachers; the influence of cultural commodities like textbooks, television shows, and popular music; etc).

In the chapters ahead, I will explain and illustrate such things as "key informants," "reconstructive analysis," and the difference between "thick" field notes and "journalistic" field notes.

The West Forest Neighborhood

Pursuit of information about social routines, cultural forms, and conditions of action must be guided by some basic social theoretical models. To introduce them, let me continue with examples from the TRUST study.

On the day of my appointment at West Forest I arrived early so that I could first drive around the neighborhood. Initially, the neighborhood did not seem particularly striking in any way. There were numerous apartment complexes near the school, which, I learned, housed most of the students. These complexes looked quite decent: the sort I would expect to rent myself with my middle-class income. There were also sections of rather nice housing, with a few blocks of obviously rundown houses that were probably rented out at low rates.

A closer look at the apartment complexes, however, was revealing. Though designed for people with middle- and upper-middle-class incomes, they were now deteriorating. They were like the first Houston "slum" I had seen: some had pools, all had central air conditioning, most had microwave ovens for each unit. But there were large patches of roof that buckled with age and neglect. Some of the windows had been broken, the glass replaced with wood or cardboard. Apartment owners clearly desired new tenants, as most of the complexes displayed large signs announcing vacancies. These signs usually boasted certain incentives for moving in: "Free Month's Rent," "Free TV," "Free Microwave!"

Every complex had some sort of security system. Fences, bars, gates, security stations were seen everywhere. One complex even had a ring of coiled barbed wire surrounding it. When entering the office of one of these apartment complexes, I found myself facing a video camera filming my every move. The attendant told me that she made all prospective residents leave a driver's license at the desk before she would take them to see an empty apartment. "That's policy," she said. "Some guys have been raping attendants once they get them alone in an apartment."

Only a few blocks from the school was a large park, surrounded on three sides by apartment complexes. I pulled into the park and introduced myself to an official-looking woman who explained that she was in charge of it. She was an Hispanic woman, named Laticia, with a master's degree in social work from the University of Chicago. Laticia seemed eager to talk to me and soon called over an elderly woman in charge of the adventure playground to join in our conversation.

"We've been trying to change things around here, but it has been hard," said Laticia. "We work here every day but leave before dark. Once it's dark, no one should stay."

Verna, the adventure playground attendant, joined in at this point. "At about six o'clock, women come out of the apartment complexes and line up over there." She pointed to the circular drive/parking area I had come in by. "You know what they are doing?" "No," I innocently replied. "They sell sex. They line up for the men who drive in one after another, every night. They are the mothers of these children"; her arm swung back towards the adventure playground. "That's the only way they can pay the rent. Of course, some use drugs and have to pay for that."

"See those two men over there?" asked Laticia, pointing to a park corner far away from the adventure playground. "They are drug dealers. They do most of their business in the park." I looked and saw two young men loitering by a bench. "I have tried to get rid of them, but the other park attendants, who are supposed to work under me, support them." "They support them?" I asked in surprise. "Because they give money to the park," explained Laticia. "I have really tried to get them out, but there is a lot of resistance. They have bought flowers and others things for our gardens."

In time, I was to visit this park quite often, coming over after a session of observations in the school. I was impressed with Laticia and Verna and everything they were trying to do. The community was mainly populated by victims: people who could not get jobs, who never had enough money, who were constantly threatened by relatively small numbers of drug pushers and gangs. Verna had built a section of playhouses in one part of the adventure playground:

> So that these children, who often have to leave one apartment for another, can have a stable home. What happens here is that a family moves in and gets a free month's rent. Then, usually, they pay the next month's rent. At the third month they can't pay but stay until kicked out. By the fourth month they move, usually to a complex right across the road. It's like "musical apartments." Children need to feel that they have a place that is really a home to them. A home has to be stable, has to give one the feeling that they have control. You should see them look after these playhouses! They sweep their houses out and keep them real nice. Homeless people sleep in them at night and the kids decided that was okay.

Verna and Laticia had free food, donated by stores, brought into the park for distribution several times a week. They helped families who couldn't find a new place after being evicted. They ran discussion groups for older children about common problems they were experiencing, like drug use.

Verna, a volunteer well into her 70s and an enthusiastic disciple of Piagetian psychology, told children stories from Hispanic and Spanish cultures so that they could develop some pride in their own histories. The adventure playground was filled with statues and paintings that were either made by the kids or had some significance within their cultural heritage. African-American heros had their photographs tacked onto some of the trees as well. Laticia liked to explain the origin of her son's name to park children: "Nelson" was named after Nelson Mandela.

Laticia and Verna were politically astute idealists. Two of their goals were to organize the adults of the community to rid it of drug pushers, and to establish a garden for area residents to grow their own food on park soil. They were having some success; Laticia proudly pointed to a large vegetable garden at one end of the park. But their work was dangerous. A murder had occurred in the park a month before my arrival. A homeless person, sleeping there, was killed at night, and no one knew why. Verna, elderly and frail, was herself thrown into a puddle by a couple of men as she left work one evening.

Laticia received continuous threats from drug dealers and their friends. She told me of a recent morning after she had chased some drug dealers out of the park. She came to work that morning to find her office broken into and wantonly trashed. A large Bowie knife was thrust into the door. "They were warning me," she said with unbelievable calm.

My Introduction to Project TRUST

Later during my first morning at West Forest, I met with Robert and his principal. TRUST was designed for use with children from this neighborhood. Teacher morale was low because of frequent classroom disruptions, so one of the TRUST objectives was simply to remove those students who made teaching so hard. Robert was well aware of the fact that extraction policies often damage students through stigmatization, but he thought this risk could be ameliorated by keeping the TRUST students up-to-date on their academic programs and returning them to the normal classrooms as soon as possible. He thought the TRUST students genuinely needed special lessons to improve their conflict resolution skills and to raise their self-awareness and self-esteem. The balance of costs and benefits, he hoped, would fall in favor of benefits for all concerned.

I met the teacher hired to teach TRUST: Alfred. Alfred was a young Caucasian male with some previous experience in counseling. Like Laticia and Verna, he was an idealist and a humanist, eager to help his students. His plan for TRUST included the alternation of daily lessons and workshops on self-awareness and conflict resolution with periods of individualized work on academic lessons. Alfred was expected to keep his students on their academic tracks and to administer state-mandated achievement tests on schedule.

It was simple for the school administration to explain the purpose of my job: find out whether or not TRUST worked. For me, the purpose was more complex. To find out whether or not TRUST worked in the school's terms meant several things: are disruption rates curbed by TRUST (easy to determine), are conflict-resolution skills successfully learned by TRUST students (harder), is the self-esteem of the TRUST student raised (still harder)?

Additionally, no answer to these questions would make much sense without asking more fundamental questions: why do TRUST students disrupt classes, what is the meaning of their disruptions to them, whether TRUST lessons curb disruptions, and what is being learned in the TRUST classroom?

These broader questions meant that I would have to observe the TRUST classroom very intensively, observe other classrooms in the school less intensively, and gain some knowledge of the culture of the community surrounding TRUST through visits to the homes and observations of the park.

Understanding the Object of Inquiry

In the West Forest study my job was first to discover what was taking place in the TRUST classroom. Then I had to assess the significance of what was taking place for the students involved: what sorts of "lessons" they were learning on both overt and covert levels, what impact was made on their identities and futures. I had to seek explanations of what was occurring within the TRUST classroom as well, and this would force me to learn about the culture of these students' homes and neighborhood, to learn about the rules and culture adhered to by school personnel, and to relate these things to the classroom routines.

The object of my study, then, could be portrayed through the imagery of a focal region within a naturally occurring stream of social life, surrounded by a complex social context. The focal region is the ongoing social routines of a single social site: the TRUST classroom. The surrounding regions include the culture and social practices of larger geographic areas from which the TRUST actors come and to which they return. They also include nongeographic structures—such as the economy, the media, and the political system—that condition action within West Forest and its community. Figure 2.1 provides a graphic representation of what was to be investigated in the TRUST study.

Sites, Settings, Locales, and the Social System

We may abstract from the situation at West Forest to arrive at a few useful concepts for all research methodology.

Figure 2.1: The TRUST Study

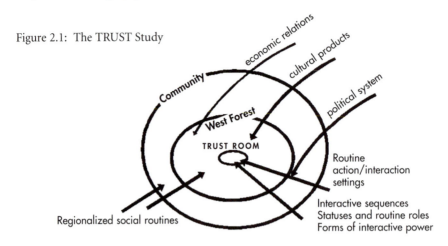

Sites

In West Forest, the object of primary interest for me was the TRUST classroom. That is where I was to spend most of my observation time. The TRUST classroom is a good example of a social site. Social sites are regions within society in which routine activities, usually including interactions, take place. Social sites are delimited both geographically and temporally: they exist within specific geographical areas, and humans interact within them at specifiable times. When human beings coordinate their activities with each other in some manner that relates to geography and time, we have a social site. The TRUST classroom involved coordinated activities between students and teacher during certain hours of the workweek and was therefore a "site."

"Site" is a loose term. The entire West Forest school could have been my "site," or the entire community. The term is rather like a template or lens to place over complex social life, which must then have its size and focus adjusted to meet one's interests.

Settings

A related term that does not, in my usage, imply geographical boundaries, is that of setting. Within the TRUST classroom, the rules through which actors coordinated their activities with one another frequently changed. A period of time characterized by quiet work on the part of students would be followed by temporal periods during which the teacher taught at the blackboard, periods during which students and teacher got into conflicts with each other, and periods during which all actors joked together without any particular task under pursuit.

Every time individuals interact with each other, certain shared understandings set boundaries on the expected behavior. During a joking session, one does not expect serious talk. During a conflict, one does not expect task-oriented behavior. These tacit, shared understandings shift frequently during normal social life, and each one is called a "setting."

A setting, then, is not something directly observable. It is defined by a tacit understanding shared by actors that makes their interactions possible. Settings shift when one actor signals the desire to change to a different type of interaction and other actors consent to the change. Often, actors will negotiate for a setting change that other actors only partially agree to. Over a short period of time, such tacit negotiations produce a consensus between the actors on a new setting through which to continue interaction.

A typical social site will be characterized by fairly predictable settings. Many different conditions will explain the usual course of settings constructed by actors on a single social site: institutional rules (like school and classroom rules); relations between the site in question and other nearby sites to which actors routinely go and from which they routinely come; and broadly distributed cultural, economic, and political conditions that influence the coordination of action on sites throughout an entire society.

Locales

Thus, whatever took place in the TRUST classroom was influenced by many things originating outside the classroom itself. The routines and rules pertaining to West Forest school comprised an obvious set of such influences. The culture and social activities taking place in the neighborhoods surrounding West Forest provided another example. These geographically wider areas surrounding the classroom are examples of what sociologists and cultural geographers call "locales." About any social site, one will find related sites that form a sort of minisocial system.

Anthony Giddens explains the relationship between settings and locales through the idea of "regionalized social action." Because the routines found in one social site are influenced by, and themselves influence, routines found in nearby sites, social action becomes "regionalized." The relationship between settings typifying one site to settings typifying nearby, related, sites, can be explained by "modes of regionalization which channel, and are channelled by, the time-space paths that the members of a community or society follow in their day to day activities. Such paths are strongly influenced by, and also reproduce, basic institutional parameters of the social systems in which they are implicated" (Giddens 1984: 142–3). The patterns generated by students and teachers coming to West Forest school each morning and leaving each evening are "time-space paths" displaying some regularity. A "region," a "locale"— consisting of typical settings distributed about a series of geographically near and socially related sites—is produced in this way.

Once again we find a loose term, "locale," suitable for the metaphors of the template and the lens. Locales can be large or small, focused or blurred: it all depends upon what site one has first selected as well as the nature of one's research questions.

Social Systems

Finally, the social patterns one finds within sites and their surrounding regions are partially conditioned by very widely distributed conditions. Many of these broadly distributed conditions do not originate in any specific geographic location; the economic system of a particular society is a good example of this sort of condition. An economy does not originate on one site but rather shapes activities throughout a large number of sites: a "society." The political system is another example of this sort of condition.

There is another category of broadly distributed conditions that does involve specific sites of origin. This category has to do with the cultural industry of a society. Cultural products like books, films, videos, music, and video games have become increasingly important. They have widely distributed influence but can be traced to specific sites, like publishing companies or Hollywood. Such sites are not part of the locale surrounding most of the sites they affect, because they exert their influences from afar and do not depend on the movement of actors ("time-space paths") from one site to another.

Such broadly distributed conditions are part of the social system(s). To understand the concept of social system it is helpful to remember what we mean by "settings." Social settings are constructed by actors when they meet each other face-to-face and negotiate an understanding of what form their interactions should take. Social settings are brought off by "social integration," which, in its sociological sense, does not refer to mixing populations of people coming from diverse racial and cultural backgrounds. Rather, social integration refers to the coordination of interaction face-to-face. Whenever a "setting" can be said to exist, social integration has occurred, because actors have established an understanding, face-to-face, through which their activities are coordinated.

The concept of social system, on the other hand, has to do with the coordination of action between groups of actors separated in space and time. This sort of action coordination is termed "system integration," as opposed to social integration. The economy is a good example of system integration. Economic activity is certainly coordinated throughout an entire society. That is why we can use dollars or pounds in any appropriate site within American or British society. That is also why we have such things as slumps, booms, and stock market panics.

The scale of this sort of coordination does not, and cannot, depend on face-to-face interactions alone. Actors using money in any way are not free to "negotiate" many aspects of their interaction. A system condition places limits on the negotiations that can accompany the most fundamental features of buying and selling (the "worth" and meaning of the money used, the amounts at hand, for examples). Use of money in economic transactions coordinates action between people who never meet each other. Later in this book we will look more carefully at the role of the economy in system integration as well as at the similar role played by legal and political institutions.

The last sentence of the Giddens quotation above reads: "Such paths [time-space paths] are strongly influenced by, and also reproduce, basic institutional parameters of the social systems in which they are implicated." Giddens is writing about time-space paths, the patterns of social action, that one will find within and about any social site. His sentence emphasizes the role played by system relations within any setting and locale. Economic, political, and cultural structures that are extended broadly throughout an entire society always influence any specific social routines one may observe. They play a big role in the establishment of locales or "regionalized" social action.

Giddens's quotation refers to something else important to our theory: actors are not forced to act by conditions; instead, they are rather strongly influenced (in the case of cultural conditions) or resourced/constrained (in the case of laws and economic conditions) to act in broadly predictable ways. Conditions that *resource* and/or *constrain* action operate *externally* to an actor's volition. They are conditions (like the physical environment, available money, and laws) that have to be coped with regardless of an actor's beliefs, values, and social identity.

Conditions that *influence* operate internally to actors' volitions by helping to constitute their values, beliefs, and personal identity. With every act, actors draw upon cultural themes they are familiar with so that the act will uphold certain values, be consistent with certain beliefs, and reclaim certain social identities.

In neither the case of external nor internal conditions are actors compelled to act as they do. A social act could always have been otherwise, regardless of the conditions under which it was performed. This is why Giddens uses the term "reproduce" in his statement. By acting in accordance with economic, political, or cultural conditions, actors "reproduce" system relations. There is always some degree of freedom for acting otherwise: acting against conditions rather than in conformity with them. The "social system" only exists through continuous reproduction: continuous human activity that affirms the basic form of such conditions rather than challenges them. Of course, every social act makes some sort of innovation and adds something new to system milieu. But social systems exist because people generally make only very small innovations when they act. The general form of system milieu is reproduced during the course of normal social routines. As we will see in future chapters, power relations are responsible for keeping most social action within bounds.

SUMMARY OF THE CORE CONCEPTS

Many terms were introduced in the above section, and it would not hurt to summarize their meanings here:

- *Social Sites* are specific spatial and temporal regions within society where people interact. Usually, a social site will be characterized by routine activities.
- *Social Settings* are tacit understandings reached between actors concerning the type of interaction they will engage in. Settings are not observable and do not depend on a physical surrounding or even on the social site within which they are constructed.

But settings are usually influenced, conditioned by many factors associated with the physical surroundings.

- *Locales* are patterned activities taking place in areas surrounding a social site. They both are influenced by the social sites they contain and influence these sites.
- *Social Systems* are the result of external and internal influences on action that are very broadly distributed throughout a society. They are reproduced through patterned activity stretching across wide reaches of space and time.
- *Social Integration* is achieved whenever a setting is constructed. It is the coordination of action between people through face-to-face contact. People frequently negotiate settings and shift old settings into new ones when their negotiations are successful.
- *System Integration* is achieved when a social system is established. System integration is the coordination of action between actors separated in space and time.
- *Reproduction* occurs when people act consistently with respect to broadly distributed conditions. Actors are always free, in principle, to act against such conditions—to challenge them or transform them. This is why the concept of social system must not be thought of as something existing outside of human activity. Social systems are human activities that have become patterned. To exist they must be continuously reproduced.

It is helpful to diagram these core concepts (see Figure 2.2) so that readers may retain them in visual form. Readers should remember that no diagram is going to do more than roughly represent the ideas discussed above.

THE CORE CONCEPTS AND SOCIAL RESEARCH

All social research will in some way involve an interest in social action and its conditions, as I have said repeatedly throughout this chapter. Qualitative social research usually employs these concepts more directly than other types, but other forms of research come down, ultimately, to the same set of ideas.

So What about Interview-only Studies?

There are many qualitative studies that aim to study the attitudes, beliefs, and experiences of individuals through qualitative interviews alone. Such studies might seem to be unconcerned with social action taking place within sites and locales that are influenced by social systems. A student of mine, for example, once conducted case studies on the understanding certain males have of "masculinity." Another student of mine is currently studying male attitudes toward "intimacy," and another has studied the long-term coping strategies of therapists to the suicide of a client. Another student's study of religious experience is also an example. What significance do action, site, locale, and system have to studies like these?

The answer is that such studies are addressed to social action but seek information

Figure 2.2 System Relations

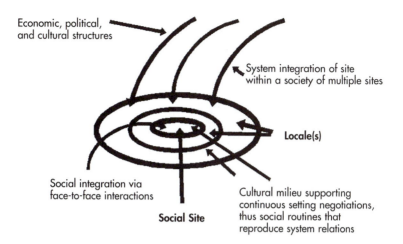

Economic, political, and cultural structures

System integration of site within a society of multiple sites

Locale(s)

Social integration via face-to-face interactions

Social Site

Cultural milieu supporting continuous setting negotiations, thus social routines that reproduce system relations

about cultural schema that subjects regularly draw upon in many (usually not all) social situations. A particular way of understanding "masculinity," for example, conditions many diverse specific acts produced by a subject within many different locations. Interviews aimed at eliciting the articulation of a masculinity construct abstract from actual social sites and contexts in order to discover cultural schemes of general deployment. The significance of a study on masculinity constructs lies in the situated social acts produced by people who hold to the constructs.

The same can be said about studies of "pure subjective experience," such as my student's study of religious experience. As soon as a subject starts to talk about an experience, cultural schema are inevitably employed. Such schema are related to activities that the subject takes part in, or could in principle take part in. There is no such thing as a pure representation of subjective experience: schema must always be used, and such schema will be closely tied to contexts of social action. At the very least, a person discussing highly subjective and almost ineffable experiences will have to employ metaphors rooted in cultural forms of life.

In fact, the most effective way to use qualitative interviews with subjects is to get them to describe events they remember taking part in: to begin at a concrete level where a specific action situation is recalled and then to work toward articulations of interpretive schema that the subject applies in many diverse situations (see chapter ten).

QUANTITATIVE RESEARCH

Experimental research, survey research, and all other forms of inquiry that employ "variables" may also not seem to be focused on social action and its contexts. But once again this is due to the level of abstraction employed by the researcher when formulating variables. Test scores, demographic data, drop-out rates, performance measures, and other items commonly studied by quantitative researchers originate as abstractions from either actual social action or from its conditions. The significance of such studies always comes back to specific action contexts: to making curriculum changes in order to raise test scores, to making organizational changes so that workers may be more empowered, to simply understanding voting or consumer behavior.

FIVE RECOMMENDED STAGES FOR CRITICAL QUALITATIVE RESEARCH

This book is focused on critical qualitative research and will not address the interesting question of how critical epistemology and social theory might inform quantitative research. Actual quantitative methods are not threatened by critical methodology, but the ultimate meaning of such methods would take on a different significance. Certain terms commonly used in quantitative research would probably be changed if these methods were relocated within a critical framework, terms like "cause." The concept of "variable," as another example, makes good sense in physical science but connotes inappropriate imagery when it comes to social research because the freedom of people to act otherwise in any situation is lost with such a term. I will say little more about quantitative methods in this book, however, in order to concentrate on qualitative techniques.

In this last section of chapter two, I outline five stages I have recommended elsewhere, in collaboration with Michael Apple, for conducting critical qualitative research (Carspecken and Apple 1992). The rest of the book is basically organized as a sequential discussion of each stage. Some chapters, like chapters four and twelve, are devoted entirely to theoretical issues bridging all five stages.

The five stages of critical qualitative research are closely related to the core concepts discussed above. They are designed to study social action taking place in one or more social sites and to explain this action through examining locales and social systems intertwined with the site of interest. They are also designed to assess the subjective experiences common to actors on the site and to determine the significance of the activities discovered with respect to the social system at large. Issues of power and inequality necessarily permeate social research of any type and at any stage. The models presented within the following chapters will help researchers who strive to spot and analyze power relations.

Portions of this five-stage scheme may be used separately if one wishes to conduct an interview-only study or to study the relation between a social site and its locale with only marginal consideration of system relations. Thus the five-stage scheme is meant to be generally applicable to most qualitative research designs.

The five stages I recommend are not meant to be hard and fast, to be followed one after the other without ever returning to an earlier stage. Like many authors on qualitative research (LeCompte and Preissle 1993; Spradley 1980; Werner and Schoepfle 1987), I strongly recommend a loosely cyclical use of the stages. One begins with the first three in a fairly sequential manner, but soon starts to repeat earlier steps in light of findings delivered through preliminary analysis.

Here, then, are the five stages in outline.

Preliminary Steps: Creating a list of research questions, a list of specific items for study, and examining researcher value orientations

The first two of these preliminary steps have been described above. Once a researcher becomes interested in a social site, a group of people, or a social problem, it is necessary to brainstorm a list of questions. These questions should be general, broad, comprehensive, and flexible. They should not be too precise. They can be changed at any point during a qualitative study.

Next, a list of specific tems for examination should be produced. Write down what information you will have to collect in order to satisfy your questions. Usually, this list will include the specification of social routines to study both intensively and journalistically; the specification of documents, laws, media products and the like to be investigated; and the specification of actors who will have to be interviewed.

Finally, it is a good idea to explore your value orientations *before* entering the field to put a check on biases. I did not do this in my TRUST study, but the study would have been strengthened if I had. It is becoming more and more acceptable to "come clean" (LeCompte and Preissle 1993) on your own biases in a research report so that readers may question your findings and, to a certain extent, "see behind" the values that might govern your analysis and report. Discovering your own biases is a process that continues throughout a research project by using such methods as keeping a subjective journal during field work—a special notebook in which you daily write down feelings experienced. Other methods are well described in future chapters: undergoing peer debriefing sessions and conducting member checks.

It is also a good idea to explore your value orientations at the very start of your study. I have my doctoral students undergo an intensive qualitative interview with me to this end before they start field work. We go through the transcript of their interview together, and sometimes an analysis of it is included in the dissertation. This process of having a peer or supervisor interview you on the things you expect to find *before* you enter the field greatly helps to raise awareness of your own biases and check for them while compiling your field notes and formulating your research questions.

Stage One: Compiling the primary record through the collection of monological data

In stage one, the researcher makes herself as unobtrusive as possible within a social site to observe interactions. A primary record is built up through note taking, audio taping, and, if desired, video taping. An intensive set of notes is built up for the site of focus and a looser journal kept on observations and conversations made by frequenting the locale of the site.

The information collected in this way is "monological" in nature because the researcher "speaks" alone when writing the primary record. The researcher does not involve the people under study in any penetrating dialogue but rather takes a purely third-person position in relation to them: describing them from the perspective of an uninvolved observer. Reasons for using monological techniques during the first stage are given in chapter three.

Stage Two: Preliminary reconstructive analysis

In stage two, the researcher begins to analyze the primary record as it has been built up so far. A variety of techniques are employed (see chapters six through nine) to determine interaction patterns, their meanings, power relations, roles, interactive sequences, evidence of embodied meaning, intersubjective structures, and other items discussed later on in this book. The analysis is reconstructive because it articulates those cultural themes and system factors that are not observable and that are usually unarticulated by the actors themselves. Putting previously unarticulated factors into linguistic representation is "reconstructive": it takes conditions of action constructed by people on nondiscursive levels of awareness and reconstructs them linguistically. Reconstructive analysis always contains an element of uncertainty, or indeterminacy, but boundaries exist on the possibilities, boundaries that the researcher must discover and elucidate.

Stage Three: Dialogical data generation

In stage three, the researcher ceases to be the only voice allowed in building up a primary record. Here, the idea is to begin conversing intensively with the subjects of one's study through special techniques of interviewing and the use of discussion groups. Stage three generates data with people rather than records information about them. It is crucial to critical qualitative research because, if used properly, it democratizes the research process. Such new data, or information, will often challenge information collected in stage one and analyzed in stage two. But there are good reasons, discussed in future chapters, for delaying dialogical data generation until a primary record has been developed and partially analyzed.

Stage Four: Discovering system relations

In stage four, one examines the relationship between the social site of focused interest and other specific social sites bearing some relation to it. These include sites within the immediate locale and sites that produce cultural products like TV shows, movies, and books. There are a number of techniques and some useful theoretical models that may be employed to discover such system relations.

Stage Five: Using system relations to explain findings

In stage five, the level of inference goes up appreciably as one seeks to explain one's findings in stages one through four by reference to the broadest system features. A number of key social theoretical concepts, discussed in chapters twelve and thirteen, make it possible to link reconstructive analysis with system theories. If successful, a critical researcher is able to suggest reasons for the experiences and cultural forms she reconstructed having to do with the class, race, gender, and political structures of society. Often, it is this fifth stage that really gives one's study its force and makes it a contribution to real social change.

Figure 2.3 summarizes the five stages of critical qualitative research.

Figure 2.3: Five Stages for Critical Qualitative Research

PRELIMINARY STEPS

1. **Stage One:** Compiling the primary record
2. **Stage Two:** Preliminary reconstructive analysis
3. **Stage Three:** Dialogical data generation
4. **Stage Four:** Describing system relations
5. **Stage Five:** System relations as explanations of findings

3

Stage One: Building a Primary Record

Items covered in Chapter 3:

- Compiling a thick record

- Keeping a field journal

- Doing passive observation

- Selecting periods for intensive observation

- Rationale for passive observation

This chapter describes what a primary record is and how to construct a "valid" one. It will beg a number of hot questions currently under debate by methodological theorists. What is meant by a "valid," "unbiased" record? What sense should be given to "objectivity" and how should it be distinguished from "subjectivity"?

Though begged in this chapter, these and other questions will not be addressed until the next chapter on critical epistemology. Rather than present many seemingly abstract arguments all at once, I thought it would be best to return to my TRUST study at this point, show through its example how a primary record can be constructed, and give some tips on keeping one's record as trustworthy as possible. Much of the epistemological justification for conducting passive observations and writing records in the manner I suggest will be given in the next chapter.

THICK DESCRIPTION AND FIELD JOURNALS

When I first visited the TRUST classroom, I was struck by the complexity of the interactions taking place. Many things were happening all at once. Many things seemed subtle, such as eye movements and body posturing, that are hard to record. Of course,

I also realized that what was taking place in this room could only be understood through observing many other things, like the other classrooms in the school, the counseling room, the office and teacher's lounge, and the homes and neighborhoods of the students.

I decided to produce a thick record of classroom activities and a "not-so-thick," journalistic record of events in the corridors, teachers' lounge, homes, neighborhood, and park. Therefore, I began with two separate notebooks that I took with me each day: a notebook for thick descriptions of classroom interaction and a notebook to record things seen and heard during my visits to the cafeteria, lounge, park, and other sites. I call this second kind of notebook a field journal, the first kind I call the primary record. I use the phrase "primary record" because most of your analysis will be focused on the thick notes, which serve as a sort of "data anchor" for the less intensive notes compiled in the journal. In addition, the term "primary" helps to distinguish between your thick observation notes, which will be typed into a series of word processor files, and copies of these same notes to which codes, commentary, and sections of expanded analysis will have been added during stage two.

It is standard to make entries in the second notebook, the "field journal," some time after the events described took place. This recording from memory can be done quite soon after one has observed or taken part in some activity; grab a chair or a bench for twenty minutes after spending time in a lounge or cafeteria to jot down what you remember. The notebook for intensive observations, however, can be used during the observation period so that a lot of detail can be captured.

An Example of Thick Description

Here is an excerpt from my typed record of intensive observations:
Date: 2/6

Diagram of TRUST Room (Using "line draw" on word processor)

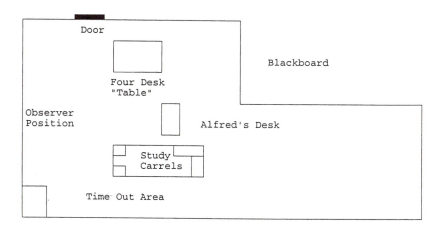

Context Notes

Arrived at 9:30 and waited for Alfred. Samuel in time-out area, reading a book and waiting for Alfred. He looks sleepy when he comes out.

Ricardo [another TRUST student] at home over a glue incident. Had poured glue all over his arms and got sent home for it. Also had hit mother. Vice principal expressed his view that Ricardo might have to be sent elsewhere, that TRUST was not working for him. I learned later in the day that Ricardo's mother had taken him to see a prison to show him what could happen to him if he didn't start "acting better." Mary is taking a standardized test with her normal classroom and thus out of TRUST. Thus, only Samuel here.

Thick record:

9:37

[1]A: Alfred enters room, casts a glance towards Samuel and then towards me, moves towards "table" made of four desks shoved together and shuffles some papers about.

[Observer Comment: *I wonder if he is very conscious of me at this time. He didn't acknowledge my presence but did look at me—same with Samuel. He seems to be collecting his thoughts or something as he shuffles papers.*]

9:38

[2] A: Alfred looks up in Samuel's direction with placid, smooth facial features.

[OC: *as if bland, nonchalant, "no big deal."*]

[3] A: *Samuel, let's go now and take that test.* Addresses Samuel in matter of fact way, as if "no big deal, time to take the test, as we both know."

[4] S: Samuel frowns. His body tightens in chair. Raises head and chest up. Lips tight.

[5] S: *I'm not taking that test, it's too hard.* Tone implies firm stance but no sharp tones, not loud.

[OC: As if: *"I'm just not taking it, it's simply too hard, so that's that."*]

[6] A: *You've got to take it.* Has moved three steps toward Samuel. Voice firm, not loud, not sharp; calm.

[OC: As if *"you've got to take it and that's that."*]

[7] S: *I'm not doing it, it's too hard.* Tone as if becoming angry, or desperate. Eyes have shifted away from Alfred and toward wall behind him. Body tighter, arms about chest.

[8] (Silence)

By the way, the numbers I put in brackets before particular acts are not part of the thick record but were added later on so that I could refer to sections of the record when writing about it. Do not attempt to take field notes with numbers like these.

Principles of Thick Description

First, notice that these notes are indeed pretty "thick," which means that they capture a lot of detail. Remember that not all field notes need to be taken this thickly. It is necessary, for the analytic methods I advocate, to compile many sets of notes with this amount of detail for selected periods of time in selected sites. Below I will suggest some principles to use for deciding when to take notes this thickly and when to take them more sketchily. In this section, however, I will indicate some of the basic features of thick description itself.

Components and Qualities of Thick Description

1. *Speech acts, body movements, and body postures* were recorded as thickly as possible in the example above. This segment was produced as all my thick field notes are: from both written notes and a tape recording.
2. *A low-inference vocabulary* is used. Where normative or subjective inferences are suggested terms like "as if," "appears to be," and "it seems" are used to qualify them.
3. *The time is recorded quite frequently.* This is important for one can only retain a sense of the time periods involved in a segment of interaction if the time is actually recorded. Without a record of the time one can easily get a greatly distorted impression of the time intervals involved.
4. *Occasional use of brackets and the "OC" code* are employed. The "OC" code stands for "observer comment." It is often a good idea to insert speculations about the meaning of what is occurring in an interaction right into the primary record. But this must be done in a way that clearly distinguishes speculations from the objective-referenced data. I use brackets, OC, and the indentation of such comments below my descriptions. Later on other things will be included within brackets inserted into the primary record, which is why the OC code is necessary in my scheme.
5. *Context information* is recorded before the thick description per se is begun. This includes time of arrival at the research site, reasons for only one student in the classroom this day, and comments made to me by the vice principal when on my way to the classroom.
6. *Verbatim speech acts are put in italics.*
7. *The record is typed into a word processor.* This is important for the stages to follow. Word processors make it easy to add commentary, copy out sections of the primary record to illustrate various points made in the final write-up, and use a coding scheme. I use one word processing file for each day of field notes. At this time, use of word processing is virtually a necessity for qualitative research.
8. *A simple diagram* is entered into the record. Clearly, diagrams greatly help when one is describing areas of the site or the movement of people from one area to another. Most word processing programs these days include a rudimentary "draw" utility, making it easy to diagram sites and people's positions within them.

When to Use Thick Description

Usually it will not be practical to construct an entire set of field notes as thickly as the notes of my example are. As I have already mentioned, it is important to produce selective sets of thick notes. In most qualitative research projects, one will spend a lot of time moving about the general locale to get an idea of what goes on where. The field journal should be kept for taking general notes on what one learns. Within the locale, one or more sites will probably be of primary interest in the study, and selected periods of intensive observation should be made for the purpose of generating thick field notes.

One can also conduct periods of intensive observation with the purpose of producing "quite thick" field notes as well: write down observations in a separate notebook as thickly as you can, run a tape recorder, but only type the written notes into the computer rather than running the tape as well. This way you will always have the option of returning to the tape to give more detail to your notes if your analysis requires it. So initially, only a few representative periods of observation need be typed into the computer in a very thick manner, with all speech acts recorded verbatim. Later on, during stage two, one can return to "quite thick" notes to thicken them with detail from the tape recorder if this becomes important to the analysis.

I observed the TRUST classroom intensively on twenty separate occasions of two hours duration each. Of these, eight were initially typed into the computer with use of my tape recorder to produce the sort of thick record exemplified above. Twelve were typed into the computer as "quite thick" records, each of which had a corresponding tape recording I could use if necessary. As it turned out, analysis of the data did require going back to some of the tape recordings to add detail to these quite thick records.

Thick description must be considered the "ideal case" for meeting validity requirements of objectivity, as discussed in the next two chapters. The sections of thick record compiled in one's primary record can be used to "ground" inferences made on less thickly compiled notes, for these often display the same patterns of behavior captured thickly. When less formal observations and less thickly recorded formal observations are included in one's field notes, they should approximate the standards of thick description as much as possible by using a low inference vocabulary, by getting speech acts down as verbatim as one can, and by distinguishing between objective-referenced data and observer comments.

Doing Passive Observation

A few practical suggestions for conducting passive observations can be made here without repeating much of what already has been published on this topic (good sources on observation methods include Spradley 1980; Goetz and LeCompte 1984; Bernard 1988). Most important is the use of a flexible observation schedule to disrupt the tendency for unnoticed biases to guide composition of the primary record.

The Method of Priority Observation

The technique I usually use can be termed "the method of priority observation." I take one person in the setting and record everything that person does and says as thickly as possible as a first priority. I record everything other people do and say in interaction with this person as a second priority, and I record everything else happening in the setting as a third priority.

Roughly every five minutes, I shift to a new individual as my "priority person." If an event occurs during the observation period that seems "important" to the study for whatever reason (usually because it is a conflict, a disruption, a deviation from apparent routines, or an uncommon but important intervention from an authority figure), I will momentarily end my focus on one individual in order to capture this event for the record. But once such events are over I return to the priority observation schedule.

If there are few people interacting in the site of interest, this method will soon give every one of them priority position for a time. If there are many people interacting, you will have to choose a smaller number of people sprinkled geographically about the site. Sometimes you will be primarily interested in certain groups within a site of many people: one or two work groups, friendship groups, or demographic categories of people like females, blacks, the elderly, and so on. Then the method of priority observation can be employed for members of these groups only.

After a number of initial observations have been conducted, you can take a category of behavior for primary recording. Focus mainly on body postures and gestures for a time, switch to intonation patterns, switch to facial and eye movements, and so on.

Other Tips for Compiling a Thick Record

One's first intensive observations ought to be typed into the computer thickly to help sharpen one's awareness of events that may occur routinely. After that, every third or fourth intensive observation may be entered into the computer with the aid of tape recordings.

Another practical suggestion is to choose an appropriate schedule for entering and exiting the field. I have found that observation periods longer than two hours will produce burnout when a thick record is being compiled. Choose two-hour blocks at different times of the day so as to catch the effects of time and organizational routine on interactions.

In terms of how many observation sessions to conduct, I can only say that this will vary a good deal according to the site one is investigating and the research questions one has in mind. I suggest you continue with stage one until you find yourself recording the same basic routines over and over again. At this point you have probably compiled an extensive enough primary record to move ahead with the next stages of inquiry. Make sure that you allowed time for the subjects to become accustomed to your presence and to make sure that you have solid information on body movements, vocal tones, and facial expressions in addition to verbatim speech acts. If you have met these conditions, it is probably time to move on to stages two and three. Often one will begin stage two with some initial reconstructions and then find from the analysis that more observations should be made focused on activities, times, or individuals inadequately represented in the primary record to this point.

Field Journal Notes vs. Thick Description

In your research design, you ought to carefully select certain sites and certain time periods for generating as thick a primary record as possible and then select other time periods and settings for constructing less formal field notes that will bear some relation to the thick record. In the TRUST study, the TRUST classroom was an obvious choice for intensive observations and thick description because the purpose of the study was to determine the nature of interactions within this classroom. The school corridors, teachers lounge, cafeteria, administration offices, and nearby park were good choices for constructing a less formal record.

Journalistic notes will be greatly aided through the use of key informants. I do not like the term "informant" because of the connotation of betrayal it carries. But informant has become a traditional term in the ethnographer's lexicon so we are basically stuck with it. For ethnographers, an informant is someone living on the site or in the culture of interest who is well connected and highly articulate. A good informant can tell you much about what goes on within a locale and why. In the TRUST study I often asked the park workers, Verna and Laticia, questions about the community, learning a lot from their answers; they were informants for my study. I also asked my former student Robert many questions about what went on in the school of West Forest; he, too, served as an informant for my study. I recorded my conversations with Verna, Laticia, and Robert in my field journal, along with my own impressions of nonintensively observed events.

Example of Field Journal Entries

In the TRUST study, I spent a fair amount of time chatting informally with teachers in the lounge, with administrators in the principal's office, and with various students and school personnel in the corridors of the school. I also spent time in the park observing the same children I was studying within the TRUST classroom. It would not have been possible to make a thick record of these less formal observations, but it was important to write down what I remembered from them as soon as possible later on in the day.

Here is an example of what such field journal entries look like, after typed into the computer.

First Journal Notes Typed into Computer
First meeting on the 22nd of January. From notebook 1.
Met Marilyn and Sue (counselors), Janet (principal), Louise, Alfred.
The school has 841 students—8th year there for Janet (principal).
TRUST began in September. At the end of October the first students entered the program.

*Those present commented that disruption referrals have gone down since TRUST began
because it is viewed as a stigma to go there. Getting assigned to TRUST is the end of a
long process of referrals, monitored by Robert in his role as vice principal.*

*Last year at this same date Robert had 600 referrals, this year he has had only half
that number.*

The teacher is brand new as a classroom teacher (Alfred).

*He observed in the cafeteria for several months as part of the process of choosing children
for the program.*

*The first student has a supportive family and did very well in the program. He moved
out after several months, now sees Alfred regularly at lunch time and has not been
disruptive to the extent that he was. The goal was to improve his self-esteem and his
coping mechanisms.*

*The first student said that he now "cares" whether he is good or bad, whereas before he
did not care.*

*TRUST began with Robert noting that last year he had 1,400 referrals for discipline prob-
lems. Thirty students were what he termed "frequent fliers"—taking the bulk of
the referrals.*

*West Forest also runs parenting classes at the school. Not brilliantly attended and parents
who most need it do not come.*

*They mentioned a "three-strike" system and "project Charley"—I will have to find out
what these are.*

In the classroom they do regular school work and also affective domain work.

*Mention of the discrepancy between forms of discipline and authority forms in the home
and in the school.*

They also have a "resource room" for students with learning disabilities.

These are typical field journal notes. They were partially written into my field journal
while talking with the school staff, with more comments written in shortly afterwards.
Comments are sketchy and jump from topic to topic. No verbatim speech acts were
captured in these particular notes, though sometimes it is possible to get an exact
quotation down.

RATIONALE FOR STAGE ONE: PASSIVE OBSERVATION

Whether interest is focused on a social site or a group of people transversing several
sites, it is best to begin a study in as nonobtrusive a manner as possible, which usually
comes down to passively conducting observations for a period of time. It is best to
begin a study in this way in order to reduce the effects of researcher presence on
routine activities as much as possible at first.

Of course, some studies cannot begin in this way. To study a group of people with
whom you have no prior relationship and who are involved in activities that would
lead them to mistrust strangers (such as a drug culture), one would have to interact a
good deal with the subjects to win and maintain their trust. In these cases, however, it

is necessary to take the stance of a student who has little to contribute and much to learn. Be conversant and get accepted by the group, but let them lead the action in every way. Be sure to set aside periods of time in which to take notes and observe passively whenever possible.

Reasons for Beginning with Passive Observation

The effect a researcher has on the events she wishes to study is known as the "Hawthorn effect" because of the famous study conducted on the Hawthorn plant during the 1920s. In this study, the mere presence of observers greatly affected the way in which their subjects behaved. Since the Hawthorn study was designed to measure the effect of certain "variables" on work performance, an effect produced by the presence of researchers destroyed the validity of the study.

Most qualitative studies, however, are not designed to measure the effects of independent variables on dependent variables. The concept of "variable" is not appropriate in qualitative research, according to this methodological, social, and philosophical theory. Action is conditioned, not determined. Analysis must focus on actions and their conditions, not on "variables."

Reconstructive analysis (stage two) focuses on one category of action conditions: cultural milieu or the norms, values, and beliefs of the people being studied. For this reason a Hawthorn effect is not damaging to a qualitative project. Alterations in behavior brought about by the presence of a researcher usually do not correspond to alterations in cultural milieu. Actors under investigation adapt the same cultural themes to the presence of the researcher and produce different behavior accordingly. Therefore, if properly conducted, reconstructive analysis and the analysis of system relations will not suffer from Hawthorn effects. The effects of a researcher on those being researched can even greatly clarify what one is after: the reconstruction of cultural forms.

It is extremely helpful, however, to produce a thick record of social routines in as naturalistic a form as possible to reduce analytic complications brought about by Hawthorn effects. This is why I suggest passive observation first, and more interactive modes of generating data later on, after a thick primary record has been constructed. It is not the fact that the researcher's presence changes behaviors that is the problem, but rather that it is important to know *how behaviors have changed* if one's reconstructions are going to be penetrating. In fact, the best reason for getting a thick record down before fully engaging with the subjects of study is to be able to compare two sets of data later on: the data collected in stage one as a passive observer and the data collected in stage three as a facilitator of talk and discussion. Contrasts between these two types of data can be extremely revealing.

CHAPTER CONCLUSION

This chapter has explained and illustrated what a primary record is in field research. Primary records should be built up in both thick and "not so thick," more journalistic, form. Thick records consist of highly detailed accounts of observed activity that include all speech acts in verbatim form and many observations of body movements and postures. Less thick records consist of impressions gathered during informal observation periods and conversations with key informants. The field journal looks a lot like a personal diary.

As an end to this chapter I will include another section of thick notes, continuing the interaction between Samuel and Alfred as they argued about taking a test:

[8] (Silence)

[9] S: *I can't do it. I don't get any help around here!* Loud voice. As if mixture of complaining and anger.

[10] (Silence)

9:44

[11] S: Samuel throws test on the floor. Hums a cheerful song. Arms still about chest but not as tightly drawn. Has turned to a new direction and is looking up toward ceiling/wall intersection.

[12] A: No response from Alfred.

[13] S: He moves around a lot. Gets up, takes his chair over to Ricardo's 4-desk table chair near Alfred and trades them. Kicks test on way back. Sits at carrel looking very bored. Did not make eye contact with Alfred, though moved close to him when getting chair.

[14] A: No response from Alfred even though this was a series of violations of class rules.

9:56

[15] A: *Samuel.* Very calm voice, gentle but as if mildly authoritative.

[16] A: Alfred has sat down upon table now.

[17] S: *What?* As if irritated.

[18] A: *Would you come up here please?* (over to the four desk table, from here on called the "table").

[19] A: Alfred has placed his hands on his hips, still sitting on table.

[20] S: He comes up with jacket pulled over head, looks at blackboard.

[21] S: *What?* Sharp and irritable type tone. Jacket still over head. Sitting down in chair as in a slouch with legs spread and extended.

[22] A: *We're at a very critical point now, aren't we?* Alfred remains calm in tone, looking at Samuel but Samuel not looking back.

[23] S: Samuel pulls jacket away from eyes but still does not look at Alfred. He pulls jacket down as if angry; a sudden, rapid, crisp movement.

[24] S: *I don't know what you're talking about.* Said almost as if disgusted.

[25] A: comments missed—something like what has just been going on?

[26] S: *(garbled) ... the test and I ain't going to do it.*

[27] A: *We're at a critical point (garbled).* Tone still calm.

[OC: As if, *"You know what is going on as well as I do, you are just refusing to talk about it. But I am patient."* Also, *"Things have gone too far and something bad is just going to have to happen unless we discuss it."*]

[28] S: *WHAT?!* Very loud, irritated, disgusted.

[29] A: *We're at a critical point (garbled).* Very calm.

[30] S: Samuel slouches on desk.

[31] A: *Sit up, please.*

[32] S: Samuel complains—words missed

[33] A: *You can sit up, though.*

[OC: Alfred's tone implies acceptance. "Though" said in way indicating acceptance of whatever complaint Samuel made but as a way to point out that, nevertheless, Samuel could sit up.]

10:07

[34] S: Samuel sits up as if annoyed at having to do so.

[35] (pause) Then Alfred says something about trying to get work accomplished.

[36] (silence)

[37] A: *Are you upset about home?* Tone implies calm: "reasonable."

4

Validity Claims and Three Ontological Realms

Items covered in Chapter 4:

- Definition of "validity claim"

- Validity claims in everyday life

- Objective, subjective, and normative-evaluative claims

- Objectivity vs. reality (optional)

- Multiple realities?

- Layers of subjectivity

- Ontological uncertainty (optional)

- Operational definitions vs. face-to-face interviewing

- The rationality of value claims

- "Meaning" and norms as explanatory concepts

- Normative truth claims

- Ending exercise

Now it is time to address some of those "hot questions" I mentioned at the beginning of the last chapter: what criteria exist by which to construct a "trustworthy" primary record? What criteria should be employed to make "valid" inferences on a primary record when analyzing data?

What Is "Validity"?

To answer these questions we will have to understand what "validity" means from a critical perspective. In traditional philosophy, validity refers to the soundness of arguments rather than to the truth of statements. For example, the following syllogism is valid but not true: "All horses have two heads, Lester is a horse, therefore Lester has two heads." If the premises were true, then the conclusion would also be true. Thus the argument is valid.

Critical epistemology borrows extensively from the American pragmatist school of philosophy, which defined truth in terms of consensus to truth claims. A truth claim is an assertion that something is right or wrong, good or bad, correct or incorrect. According to pragmatist philosophers like Dewey, Peirce, and James, the truth of the statement "All horses have two heads" can only be determined through the ability of this statement to win the agreement of a cultural community. Such community agreements can never settle a truth claim once and for all: a community consenting to any assertion (like "All horses have two heads," or "Lester is a horse") during one historical period may come to disagree with it during a later historical period. Thus all truth claims are fallible: They might come to be regarded as wrong during a later historical period or after one cultural group experiences contact with another.

The critical epistemology that has reached most rigorous formulation to date is that developed by Jurgen Habermas (1981, 1987b), who has borrowed some of these pragmatist ideas. With truth, what should be concentrated upon is not whether they are true or false in the traditional sense but rather whether they meet certain validity conditions necessary to win consensus. Truth claims should be translated into validity claims when they are to be carefully examined.

When truth claims are made, their ability to win the consensus of a cultural group is partly determined by certain universal standards; standards that are not culturally specific but that are rather rooted in the structures of human communication. These standards never give us an answer to the specific contents of a truth claim but rather give us criteria for determining whether or not a truth claim is valid in form.

Pragmatists suggest a different understanding of validity than what one will find in traditional logic and philosophy. Because truth itself depends on consensus, validity issues are not simply limited to the logic of an argument. Indeed, validity issues extend right into the premises of an argument. Whether a horse has two heads will depend on how a culture understands the terms "head" and "horse." However, cultural understandings of "head," "horse," and all other semantic categories are themselves rooted in social routines and in the necessity of achieving agreements to coordinate activities between people in everyday life. Thus, all cultural categories used in everyday contexts must be ones that are successful in human communication and in the coordination of human action. Pragmatists argue that a single, real, world exists independently from any cultural categories used to describe it and to act in relation to it. The real world is said to "resist" human activity so that only some types of cultural constructions are possible. If we claim that broken glass is not sharp and act toward broken glass in relation to this claim, "real" broken glass will "resist" our assertion and force us to change it (by cutting us!).

Thus, truth claims will be regulated from various directions, setting limits on the possible claims any culture could construct. One direction of regulation occurs from the conditions that must be met for people to understand each other and to argue their truth claims in an effort to win consensus. This direction gives us validity criteria. Another type of regulation or limitation on cultural truth claims comes from the direction of a real objective world that "resists" human action, making only some formulations possible (e.g.; broken glass is sharp and can cut). Yet another type of regulation, it can be argued, comes from universal forms of human experience and motivation: a set of universal human interests limiting truth claims of the normative-evaluative type (see below).

Critical epistemology focuses on validity more than truth, although criticalists tend to agree on the existence of a single objective reality that can only be represented in language and symbol systems mediated by power relations. Criticalists also implicitly agree, I think, in some set of universal human interests such as the value of democratic social forms (see below). It is the nature of validity, however, rather than truth that gives critical epistemology its methodological rigor. Validity, you will remember, is regarded by pragmatists and criticalists alike as inhering in the structures of communication. A truth claim cannot be conveyed to another person without these structures, and it will be understood as either a valid or an invalid claim according to how well it meets validity criteria derivable from the basics of communication itself.

Thus, a rule of thumb in critical epistemology could be phrased like this: whenever considering a truth claim, examine the validity conditions associated with it. What procedures have to be followed to try to win the consensus of any cultural group to the claim? Even more fundamentally, what procedures have to be followed and what conditions satisfied to ensure that other people simply understand the claim? Simply understanding another human being will entail processes fundamental to the theory of validity.

If a claim is made and supported in a way that meets its validity conditions, then it is to be regarded as "true" as long as it wins the consensus of potentially any cultural group. If groups disagree over the claim, then arguments should proceed that meet its validity conditions. This includes efforts made by disputants to understand the claim in an identical way. Such efforts can lead to debates over the appropriateness of cultural terms and categories for describing objective and subjective reality.

VALIDITY CLAIMS AND SOCIAL RESEARCH

A research report consists of a series of *validity claims:* claims that the data or field records produced are true to what occurred, claims that the analysis performed on the data was conducted correctly, and claims that the conceptual basis of the analytic techniques used is sound.

Remember the distinction between truth claims and validity claims. In critical social research, we immediately translate truth claims into validity claims, understanding that some of the content of any truth claim is going to be culturally bound. Our aim is to produce truth claims that have met their validity requirements and that are therefore well supported. We never claim to have the final "truth" of any issue pinned down, however, because we agree with the pragmatists that any assertion will always be fallible. We do think that following the validity requirements of any truth claim carefully will give us research findings that point toward truth; certain sections in this chapter will make this idea clearer. Critical methodologists are not "relativists";

we do not think that different cultures "construct" entirely different worlds and thus entirely different "truths." We acknowledge the mediation of culture in all truth claims, but we point out that all human beings, wittingly or not, assume a common reality whenever any attempt is made to reach understandings. This assumption is required by the structures of human communication. Moreover, empirical evidence supports this assumption that a common reality exists, because fundamental communication problems that could be expected if the case were otherwise have not generally occurred when diverse cultures come into contact with each other. I argue this more thoroughly in certain "optional reading" sections below.

VALIDITY CLAIMS IN EVERYDAY LIFE

Critical research methodology is distinctive from other approaches in that it traces the origin of our concept of validity back to everyday human interaction. This is true, at least, for the specific brand of critical methodology I advocate, which draws heavily from Habermas's work on validity (McCarthy 1978; Habermas 1981; 1987a, 1987b, 1988). The validity claims made by a researcher do not differ in nature from validity claims made by all people in everyday contexts. If we can understand the central role played by validity claims in normal human communications, we will then be able to formulate the special requirements that a social researcher conducting formal inquiries into social processes must employ to produce a trustworthy account.

In this chapter I will first illustrate the presence of validity claims in everyday human communication by examining more of the interaction between Alfred and Samuel in the TRUST classroom. Then I will use an exercise to produce some formal definitions of truth claims so that basic principles of epistemology, "critical epistemology," may be formulated. These principles will be used throughout the rest of this book both to specify the validity requirements that researchers should strive to meet and to construct a number of analytic models useful for qualitative data analysis.

Communicative Validity Claims

Let us begin by returning to the interaction between Alfred and Samuel in the TRUST classroom that I used to illustrate thick description in the last chapter. Alfred had asked Samuel to take a test, and Samuel refused. Alfred next changed the setting from one of a confrontation between teacher and pupil over taking a test toward one of an adult and a child discussing the pupil's problems. He did this by asking Samuel, in [37], whether he was upset about something taking place in his home.

Just below I will continue the notes. As the interaction proceeds, Samuel and Alfred develop an "interactive rhythm" that has the form of a tacit debate. As you read through the notes, pay close attention to Samuel's defensive strategies. Alfred is overtly asking Samuel questions about his mother and his feelings, but many of Alfred's questions also convey an under-articulated challenge to the response Samuel provided moments before. Samuel's responses are more oriented toward the background challenges Alfred is making than to the explicit questions Alfred asks. He defends himself from Alfred's challenges by referencing a number of tacit counterclaims.

Alfred's tacit claims bear a "field" characteristic that is more fully explained in chapter six. For now, simply note that a "meaning field" consists of *possible* claims referenced by an act of meaning. Neither the researcher nor Samuel can know for sure what Alfred *intends* by his remarks, but both the researcher and Samuel ascertain a field of possible meanings from Alfred. Samuel responds by focusing on one of the possible background claims in Alfred's challenging questions. Thus, he interprets the gist of Alfred's question and then defends himself against a tacit challenge carried by that interpretation.

Remember that a validity claim can always be derived from a truth claim: an assertion (explicit or implicit) that could be judged to be true or false, right or wrong, good or bad, correct or incorrect. Your job in this exercise is to articulate some of Samuel's counter truth claims (which we will translate as "validity claims" by focusing on the conditions that would have to be met to affirm them). To make the task more clear, I have embedded my own articulations of Alfred's tacit validity claims within the notes, using brackets and indentation to separate my interpretations from the actual field-notes. Your job is to articulate Samuel's counterclaims in much the same way.

Articulating Validity Claims from Field Notes

Here is the exercise. Remember that the bracketed comments after Alfred's speech acts are my reconstructions. You should produce articulations of Samuel's tacit claims in a similar manner. The next step is to try to devise a scheme for categorizing types of validity claims: the claims exemplified by this interaction fall into different categories, and I want you to try to figure out what these categories are.

Field Note Excerpt: Samuel and Alfred in Tacit Debate

[37] A: *Are you upset about home?* Tone implies calm: "reasonable."
  [*I think you are probably feeling upset because of things that happened at home; bad things happen at your home.*]

[38] S: *No.* Said in new tone, not angry or irritated, but as if a little defensive with intonation up by end of word.
  [*What are the possible, tacit validity claims?*]

[39] A: *No? Was mom home last night?*
  [*I don't believe you; You are not being honest with me; your mother often leaves home and/or your mother should not often leave home and/or some mothers stay at home with their children, some mothers leave their children, this is upsetting to the children, your mother is the kind that leaves her children at home.*]

[40] S: *Yeah.* Same sort of tone: intonation up at end of word.
  [*What are the possible, tacit validity claims?*]

[41] A: *Yeah?* As if not believing.
  [*I don't believe you, you are hiding the truth.*]

[42] S: *Yeah. And then she left.* Samuel's voice has become softer, his shoulders slump forward slightly and he looks down.

[*What are the possible, tacit validity claims?*]

[43] A: *And then she left? Where did she go this time?* Alfred has shifted over slightly on table toward Samuel.

[*Just as I suspected, your mother frequently leaves you to go out, as we both know.*]

[44] S: *She left to work on the car.* Tone implies defensive posture still. Samuel's body has straightened, eyes up but looking away from Alfred.

[*What are the possible, tacit validity claims?*]

[45] A: *Left to work on the car?* (pause) *Do you believe that's what she did?*

[*We both know she didn't go to work on the car, your mother lied to you, where she went was "bad," you are not being honest with me.*]

[46] S: *Umm.* Affirmative tone. Samuel looks at Alfred, puckering lips forward.

[*What are the possible, tacit validity claims?*]

[47] A: (something like, *do you like it when she does that?*)

[*I know you don't like it when she does that, and/or most kids wouldn't like their mothers to do that, and/or it is okay to feel bad about that so let's talk about it.*]

[48] S: *I don't care.* Eyes looking downish and away.

[*What are the possible, tacit validity claims?*]

[49] A: *You don't care (garbled—what she does)*

[*Tell me more about that, or, we both know you must care.*]

[50] S: *Umm.* Affirmative. Samuel is still looking away, looking up now.

[*What are the possible, tacit validity claims?*]

[51] A: *Why don't you care what she does?*

[*It is unusual not to care what your mother does, and/or, could you tell me more about not-caring, and/or I don't believe you don't care: prove it to me.*]

[52] S: *She can do what she wants.* Emphasis on "she."

[What are the possible, tacit validity claims?]

[53] A: *Uh umm, but how do you feel about it?*

[*It is okay to talk about how your mother's actions affect you without judging her, feelings are separate from judgments, and/or you have rights too.*]

[54] S: *I don't care.*

[*What are the possible, tacit validity claims?*]

[55] A: *You don't care being left with grandma then?* (pause, another remark that is garbled)

[Note: Grandma was very harsh with Samuel.]

[*You have told me in the past that you do not like being left with grandma, I don't believe you, we both know you are not being honest about this.*]

[56] S: *I don't care what I do anymore.* Emphasis on "I." Samuel has taken on more and more of a sort of "hopeless" posture during the last several interactions. He has resumed his slump and his eyes are cast toward the floor.

[What are the possible, tacit validity claims?]

[57] A: *Why don't you care what you do anymore?*

[58] S: (silence)

[59] A: *Why don't you care?*

Of course, we will continue with this interaction later on and see where it goes. In fact, we will subject these same interactions to more intensive forms of analysis in later chapters. But for the present you should have attempted to reconstruct some of Samuel's counterclaims; here are my ideas on them.

Samuel defends his position for a while in the beginning by making the following counterclaims: "My mother did not do anything last night that is unusual or worthy of discussion" [40], "My mother did work on the car" [46], "Mothers, like all people, have the right to do what they want" [52], "My mother did leave last night but this did not affect me emotionally" [54].

Alfred keeps pressing Samuel on these counterclaims until Samuel shifts the setting from a discussion of his mother to a discussion about himself [56]. The bid for a *setting shift* (chapters two and six) involves new tacit counterclaims: "I do feel unhappy, but this has to do with my own nature, not with anything my mother or grandmother do."

In terms of validity categories, Samuel defends himself by asserting that a certain objective event did in truth take place (his mother did in fact work on the car), asserting that his feelings are of such and such a nature (he did not have any significant feelings about his mother's behavior, he does have generally negative feelings about himself), and that certain norms and values deserve general recognition (mothers, all people, have the right to do what they want and should not be judged for doing what they want). So we have claims pertaining to objective-like events, subjective states, and claims about what is good and bad. In this chapter, these three categories of claim will be given formal names, fully fleshed out, and linked to an ontological framework.

Ontological Categories and Validity Claims

As a second exercise, I want you to read through the list of statements presented below and consider the nature of the validity claim each *explicitly* makes. Do not worry too much about what is backgrounded in the case of these statements. I will then discuss each statement in turn, providing a fair amount of detail on each ontological category illustrated and its philosophical/methodological ramifications. At times the discussion becomes rather dense, and I have put "optional reading" at the end of certain section headings. If you wish, you can skip the dense sections marked as optional reading.

Once again, readers must know that the inspiration for this chapter comes from the work of Jurgen Habermas and his theory of communicative action (1981, 1987a, 1987b). Habermas has given us the theory of ontological categories as universal features of human communication. However, I have modified Habermas slightly here and there in this discussion and have developed certain methodological implications of his ideas in ways left untreated by him. In addition, the manner in which I present

Habermas's theory of three ontological categories is very different from the manner in which Habermas presents his own views. I believe that my presentation is more accessible than what one will find in Habermas's books. Many students and professors have not read Habermas carefully because of his habit of pitching arguments at very high levels of abstraction. Many people find Habermas's exceedingly dense style of writing difficult to penetrate. My own presentation is meant to be much more accessible.

Each statement below is typical of statements people make every day. Each is also typical in basic form of the sorts of statements one can find in research hypotheses and research conclusions. Each statement is an *assertion,* which is to say that each makes a claim about reality that one could be asked to defend. To simplify things, I have made most of these statements assertions of "fact" (a statement that such and such is the case) and have put in no explicit statements of law or of general relationship between two or more items. I do not include statements like "poverty is a cause of crime" or "constructivist pedagogy produces more creative individuals than traditional pedagogy." We must be clear about validity claims accompanying statements of the factual sort before we can begin to understand validity claims involved in assertions of general relations between terms. However, my discussion of the last of these seven statements will require considerations of social regularities: of the relationship between patterned and predictable activity to conditions that help to explain the regularities one may observe.

Seven Statements and Their Presuppositions

Please read each statement below. Imagine yourself asserting each in a situation where you would believe it to be valid, and then ask yourself how you could go about defending the statement if someone expressed disagreement with it. Ask yourself what arguments or procedures you would use to support the validity of each statement if you were convinced it were true but someone disagreed. See whether these statements can be grouped into categories determined by the manner in which one would have to support their claim to be valid or true.

1. There are four, and only four, chairs in my office today.
2. There are three males and five females in the corridor at this time.
3. Your next-door neighbor likes you.
4. Bill is angry, he just doesn't know he is.
5. Eighty-six people committed suicide in Houston last year.
6. Poverty is bad.
7. Generally speaking, American people will avoid eye contact with strangers on elevators.

I will now discuss each statement in turn.

1. *There are four, and only four, chairs in my office today.*

For most people in everyday contexts of life, this statement may easily be determined as either true or false through simple observation and counting procedures. This holds for scientists as well. Observation and counting are the two processes required to justify this statement. If someone disagrees, we could invite them to observe and count. If that is impossible, we could probably convince them by taking a picture or having any number of other people observe, count, and report their findings to the disbeliever.

Prerequisites for defending statements based on observation and measurement

Some of you, however, have probably already thought, "But we must be sure we have a common definition of 'chair.' The person who does not agree with the statement may have a different idea of what a chair is than we do." This is basically true, and it qualifies our assertion that the truth or falsity of statement (1) is determinable with certainty. Another qualification is the process of counting: we must be clear on what we mean by "four." Both of these two qualifications are usually not given much weight if a statement like (1) is made between people sharing the same language and culture. If cultural differences explicitly enter into the context of making a statement like this one, efforts would have to be made to convey the concepts of "chair," "number," and "counting" to the members of the other cultural group. If a consensus may be reached on the terms and procedures, the statement could then be determined as true or false with high levels of certainty by all those involved through using observation and counting procedures.

The general significance of these two qualifications can be stated concisely:

1. Validity claims based on observation and measurement procedures amount to claims that all other people would agree with the statement made if they were present to observe and conduct the same measurement procedures as employed by the person making the claim.
2. Agreement of this kind, however, presupposes a shared object-term (in this case "chair") and a shared measurement procedure (in this case counting and the concept of number underlying it).
3. Therefore, disagreements on validity claims of this sort can be adjudicated through repeated observations and measurements, and/or through
4. Discussions of the object-terms and measurement procedures employed in order to obtain consensus with respect to them.

Yet another qualification may have occurred to you, the possibility of having hallucinations. What if I see four chairs in my office and everyone else who comes in states that they see three? If we seem to agree on our definition of chair and if we share a language with totally isomorphic conceptions of number and counting (some cultures have only four number terms: one, two, three, and more than three), then probably it would be decided that I see things that are not "really there." This would mean that I had had an "hallucination," or that my eyes malfunction in some systematic way, or that I was daydreaming at the time, or that I am "crazy."

The general significance of this third qualification is the emphasis it places on processes of reaching agreement on validity claims about observable objects. In everyday contexts, disagreement on claims about the object-world that cannot be resolved, either through repeated observations or discussions of terms and measurements, will lead to the claim that one of the disputants has observed things that "are not really there." Cultures have terms for explaining such rare instances of disagreement: "hallucination," "insanity," "stupidity," and so on will all do the job depending on circumstances.

The First Ontological Category: Objectivity

Statement (1) presupposes an ontological category: "objectivity" or the "objective realm." When truth claims like (1) are made in everyday contexts of life, as well as in scientific research, they are made against the presupposition that other people could observe in the same way as the observer to arrive at an agreement with the statement. This presupposition is an ontological one in that it frames the concept of "chair," or, in general terms, the concept of a "sense object," in a particular way. One must believe that sense objects *exist* in such a way as to be open to multiple observers who will agree on their existence if they share certain features of a language and a culture. To say that objective-realm entities *exist* is to say that they are accessible to multiple observers.

The Appearance vs. Reality Distinction

Following Habermas, we note that a contrast between "appearance and reality" is a feature of the objective realm. In a disagreement, people will reference an assumption that there is one objective reality about which they are trying to establish an agreement. A disagreement means that an error occurred in the observation of this one reality or that the terms used to describe this one reality differ between parties. If the latter is deemed to be the case, the reality of the object will be appealed to in redefining or rearranging observation terms so that a consensus may be reached. Finally, if repeated observations and/or discussions of terms fail to produce consensus, it will usually be assumed that one party has experienced a false appearance. For this party, appearance and reality do not match, and cultures provide reasons for such mismatches with terms like "hallucination."

In some cultural communities, notably some academic ones, a failure at consensus over objective-referenced truth claims can result in alternative configurations of the appearance vs. reality distinction. One such community, "social constructivists" (Guba 1990a; Lincoln 1990), would explain lack of consensus on objective claims by arguing that there is no difference between "reality" and "appearance." A lack of consensus can occur between people of diverse cultural backgrounds because the frameworks employed by each group are incommensurable with each other; no mere discussion of object terms will resolve the disagreement.

I will discuss this idea again a little later on in a section in this chapter on "multiple realities." Let us note here, however, that this alternative view acknowledges that people sharing a single cultural framework must act as if there is a shared reality and that minor disagreements between people of the same group will employ the appearance vs. reality distinction, even if it has no *ultimate* ontological foundation (even if, ultimately, there is no single, common reality).

Definition of the Objective Ontological Category: "The" World

The objective category is presupposed by all statements that can be understood and then judged as true or false according to the principle of multiple access. Objective-referenced truth claims are claims that others would agree with one's observations and thus depend upon a presupposed ontological category to which all humans in principle have access through their senses. This category is structured through the opposition between appearance and reality. Because this category is structured fundamentally according to the principle of multiple access, it involves a notion of *the* world—a single world which is "the same" for all people (McCarthy 1978). When different ways of interpreting this same world are pointed out, this is explained through the appearance vs. reality distinction.

Fine Points: Objectivity vs. Reality (Optional Reading)

Note that I am not saying that there is an objective realm that really exists outside of all human efforts to know and describe it in what I have said so far. Up to this point I have only written of the objective *category* and have merely associated it with one type of truth claim. Throughout this book I will frequently use the phrase "objective realm," but this must be understood to be an ontological *presupposition* that is unavoidable when making certain types of truth claims. It is a necessary presupposition in human communication.

But this does not mean that objectivity exists aside from, independently of, human culture, language, and knowledge. The reader may accept all that has been said about objectivity so far and remain agnostic on the question of whether an objective reality exists aside from human references to it. The point that must be understood, however, is that certain types of truth claim depend on references to a realm of objects to which humans have multiple access. Within any particular culture or discourse, an objective realm is constructed as a world of objects to which all have direct access. The question of whether or not "real" objects ultimately structure the possible ways of constructing an objective realm is not an issue at this point. One can take either a realist position, a constructivist position, or remain agnostic.

Another fine point can be noted here. My references to the senses and to "sense objects" are not essential to the objective category. The concept of "sense" is not, in fact, central to the objective realm, only multiple access is. In western culture, multiple access has increasingly become understood as dependent on the senses of sight, hearing, touch, smell, and taste, but in other cultures this is not necessarily so. The distinction westerners commonly make between a behavior (which is observable through the senses) and the subjective state of the actor (which is not observable as such) is not necessarily universal to all cultures. "He is mad" might be an objectively framed assertion for members of a different cultural group if there is a consensus within this group that certain modes of acting simply *are* "being mad."

But cultures that seem, from our perspective, to "conflate" subjective and objective terms still use the category of multiple access, still presuppose the objective realm in a large number of day-to-day communications. In the case of our example, "madness" would be an objective-referenced term for the culture in question. Many additional fine points emerge from this but will not be examined here due to lack of space.

2. *There are three males and five females in the corridor at this time.*

Statement (2) may have caused many of you to think, "Oh, he is trying to trick us! What about medically induced sex changes?" Sex changes are these days well-known occurrences. We are used to such statements as this one: "A person may appear to be a woman, even when undressed, when in fact she is a man!" and we find no problem in understanding such remarks. People living during the early part of this century and during the centuries before, of course, would not have found such remarks readily intelligible.

The reason I put statement (2) into the list was to illustrate further the dependency of objective-realm validity claims on shared cultural terms and definitions and to show once again how the appearance vs. reality distinction enters into play with all objective-realm statements. Statement (2) illustrates how, within a single culture, different social contexts may produce different ways of characterizing the "same" object.

During the course of our everyday lives, we are usually able to determine whether a new acquaintance is male or female. In fact, it commonly produces a feeling of discomfort if one is not able to determine the gender of the other person. Not "knowing" the gender of someone else makes it difficult to interpret what s/he expresses toward you and difficult to know how to act toward her/him.

Since the advent of genetic theory and surgical/biochemical techniques for bringing about sex changes, the definition of male and female has undergone certain changes. Olympic Games officials now use chromosome tests to determine the "real sex" of contestants; a person with whom you would interact as a female in the grocery store might be considered a male by Olympic Games officials.

Note that it would be sterile to ask which understanding of gender is the "correct" one. In most social contexts, chromosomes play no part in the validity of judgments regarding gender. Whatever the chromosomes, a social researcher will be able to determine the gender composition of a social setting, objectively, in terms of how gender is constructed by interactions. The social researcher will be interested in the objective-referenced gender claims of the population under study, and these will almost always command a consensus within the group, regardless of chromosomes.

In one sense, then, gender is a category characterized by "multiple realities." In some settings one way of defining gender prevails, in other settings a different way prevails. Thus the same person might be regarded as male in one setting and, female in another, and it is entirely appropriate to regard such a person as being "both," depending on which context is in play. The culture, the discourse, seems to construct the objective realm.

Multiple Realities? (Optional Reading)

Some writers use more extreme examples than that of gender to argue for the existence of "multiple realities," where multiple *objective* realities is meant. It was long believed, apparently incorrectly, that Eskimo language employs many different terms to refer to those perceptual phenomena that English speakers simply classify as "snow." Recently I read that Eskimo language has only two or three terms for "snow," but let us stick with the myth to illustrate a general point. Would Eskimos also perceive "snow" differently than us, if they had so many different terms referenced to it?

In the work of Benjamin Whorf, Navaho language is described as embedding vastly different concepts of time than do Western European languages. Do Navahos experience time differently? Does language construct the world, simply interpret it, or directly represent it?

For our purposes, the ultimate ramifications of this question may be shelved; they will not affect our social theory or our research methodology. All we need to be clear on is the manner in which an objective realm is presupposed by certain common types of truth claims and references. When presupposed, the principle of multiple access and the appearance vs. reality distinction are unavoidably put into play. When a social researcher encounters situations in which a population of people—like Eskimos, Navahos, Olympic Games officials, or grocery store shoppers—describes or references an objective entity differently than the researcher ordinarily does, this must be noted as an interesting finding. The manner in which the claim is made, the terms and procedures associated with it, must be learned. This sort of finding is not uncommon in field work and could be superficially described as the discovery of "multiple realities," multiple objective realms experienced by diverse cultural groups.

However, in all the examples given above, the description of multiple realities given by the researcher references a new, single, objective realm. The gender example is intelligible only if we take the case of "the same person" who is defined male in one context, female in another. A reference is made to "same person" such that this entity preserves its identity across the two "realities" described. Gender no longer refers to an essential feature of the entity, but to one of its qualities.

Similarly, the example of Eskimo language is intelligible only through the assumption that the "same thing" is divided up in different ways by different languages and/or interpretative schemes. To convey the general idea of a contrast between Eskimo and English language regarding "snow," a range of objective entities is presupposed to be in essence "the same," although interpreted and categorized differently. For English speakers, Eskimos must be understood as having names for "different types of snow" (crusty, fluffy, icy, dry, wet, etc.), while English speakers have a name for what is common to all these types.

Thus the concept of "multiple realities," particularly where it refers to objective-realm entities, is most immediately intelligible through the appearance vs. reality distinction. Every time someone translates one system of constructing objectivity into another system, or even simply provides the general idea of where the two systems differ, *new* objective entities are referenced in such a way as to underlie both systems. Qualities keep splitting off from some presupposed essence. When describing multiple objective realities, a single objective reality is referenced necessarily, and the description takes the form of *different appearances rendered through different interpretative schemes of the* same *reality.*

Now, imagine a prolonged debate over features of objective reality in which all cultures of the world participate. Eventually, a common set of object terms is constructed to which all parties agree. Do we now have a perfect correspondence between objective reality and our system of symbols? The answer is that we could never know. Science has basically attempted this very feat by producing a specialized language into which a few members of every cultural group in the world are socialized. But scientific language is still a cultural language: it is still highly possible (probable, in fact) that scientific cultures of the future will discard current terms and invent new ones that give better problem-solving power. This fallible feature of all object symbol systems can never be removed.

Extreme versions of relativism argue from this point that the "same reality" referred to, necessarily, in every effort to communicate about entities possessing the quality of multiple access is nothing but a "flux." It has no form or qualities in itself and will have none until a symbol system is imprinted upon it.

But one can question this idea of a formless flux. Objective reality does seem to "resist" human action and thought: not just any system of representation works for dealing with the world of multiple access. Moreover, the concept of "flux" is itself dependent on shared perceptual experiences. It is a metaphorical concept that brings "blurs" and "mists" and other shared phenomena to mind. It is usually used as an ontological concept, referring to a reality independent of human experience and knowledge that is, however, "formless" and "shapeless" in essence. Philosophically, this is a very problematical idea, one rejected by most critical theorists.

3. *Your next-door neighbor likes you.*

Probably you have noted that this statement is not knowable with certainty, at least in the same way that the number of chairs in a room is. Novels and films are often based on the quite common social phenomena of deception: false lovers convince their victims of undying affection, only to run off with the money after the marriage ceremony; double agents dupe their colleagues into believing them loyal and beyond suspicion, only to place the blueprints of a new weapon system into the hands of the enemy.

Statement number (3) similarly brings the possibility of deception to mind. The state of "liking" someone is not an objective-referenced phenomenon; it is not characterized by multiple access. For you to defend this statement against the counter-claims of another you could only point out consistent, objectively accessible, modes of behavior which your neighbor exhibits toward you, and these modes of behavior would have to be culturally defined as *indications* of "liking." Your antagonist, however, could in principle agree that the modes of behavior you draw attention to are in fact consistently exhibited by your neighbor, agree that such modes of behavior generally indicate "liking," but still dispute your claim by saying something like: "But I believe she is just *acting* that way."

"Liking" cannot be reduced to the objectively observable behaviors that a particular culture will take as its indicators. The existence of a state of "liking" differs in kind from the existence of "chairs." The latter kind of existing is structured by multiple access, the former is structured differently: no amount of repeated observations could absolutely settle the question of whether or not your neighbor likes you, no matter how tight the agreement on what "liking" means.

The Second Ontological Category: Subjectivity

Many statements made in the course of daily life and in the course of a research project concern emotions, desires, intentions, levels of awareness, and so on, to which an outside observer can never have direct access. All such items are understood against the background of an ontological category characterized by privileged access rather than multiple access. I have privileged access to my own subjective domain in that I may conceal or reveal it to others. When revealing my subjective states, moreover, others must assume that I am being honest in my disclosures if they are to feel any degree of certainty with respect to my feelings.

The act of disclosure is not the subjective state disclosed; it is a representation of it. All actors have a certain amount of control over what they reveal of their realm of privileged access and what they conceal.

What about the relatively common experience of "giving yourself away," blurting out a self-disclosing statement before you could stop yourself, or betraying a state of nervousness you wish to conceal through shaking fingers and trembling voice? Even in cases like these, the fundamental structure of privileged access is in play. No matter how unconvincing you may be, you always have the option of denying the significance of your shaking fingers or of giving it a different interpretation: "Sorry my fingers seem to be shaking, coffee always does that to me." If others persist in taking your self-betraying behaviors to mean exactly what you wish to conceal, the structure of the claim remains the same: "nervousness" and all other subjective-referenced terms are conceived in distinction from the behaviors we take to indicate them. The behaviors in question are objective-referenced events open to multiple access; the subjective states we associate with them must be inferred and are not by nature perceivable.

The Self-Knowledge vs. Performance Distinction

Once again you will notice a distinction between "appearance" and "reality" in play, but it is not identical to the distinction that structures the objective realm. Here, "reality" refers to one's real feelings, desires, and intentions, rather than to an object open to multiple access. "Appearance" must also be conceived differently here. Instead of referring to something akin to "sense impressions" it refers to symbolic activity which is in principle under the control of the actor. The distinction may be better expressed as that between the *self-knowledge* of the actor and her *performance* (reinterpreting Habermas slightly here: see McCarthy 1978).

Disputes taking place over objective-referenced claims are structured by the appearance vs. reality distinction, in that each disputant can ask the other to observe again or to make an effort to understand certain object-terms and measurement procedures. If these efforts at patching up a disagreement fail, one has to appeal to others for support in one's own claims. And when such support is forthcoming it is possible to claim that the second person in the dispute is experiencing a "false appearance" for whatever reason.

Disputes taking place over subjective-referenced claims are ultimately structured by the self-knowledge vs. performance distinction. The core validity claim concerns "my world," "her world," or "your world," rather than "the" world. Hence, only a self-report can approach validation of any claim that is subjective-referenced. The validity of a self-report depends upon something that only one person has control over: honesty. When people in everyday interactions reference their own subjective states, they do so alongside the claim that they are being honest. When people make claims about the subjective states of others, their claims boil down to the core claim that these others would confirm such statements if honest.

Definition of the Subjective Category: "My," "Her," "Your" World

The subjective category is presupposed by all statements that can be understood only with the concomitant understanding that privileged access to a certain form of experience is in play. Claims referenced to subjectivity are structured by the distinction between self-knowledge and performance. This makes the honesty or veracity of the actor in question central to all subjective-referenced claims. Subjective-referenced truth claims are claims that the person whose subjectivity is referred to would confirm the statement about her subjective state if she were honest in her self-disclosure. Because this category is structured fundamentally according to the principle of privileged access, it involves a notion of my world, her world, and your world. But what about the next statement?

4. *Bill is angry, he just doesn't know he is.*

Privileged access to our own subjective states is sometimes affected by processes of repression or by a paucity of cultural terms with which to describe our "real" feelings.

In fact, sometimes others might seem to have a better idea of how we "really feel" than we do. Perhaps with the skilled intervention of a counselor or therapist, Bill will realize that he is often angry without awareness of it. Without such skilled intervention, Bill may continue to express honestly his lack of anger while we continue to believe he is chronically angry; he just doesn't know he is. This seems to complicate our understanding of the second ontological category, subjectivity.

However, even in such cases as these, where what we currently consider to be unconscious psychological processes are in play (e.g., repression) or where a feeling exists that is systematically misinterpreted by an entire culture (e.g., certain modes of sexual desire in Victorian England), there is always a subjective state of awareness (distorted or not) that a person has privileged access to and that can be revealed or concealed from others. Bill believes he does not feel angry. Bill's privileged access to his own subjective state does not give him the idea that he is angry. And Bill can either conceal or reveal his lack of a feeling of anger to others.

Our statement that Bill is in fact angry but does not realize it is structured by the category of subjectivity in complex ways. It amounts to saying:

1. Bill does not in fact *experience* anger.
2. "Deep down," Bill really *is* angry.
3. Therefore a psychological process is operating "within" Bill of which he is not aware and that systematically bars him from feeling something that affects his behavior and "psychological states." Thus a distinction between "subjective state" and "psychological state" is involved.

Such claims as this one are common in western culture during this current historical period. They in fact depend upon two senses of subjectivity. One sense completely corresponds to my discussion of "Your next-door neighbor likes you." Part of the claim in sentence (4) is that Bill does not feel anger. This claim can best be supported through eliciting self-reports from Bill about what he feels. In his self-reports Bill has some amount of control, lacking to us, over whether he will be honest or dishonest. The first sense of subjectivity thus involves the concept of privileged access and the related distinction between "self-knowledge" and "performance," exactly as elucidated in the case of "Your neighbor likes you."

The second sense of subjectivity is that of the "inner" as opposed to the "outer." Different psychological and psychoanalytical theories treat this idea in different ways, but in general we can say that this sense of subjectivity refers, for Bill, to a "potential" experience of the privileged sort, which is blocked for various reasons. Removal of the blockage through a counseling or therapeutic process will result in a privileged experience of the relevant emotion on the part of the person in question. To validate this claim, the distinction between privileged access and multiple access must still be in play. We cannot claim to know that Bill "is angry" but does not acknowledge it; we can only claim that various evidence provided by Bill's behavior strongly suggests this. Our claim would receive its strongest support if Bill was brought around to saying that he now feels the anger we are talking about, after some cathartic process has taken place. This is the ultimate support possible for any claim involving layered subjectivity and it collapses into the same set of conditions described above that structure subjective-referenced claims. Bill's honesty and privileged access to his own experiences are, in the end, always *the* basic factors structuring the situation.

Fine Points: Subjectivity, Objectivity, and Ontological Uncertainty (Optional Reading)

Philosophically, statement (4) raises some interesting issues that are quite congruent with issues raised regarding the ultimate nature of objectivity. Is subjectivity something that simply occurs in an "inner realm" and then is either revealed to, or repressed from, the awareness of the subject? Or is subjectivity a construction of the cultural terms employed to describe it or represent it in performances to others? Or is there an intermediate case, that subjectivity arises and is then interpreted by the one experiencing it either accurately or inaccurately through cultural interpretative schemes? These questions are absolutely congruent with those asked above regarding the ultimate nature of objectivity.

Once again we can shelve this question and only hang onto the concept of subjectivity as a formal ontological category presupposed by certain types of truth claims and referenced in communication. Within communication, subjective states are claimed to be present as such within the privileged experience of a subject. Just as different appearances may be ascribed to "the same" object, so different interpretations may be discussed of "the same" subjective experience. But whether or not there "really is" a single subjective experience at any given time is not determined one way or the other by elucidating the formal communicative category of subjectivity.

For example, when we discuss the plight of upper-class women in Victorian English society, we might find it plausible to believe they felt "angry" more often than they could inwardly acknowledge, because "anger" was not considered a feminine attribute, a proper feeling for a "lady" to have. We might think correspondingly that Victorian upper-class women were repressed by their culture. What they called "hysteria," perhaps, was "really" suppressed anger brought about by a terribly sexist culture. To believe this is to believe that certain subjective experiences occur in essential independence from the cultural terms available with which to describe them. Our formal category of "subjectivity" and its structures, however, does not allow us any support for such a belief. Support for the idea that subjective states are independent from cultural interpretative frameworks must come from elsewhere and must make use of a distinction between "subjective states" and "psychological states," which I have so far made no effort to clarify or defend.

Now, to point out that elucidation of the formal categories of subjectivity and objectivity does not depend upon taking a position on the ultimate nature of objective and subjective phenomena is not simply to skirt a difficult issue. The fact that discovering our common use of these formal categories does not tell us anything about their absolute nature is itself a structure of communication.

This is an important point. Objective-referenced entities and subjective-referenced states come into truth claims and communicative acts as fundamentally uncertain in nature. All validity claims involving objectivity and subjectivity can be doubted in some way. This core characteristic of uncertainty in objective and subjective claims structures communication in important ways. It is a feature of what I shall later call the "uncertainty principle of meaning" and "ontological uncertainty."

5. *Eighty-six people committed suicide in Houston last year.*

I can hear many of you commenting on this statement by pointing out that suicides depend on coroners' reports, and thus any published numbers must be qualified by an unknown and unknowable amount of "coroner error." In addition, you may have considered the fact that not all deaths are brought to the attention of a coroner, so that some suicides will be missed in the official records for this reason. These are important qualifications on any assertions regarding the number of suicides that took place in a certain place at a certain time. Many "facts" in social research must be gathered with the same such limitations: the number of babies born, the number of immigrants, the number of school dropouts, etc., are all ascertainable mainly through official systems of record keeping, which are certainly subject to error.

However, this is not the reason why I placed statement (5) in with the rest. Unlike a birth, an immigrant, or a dropout, a suicide is not a wholly objectively framed category. It is a category that depends on both objective and subjective references simultaneously. A suicide occurs when a person takes her life and does so intentionally. Thus objective measurement procedures alone will never determine with absolute certainty whether a death was a suicide.

A man steps in front of you on the sidewalk, draws a pistol to his head, and fires, killing himself before your very eyes. Apparently a suicide, but could we ever be absolutely certain that he wasn't simply trying to alarm you by using what he thought was an unloaded gun? No, we cannot. Social research will often encounter objective-like terms that partially depend upon subjective-references and thus can never be validated through measurements alone.

Operational Definitions vs. Face-to-Face Interviewing

Statement (5) gives me an excuse to discuss the concept of operational definition within this scheme of ontological categories. Suicides, homicides, and certain other categories of social activity all mix observable criteria with subjective-referenced criteria in their definitions. In a court of law, the difference between a homicide and an act of manslaughter is absolutely crucial, and it is a difference that depends entirely on the subjective state of the offender during the criminal act. Standards for judging the honesty of a self-report must be routinely employed to build a case with respect to the nature of an actor's intentions. Such standards commonly concern the consistency of a person's activities over a period of time, the consistency of the account given by a person of her own behavior, and evidence of self-disclosures made to other people at various times. Such standards can never conclusively prove that a person ever acted with one intention as opposed to another, but they can certainly help build a case in support of one view over the other. That is the best that can ever be done with the subjective-references involved in any validity claim.

Social scientists, unlike lawyers, must often make decisions regarding the subjective realm without recourse to a process of closely interrogating or interviewing a subject. Any study that deals with large numbers of people, such as a survey, must deal with subjective-referenced claims without the benefit of face-to-face interactions between researcher and subjects. The usual method for dealing with this problem is the operational definition.

An *operational definition,* as discussed in chapter two, is a rigorous way of mapping a concept involving multiple ontological references onto the objective realm alone. This is done by defining a term popularly conceived in reference to subjectivity solely in terms of objective measurement procedures. This is risky. If poorly constructed, an operational definition may rob a particular concept of its significance to the researcher.

One may wish to study, for example, pedagogic factors that contribute to the enhancement of "self-esteem" in classrooms. The value of such a study is obvious: there is the consensus in our society that high self-esteem is a "good thing." But what does "self-esteem" refer to? It refers to something like one's general feelings about one's self, one's self-perceptions, or one's self-concept, and is thus a subjective-referenced affair. If we wish to conduct our study with a large sample of students, we will have to operationalize the concept of high self-esteem so that it comes to mean something like a high score on a certain attitude scale. Instrument scales produce objective phenomena, open to multiple measurements and repeated observations.

But scales designed to indicate subjective states must be carefully thought out. They will always depend on the honesty of each person filling them out as well as on a congruence between the manner in which the researcher interprets the survey questions and the manner in which the subjects do. Procedures exist to enhance the probability of getting honest responses and congruent interpretations, but there is always the risk of incorrect inferences with respect to the subjectivity of a research population when operational definitions are employed.

The general point here is that researchers must be aware of which ontological categories are at play when asking research questions and designing a method of inquiry. Operational definitions map all other ontological categories onto the single category of objectivity. Many assumptions must be made when constructing such maps. If a count of suicides is important to a particular study, an operational definition is unavoidable, but the assumptions employed must be carefully explicated and set forth.

Fortunately, in qualitative research operational definitions can usually be avoided. A good general rule for qualitative researchers is to approach the subjective realm without operationalizing. Sound interview techniques exist (described in chapter ten) that will build up a much more solid case for subjective-referenced research claims than any operational definition can provide. This is true for several reasons worth listing here:

1. In face-to-face interviewing, a larger number of checks can be brought to bear on the self-disclosures of people than can be brought to bear through instruments like attitude scales.

2. In face-to-face interviews, the problem of cultural blindness can be much better overcome than is the case with self-report instruments. Interviewing is flexible so that the researcher may continuously revise her understanding of core cultural categories employed by her subjects of study. She can alter her interview protocol after and even during every interview.

3. Only a face-to-face interview can adequately deal with the problem of layered subjectivity by facilitating the rise into awareness of subjective states routinely repressed or misinterpreted by an interviewee in most social settings. In qualitative interviews, we basically work with an heuristic understanding of the subjective states/psychological states distinction. It is extremely common to find that what people will say about their attitudes and feelings during initial stages of an interview alters a great deal by the end, and this without the use of any "leading" questions on the interviewer's part. Only some theory that differentiates between subjective states and their interpretation can explain this phenomenon well. For the qualitative researcher, evidence of alterations in self-awareness produces rich data that an instrument can never reach.

6. *Poverty is bad.*

By the time most of my students come to take my courses in research methodology, they have been trained to regard statements like (6) as "subjective," by which they mean "just opinion." Statement (6) is a value claim, and value claims are not regarded as truth claims in mainstream social science. Values are generally acknowledged to be what motivates research because, for example, studies about poverty, its causes, and its effects, will be conducted due to certain concerns held by the researcher and funding agencies. But value claims are usually excluded from the research process itself. They are not perceived as truth claims, which can be determined as valid or invalid through some sort of "scientific" procedure.

Yet at this point in the discussion, it is easy to see that value claims are not subjective, in the way I have characterized subjectivity. Privileged access is not a core principle structuring value claims. If I say: "Poverty is really bad," the only thing subjective about my statement is the implicit claim that "*I believe* poverty is really bad." Whether poverty is in fact bad can be debated without us concerning ourselves over whether I or anyone else believes it bad.

Value claims can be argued for and supported in various manners; people argue about values in structured ways all the time. Arguments over values take typical forms such that underlying structures or principles are in play. It is wrong to say that values are "just opinion." These underlying principles do not work directly with either the principle of multiple access nor the principle of privileged access. Distinctive principles are at work, and they correspond to a third ontological category implied in all value claims.

The Rationality of Value Claims

It will not be a straightforward matter to introduce this third ontological category, for the category itself is rather complex. Here we can simply define what values are.

Values may be regarded as views of what is good, bad, right, and wrong.

As my arguments proceed, a particular conception of values will emerge that renders them as a special subset of a larger category, the category I will call the "normative-evaluative realm." Values will be shown to be among several constituents of meaning, related to but distinguished from norms. But a sequence of conceptual arguments will have to be developed to bring us to a full understanding of all that is involved in the "normative-evaluative realm." These arguments will begin in the next section of this chapter but only become fully manifest by the end of the book.

Here it is important to note only that value claims are a type of truth claim or validity claim having properties distinctive from the objective and subjective realms. The manner in which values are supported or disputed in arguments consists of efforts between disputants to articulate an agreement on some value claims so that arguments may be developed from such agreements toward the value claim in dispute.

The rationality of value argumentation depends on a beginning consensus that is not supportable through the principles of either multiple access or privileged access. With a beginning consensus in place, argumentation proceeds through efforts to logically link the beginning consensus to the value position in dispute. Let me clarify this point by returning to the statement: "Poverty is bad."

Is poverty bad? Many people think so, but some people do not. Some people think that there has always been an impoverished class and always will be; there must be some reason for it; it's a "natural" state of affairs. Still other people have argued for the "positive social functions" that a certain amount of poverty fulfills. For example, it keeps a class of unemployed people ready to assume menial jobs during periods when the economy expands. Since modern society needs such a population of ready workers, poverty is not bad, according to this view. Large numbers of us, however, find poverty repugnant in every way: definitely a bad thing.

Now imagine someone asserting that poverty is not ultimately a bad thing because "there has always been poverty and always will be; it is natural." We disagree. How would argumentation proceed? Well, it could proceed in many different ways. One line of attack for us could be that of undermining the objective reference made by our opponent. Poverty has not always been in existence, because many preagricultural societies are known to exist without poverty. Nor is there any evidence that poverty will always exist. Therefore, there is no reason to think that poverty is "natural." If we argue in this way, we are putting the objective reference into dispute by assuming a shared definition of "poverty" and "natural" between ourselves and our opponent and presenting evidence structured by multiple access to deny the claims of our antagonist.

However, this strategy does not challenge the underlying idea that what is natural is good, or at least that what is natural is not bad. This strategy would leave our opponent's claim that what is natural is not bad intact, in order to argue that poverty is not good because it is not natural. To show that it is not natural is to bring up arguments structured by multiple access—objective-referenced arguments.

Another strategy, however, would be to argue that not every thing that is natural is good. This strategy would involve argumentation that is directly value argumentation and exclusive of objective or subjective issues. We might point to many things in nature that are morally repugnant to human beings and claim that humans must alter nature and establish morality through their own efforts. This strategy does not foreground the objective reference of our opponent's claim but rather foregrounds directly the value claim that what is natural is good.

But how could we convince our opponent of our point of view, since we cannot here appeal to observation procedures or anything else structured by the principle of multiple access? Well, we would have to try to convince our opponent by finding some shared ideas of what is good and bad and then show that some things that we agree to be natural fall into the "bad" category. We would have to argue one value claim by finding other value claims for which there is agreement and then proceed logically to display connections between the value claims in dispute and the value claims to which there is agreement.

This is the general nature of value rationality. It hovers around the concept of value consensus. To get an argument about any specific value claim going, one must seek to find value claims to which the parties in dispute agree and argue forth from them.

Where, however, does this process ever end? Behind every value claim in dispute are other possible value claims and behind these are yet others. No beginning point can be defended through multiple access or convincing self-reports alone. What if disputants never find a common moral ground from which to discuss specific value claims?

This question is not easily answered. It can be clarified, however. I will slowly clarify this question in future sections. For now the reader should simply hang onto the following points:

- *First:* value claims are not "just opinion," not "subjective."
- *Second:* value claims invoke a particular mode of rationality that has its own validity requirements, distinct from those pertaining to the subjective or objective realms.
- *Third:* value claims are argued by finding and articulating value agreements between the parties in dispute and then arguing from them toward the value claims in disagreement.

7. *Generally speaking, American people will avoid eye contact with strangers on elevators.*

Initially, this statement brings only the objective realm to mind. It seems that, as it stands, we could ascertain its truth or falsity through observation procedures as long as we give measurement definitions to "eye contact" and "avoid." We could also give "generally speaking" a statistical form, and then conduct studies, perhaps with concealed video cameras on elevators. In this sense, statement (7) does not significantly differ, in terms of its formal validity claim, from statements (1) and (2). And, by the way, this statement is roughly correct: Americans do tend to avoid eye contact with strangers on elevators.

But statement (7) differs from statements (1) and (2) in that it is a claim about behavioral regularities. Moreover, like most valid objective-referenced statements of social regularities, it is of little value if we do not understand *why* it is true. Regularities in the physical world are commonly explained through objective models: Why do dense objects regularly fall to the ground? Because of "gravity." Why do light bulbs regularly emit light when the switch is turned on? Because of "electromagnetic laws." What are "gravity" and "electromagnetism"? They are concepts that do not directly represent perceivable entities but that account for perceivable regularities. There is no multiple access to gravity in itself, but the concept of gravity explains regularities to which there is direct and multiple access. In addition, the concepts of gravity and elec-tromagnetism are objectivistic in nature, which means that they are located **outside** of subjectivity: they are conceived as features of *the* world, rather than as features of "my," "your," or "her" world.

But no objectivistic model is going to answer our question about why people in elevators tend to avoid eye contact. To posit a "law" or a "force" of any kind would be to miss what is going on. Social regularities are not reducible to objectively conceived models, laws, forces, and the like. Traditional physical science conceives of gravity as an objective force (or geometric structure) that exists whether or not human beings know it to exist. In social science, regularities in human behavior and interaction must be explained in terms of human knowledge, in terms of the knowledge human beings employ in order to act socially, producing regular and predictable modes of activity.

"Meaning" as an Explanatory Term

A full explanation of why people avoid eye contact on elevators will be conceptually complex, so I will concentrate on only some of the issues involved. The main thing to note is that within most cultures, prolonged eye contact generally *means* that the person staring has an intention with respect to the person being stared at.

The term "intention" is subjective. It refers to a state to which only one person has access, privileged access. But intentions are not the core explanatory terms for inter-active regularities; they are rather secondary explanatory terms for routine social interactions. Why is this so? Because it is not the intention but rather the fact that *at least two people* can spot the same set of *possible* intentions indicated in an act that accounts for the interactive regularity.

In elevators, staring at strangers is a meaningful act, and it is the "knowledge" of each person on an elevator that the possible meanings of a stare are shared by the entire group that accounts for the behavioral regularity. An intention, as well as any other subjective state, will be referenced by a meaning but will not determine it. It is the awareness of each person that others might understand the act within a certain range of ways that produces the regularity in behavior and constitutes the meanings.

Thus subjectivity is not the primary category involved, nor is objectivity. The primary category involved is going to be related to "shared meanings"; awareness of how other people might take a certain act or event.

So shared meaning is the key term of explanation here. We must be careful from the start with respect to the term "shared." Meanings are never known to be literally shared between people, because the principle of privileged access rules this out. It is always "possible meanings" that are involved in interactions. Usually, prolonged eye contact without accompanying talk on elevators means something negative; it means the person staring possibly wishes to intimidate or dominate or take advantage. Thus it is avoided unless it is followed by an intentional act of some kind. It is the range of meanings associated with eye contact in American culture that explains the behavioral regularities on elevators.

So it is the reference to possible subjective states that brings subjectivity into meaning, not actual subjective states. Thus, you can catch yourself staring at another person on an elevator and realize that this could mean, to the other, that you have some intention with respect to her. That is part of the meaning of the stare. Your next act will be made in reference to this possible meaning: you turn your eyes quickly away to show that you did not actually have any such intention. Your act of turning the eyes away is typical in your culture, not because of subjectivity per se but because of culturally constructed meanings, shared by a cultural group.

Qualitative research is always going to be concerned with meanings as one of the major categories for explaining patterned activity. Thus we shall have to become clearer about the nature of meaning. In this section I will discuss the concept of meaning to the extent required for introducing a third ontological category. This will be a provisional, partial, discussion of meaning. In later chapters more of the picture will be filled in.

"Norms" as an Explanatory Concept

Not all sociologists would emphasize meaning in their explanation of elevator behavior and other socially patterned actions. Many sociologists would instead explain elevator behavior in terms of "norms." Thus we need to understand the concept of norms and their relationship to meaning.

The term "norm" is obviously related to the word "normal." Certain modes of acting in certain situations will be regarded as "the norm" by certain cultural groups. This is an objective-referenced idea. "Normal" behavior is perceivable behavior occurring in routine ways.

Sociologists, however, have used the term "norms" to develop a concept shifted away from the objective-descriptive connotations of normal. "Norm" is a term used by sociologists in an explanatory rather than a descriptive way. People usually behave in normal ways because they follow norms. Thus when sociologists talk about norms they are not talking about "what is the norm" but rather about "what brings off the norm": what produces normal behaviors.

For a long time, sociologists conceived of norms as something people *follow* and thus as something like rules. Norms were conceived to be rules that people understand, usually on tacit, implicit, levels of awareness. Take language use as an example. Language is used according to grammatical rules, but people need to possess only a tacit, non articulated, knowledge of these rules to speak competently. If I asked you right now to tell me what the pluperfect is in the English language, many of you would have to consult your old high-school grammar books for the answer. Yet all English speakers "know" what the pluperfect in English is, including you, for we all use it continuously and competently when we speak or write. We know the rule tacitly.

Similarly, why is it normal to avoid eye contact with strangers in elevators? Because people follow a tacit rule that could be articulated as something like "Don't maintain eye contact with strangers." However, people do not usually refer to rules like this one in very explicit ways; they do not often recite highly articulated rules to themselves and then obey them. Rather, people grasp most rules of social behavior in the same way that they grasp "rules" of grammar: they understand the rule without referring to an explicit articulation of it.

Norms Are Not Rules

This view of norms does not really hold up under careful examination. I will follow certain contemporary social theorists to reject this way of conceptualizing norms (Giddens 1979, 1984). The analogy with rules does capture certain features of what norms are, but it tends to obscure certain other qualities we need to associate with norms. It is true that, *when articulated,* norms take a rule-like formulation. It is also true that many norms are learned by children through explicit, rule-like formulations taught to them. "Let her take her turn" is said so often to children that the rule of turn-taking eventually becomes internalized and tacit; almost automatic. But the norms of social life never show the rigidity of rules; they are always in a state of modification as people refine, alter, or create them anew with innovative action.

Considering norms to be in essence rules is to miss their tight connection with meaning. The concept of norms must be analytically tied to our conception of meaning. Norms are in essence formal structures of meaning. They get their rule-like structure only when articulated in language, and their articulation into language is never identical to what they are.

Norms and Meaning Conceived Together

So far, I have stated that people tend to avoid eye contact on elevators because of the meanings associated with eye contact in closed spaces within our culture. The meanings associated with eye contact are responsible for normal behavior on elevators, and these meanings are associated with the norm: "Do not stare at another's eyes unless you intend to say or do something in relation to this other."

Meaning and norms come together as related concepts through the idea of position-taking. Norms pertain to structures through which an actor tacitly takes the position of another person, and meaning depends absolutely on tacit position-taking. If you are on an elevator and you catch yourself looking toward the eyes of another person, the possible meaning of your stare will occur to you through an implicit understanding of what this stare could indicate to other people—to any person being stared at and to any person observing someone staring at another. You have "taken the position" of any anonymous member of your culture who is stared at or who sees someone else stare at another person.

Norms and meanings both involve position-taking. To understand the possible range of meanings of any social act is to take multiple positions on that act as these positions are culturally defined. Norms are core structures of position-taking. On an elevator, one understands the meaning of a stare at the same time that one understands the tacit rule, or norm, in play. To understand that one's own stare might be taken as arrogance by another (position-taking) is simultaneously to understand the norm conditioning eye contact on elevators.

Thus there is an internal connection between meaning and norms. Acts are meaningful when we can take multiple positions, tacitly, with respect to them. We can only do this, however, because of norms, cultural generalities that allow us to position-take. Patterned social behavior can be explained when cultural patterns of position-taking (i.e., norms) are understood. It is the meaning of social acts that explain their use and their tendency to form patterns.

Normative Truth Claims

We are just about ready to introduce the third ontological category. To arrive at it, we need to understand that norms are internally connected to meanings and that meanings involve position-taking. We also need to understand that the normative constituents of meaning involve validity claims of a special type.

If you are daydreaming on an elevator and suddenly discover that you have been staring, unconsciously, at the eyes of another person for some time, you will tacitly grasp the possible meanings of your stare and then turn your eyes away. The range of possible meanings that occur to you include arrogance, rudeness, sexual interest, hostility, and so on. All such meanings are constituted from an unarticulated norm that, when articulated, takes a rule-like form: "Don't stare at strangers on elevators."

Now, put yourself in the position of the other person, the one being stared at. You are on an elevator and a strange man seems to be staring right at you. You grasp a range of possible meanings for this stare: he might have a sexual interest in you, he might dislike something about you, he might be thinking of how he will follow you out of the elevator in order to rob you, he might have heard about what an exceptional person you are and be curious about you; there are many possibilities.

You will be concerned with the question of whether this stranger thinks you are aware that he is staring at you because some idea about that would clarify the meaning a great deal; limit the range of possibilities. This basically means that you will be concerned with how he is position-taking with you in order for him to get some sense of how and whether you are position-taking with him. Position-taking commonly assumes multiple to-and-fros in this way and is really quite complex!

At any rate, you do not wish to encourage anything he might be intending with respect to you, so you turn your head and look at the numbers at the top of the elevator door.

After awhile, you look back toward the man and find him *still staring at you!* Being assertive in nature, you decide to confront him about this. Let us say for argument's sake that the following interaction takes place:

"What is your problem!?"

"What do mean? I don't have a problem."

"Why are you staring at me?"

"Why shouldn't I?"

"It's rude to stare at strangers on elevators."

"No it's not!"

"Yes it is! Ask anyone! You shouldn't stare at strangers like that!"

"I stare at anyone I want to!"

What began as an uncertain grasp of possible meanings led to the articulation of a norm. The articulated norm, "It's rude to stare at strangers on elevators," juxtaposed a value ("rudeness is bad") with a rule of behavior. Our effort to justify this articulated norm when the stranger failed to consent to it might seem philosophically weak ("Ask anyone!"), but it is quite typical of many everyday arguments over norms. The underlying claim is that members of a particular cultural community regard the norm to be in place and, from this, the related claim that all members of this group should act in accordance with the norm.

Our antagonist countered with a normative claim of his own: "I stare at anyone I want to!" Underlying this articulated assertion is a more tacit normative claim that people have the right to stare at whomever they wish. Even more tacit is the tie to a value claim: "Individuals have the right to do as they wish."

Now, if our arguments were to continue, they would take the form of value-rational argumentation as described in my discussion of statement (6). We would have to seek a normative-value statement upon which we agree and argue from that toward the specific norm in dispute. We might wind up in a debate about the rights of individual choice and self-determination versus the value of conveying respect to others through conformity. It could become quite philosophical and abstract!

This sort of argumentation involves normative truth claims. Value claims are a subset of normative truth claims because value claims concern only questions of what is good, bad, right, and wrong. Norms are always tied to ideas about what is good, bad, right, and wrong, but include also ideas about what is proper, and what is appropriate; that is, what behaviors ought to be exhibited in which circumstances.

Acts of meaning will always have this normative component, will always tacitly claim that certain modes of activity are proper and certain other modes are not. As claims, the normative component of meaningful acts will call upon the other person to conform to the actor or to agree with the actor about certain things. The claim is made upon the other person, who can either accept or reject it.

Values are clear statements about what is right, wrong, good, and bad and thus are within the realm of moral claims. Norms depend upon values for their ultimate support. That is, the reasons that a person will use to justify either following or not following a norm will be of a value-moral nature. Thus disputes over norms will soon move into value arguments. But norms have to do with appropriate behaviors and are not the same as values. Norms originate in the need for conventions to exist if people are going to communicate with each other.

If you make a scoring point on my team in a soccer match and I give you a thumbs-up sign, one of the norms constituting the meaning of my act towards you simply has to do with the convention of a thumbs-up signal—our agreement as to how this signal is to be interpreted. There is nothing intrinsically value-ridden or moral in that agreement, but my act claims the convention to be in place, or claims that it should be in place.

Normative-Evaluative Claims

These are claims about what is proper, appropriate and conventional. Ultimately, they are rooted in the process of position-taking structuring meaning. Once articulated, they take on a rule-like form. As claims, they impose on others by tacitly insisting that the other should conform to a certain convention. Others can always either agree or disagree; they may either affirm or reject the tacit normative claims made towards them. Reasons for agreeing or disagreeing will involve values which concern ideas about what is right, wrong, good, and bad. Thus norms and values are distinct but internally connected.

Definition of the Normative-Evaluative Realm: "Our" World

Because many truth claims are of the normative-evaluative type, and because this category of truth claim is distinct from the principles of multiple access and privileged access, it is appropriate to talk of a new ontological category: the normative-evaluative category. Here is a definition:

> *The normative-evaluative realm* is an ontological category presupposed by all meaningful action. It consists of truth claims about what behavior is proper, appropriate, and conventional. Normative-evaluative claims can always be articulated as "should claims"; people should act in such and such ways at such and such times. Normative-evaluative claims thus concern the nature of our world rather than "the" world or "my" world.

When in dispute, normative-evaluative claims quickly move into value argumentation, requiring a consensus on some values in order to argue toward agreement on the norm or value in dispute. Values are a subset of the normative-evaluative realm.

Now, there are many fine points to be made regarding the normative-evaluative category and its relationship to objectivity and subjectivity. At this point, you will not have a full understanding of the normative-evaluative category nor of its relationship to the other two. But you should have an understanding of the distinctive nature of truth claims referencing this category, how their dependence on nondisputed value agreements backgrounds an argument on any foregrounded norms or values in dispute. Neither the principle of multiple nor of privileged access will be of direct help in structuring the support one could give for a normative-evaluative claim.

In addition, readers should now understand that the normative-evaluative category will have an essential role to play in developing a research methodology. This is because social regularities occur through the manner in which actors understand norms and values, claim them tacitly or explicitly in all interactions, and negotiate them when disputes arise.

Minimally, a researcher must understand the epistemological structures of normative-evaluative truth claims simply in order to describe and explain social regularities. Maximally, a researcher must grasp the play of values and norms in their own work as researchers and in their acts of publishing accounts of other people's lives. These issues will be returned to in future chapters.

CHAPTER SUMMARY

A truth claim is an assertion that something is true or false, right or wrong, good or bad, correct or incorrect. Critical social research borrows from pragmatist philosophy by tying the sense of "truth" to processes in which social consensus is reached. Truth claims are always fallible, even when universal consent seems to have been attained. This is because future cultures might find reasons to discard the truths of today.

Critical epistemology focuses on validity because all truth claims are communicative acts that must meet certain formal conditions to win consent. These formal conditions are validity requirements, derived from the structures of human communication. With every social act, validity claims are referenced by actors, usually in tacit rather than explicit ways. The significance of everyday validity claims for qualitative researchers will be explored in chapter six; this chapter employed seven explicit validity claims to investigate the various categories in which they appear.

The analysis of our seven statements led us to three ontological categories consistent with Jurgen Habermas's theory of communicative action.[1] Each ontological category corresponds to a type of validity claim. The three categories are:

- *the objective realm,* characterized by the principle of multiple access. Objective validity claims are associated with assertions about the world: about what is, about what took place, and about what sorts of events regularly precede other sorts of events.

- *the subjective realm,* characterized by the principle of privileged access. Subjective validity claims are associated with assertions about your, her, or my world: about feelings, intentions, and states of awareness.[2]
- *the normative/evaluative realm,* which is implicated in position-taking. Position-taking with others necessarily carries claims and assumptions about what is "proper" that soon expand into cultural understandings about what is right, wrong, good, or bad. The normative/evaluative realm has to do with our world, as it is or should be.

These formal categories will become the basis of methodological validity requirements that all researchers should strive to meet. These requirements will be given in chapters ahead.

ENDING EXERCISE

Let us end this chapter by reminding ourselves of the everyday nature of validity claims. Read the following real life story and articulate tacit validity claims associated with the actions of the participants. In this case it is not the principal action per se that carries the validity claims but rather the way the main actor accounts for the act to make it appear socially legitimate.

Exercise: A Child Hits Another with a Stone and Accounts for Herself
Suppose you spot two young children playing in your neighborhood. One is in the street, and the other is playing in a vacant field. As you watch, the child in the field picks up a stone and throws it at the child in the street, hitting her in the arm. The child in the street begins to cry and runs into the field just as a car passes by. You rush over to her to offer comfort and yell at the other child; "Don't throw stones at her! That really hurts! What if you had hit her in the head!" The stone-thrower approaches you, clearly intending to explain something.

Now, consider three possible directions in which the story could go on from here:

1. The stone-thrower says, "I hit her by accident! I was aiming at the puddle" (pointing toward a puddle in the road).
2. The stone-thrower says, "She deserved it! She hit me with a stone before you saw us" (pointing to one of his legs).
3. The stone-thrower says, "Hey I saved her life! I wanted her to move so that the car wouldn't hit her" (pointing toward the car disappearing down the road).

How are the three ontological categories, the objective, subjective, and normative realms, referenced in each possible justification provided by the child? Remember that each justification will involve all three categories of reference, but that each will configure the categories differently in terms of backgrounding and foregrounding.

Here is my analysis. Statement (1) foregrounds (emphasizes) a reference to the *intentions* of the stone thrower. That is a subjective reference. It closely backgrounds a claim that if one harms another accidentally, one is not at fault. That is a normative-evaluative claim. It also acknowledges that the stone was thrown and that it hit the second child. That is an objective reference, highly backgrounded and not in dispute.

Statement (2) foregrounds the claim that harming another is *justified* if this other first harmed one's self. This is a normative-evaluative claim. It backgrounds two other claims: that the other child actually did hit the thrower with a stone earlier on (objective claim), and that both children intended to hit each other with stones (subjective references).

Statement (3) foregrounds both the *intentions* of the thrower ("I intended to save her live"—subjective reference) and a sort of *cause-effect relationship* ("Hitting people with stones is a good way of getting them to move out of danger"—objective reference). It backgrounds the claim that it is good to save people's lives (normative-evaluuative reference).

Notes

1. Habermas emphasizes the three ontological categories discussed in this chapter: the objective, the subjective, and the "social" (normative/evaluative) realms. But Habermas acknowledges two other types of validity claims as well: the claim that a statement is meaningful, and aesthetic claims (e.g., "This picture is beautiful"). See Habermas 1981.

2. Thoughts and beliefs actually synthesize the subjective and normative/evaluative realms. One can have "private" thoughts and beliefs that one does not disclose to others and that therefore fall within a realm of privileged access. But the constitution of thoughts and beliefs require position-taking and thus normative-evaluative structures. To think is to position-take with internalized, and usually abstract, audiences. Emotions, intentions, and states of awareness only enter reflective consciousness through thinking and therefore through the normative-evaluative category. But a prereflective level of experience is referenced as soon as one becomes aware of emotions, intentions, and states of awareness, and that level of experience is pure subjectivity. The interesting thing about pure subjectivity, of course, is that it is never immediate to consciousness: it becomes represented to one's self through the symbolic forms of the normative/evaluative realm.

5

Validity Requirements for Constructing the Primary Record

Items covered in chapter 5:

- Procedures to support objective research claims
- Checking for power distortions on objective claims
- Objective inferences in qualitative research

The three ontological categories discussed in chapter four will serve us well in formulating validity requirements that must be met by qualitative researchers if they are going to produce trustworthy reports. This chapter will list and explain the validity requirements of stage one: building a primary record. It begins with a list of procedures researchers may use to support the claims of their primary record, moves into a discussion of power and its significance for making objective validity claims, and ends with a brief discussion of objectivity and inference.

OBJECTIVITY: THE PRINCIPAL CLAIM IN THE PRIMARY RECORD

Building a primary record prioritizes the objective validity claim: claims open to multiple access. The primary record is a sort of massive claim to represent what took place in a manner any observer or participant would report under ideal conditions. Since multiple access is the primary principle distinguishing the objective category of truth claim, validity requirements are all directed toward the limit case of a record to which any other person present would consent. A "limit case" is a situation that can be imagined and approximated but not usually reached. The procedures a researcher may employ to support her primary record amount to efforts to approximate the limit case of general consensus on an account of events to which there is multiple access.

As I made clear in chapter three, the principal procedures that can be employed to meet this validity requirement include: (1) passive observation of naturalistic social interaction, and (2) recording interactions in notebooks, audio tapes, and (sometimes) video tapes.

Techniques to Support Objective Validity Claims of the Researcher

The most comprehensive list of validation procedures to employ in qualitative research that I am aware of can be found in Lincoln and Guba's Naturalistic Inquiry (1985: ch. 11). I use many of the terms and techniques they present for stages one through three of this methodological scheme, but I conceptually relocate them and at times give them a slightly different rationale. Below I use both some of their terms and terms employed by others to explain methods of supporting objective claims essential to the primary record:

1. *Use multiple recording devices and multiple observers.* This is commonly termed "triangulation," although the connotation of "three points of view" carried by this term has been lost in popular usage. The point is to use more than your own senses when compiling the record. Your record is of objective events to which there is multiple access. What better way to support your necessary claim that you record what actually took place than to use several recording devices? I usually take notes with a tape recorder running and, when possible, have another observer take notes with me so that our two records may be compared.

2. *Use a flexible observation schedule* to disrupt unconscious biases in attention. I have described a good method for this in chapter three, the method of priority observation.

3. *Practice prolonged engagement* to reduce Hawthorn effects. "Prolonged engagement" is one of Lincoln and Guba's terms. It means returning to the field frequently, spending a lot of time there. It is helpful for one's objective claims, because subjects become more accustomed to the researcher's presence the more the researcher is there. They are more likely to act as if the researcher were not present if the researcher becomes a familiar part of the setting. Remember that a Hawthorn effect is the effect a researcher has on the subjects she is studying. As I said in chapter three, Hawthorn effects are not anathema to a qualitative research project. This is because subjects will change their activities in the presence of an observer but will employ the same cultural frameworks to make such changes as they employ in everyday situations; qualitative research is primarily geared to reconstruct cultural frameworks. But it is best to reduce

Hawthorn effects during the first stage of research, because they complicate data analysis.

4. *Use a low-inference vocabulary* in the written record. If I write in my field journal or thick record: "Samuel sassed Alfred and sauntered haughtily toward the door," I have included many normative-evaluative and subjective-referenced connotations that go beyond multiple access. The extent to which a wide audience would consent to this description is limited, because it carries too many references to items outside the objective realm. If I write instead what Samuel said verbatim and indicate his tone of voice and body movements, my claims are going to be much more capable of winning the consensus of anyone else observing. Often it is hard to find a term that is not overtly subjective-referenced or normative-evaluative referenced. In these cases, use expressions like "as if" and "as though" in the field notes to mark off the higher-inference portions of the record: "Samuel spoke as if he were angry." Another strategy, illustrated in chapter three, is to use brackets and "observer comments" (OC) in the notes: [OC: Samuel spoke in a way that seemed rude].

5. *Use peer-debriefing* to check possible biases in attention and vocabulary. Soon after beginning a primary record ask a colleague, a peer, to read some of your notes to see whether you are ignoring certain people, giving too much attention to others, or using a vocabulary that is higher inference than it could be.

6. *Use member checks* on the record of what took place. The term "member check" means sharing your notes with the people you are studying to see whether or not they agree with your record. Be flexible with its use. In some studies it is not a good idea to use member checks during stage one; they may induce undesired Hawthorn effects. You can reserve member checks in such studies for stages three and four, conducted after a thick set of field notes has been compiled. Stage three itself is, among other things, a sort of elaborate "member check."

In other instances, however, a very controversial event may occur that is important to record and analyze for your study. If it is controversial, people are likely to disagree on what actually occurred. Since it only took place once, you may not have conclusive evidence of what objective features of the event actually took place. Then it will be important to share your record of what occurred with various subjects soon after the event, when memories are fresh. If the subjects disagree with your perceptions, record what they have to say, and your analysis will have to take the multiple perspectives on this event into account. Often this sort of thing can be particularly revealing. It occurred in my study of Croxteth (Carspecken 1991) and I was able to make much of the fact that different groups of people perceived a certain event in diverse ways. Not being able to definitively describe what actually did take place was not that important for my analysis.

The Effects of Power on Objective-Referenced Claims

Now it is time to recall a statement made in chapter one: the pragmatic theory of truth adopted by critical researchers presupposes equal power relations—democratic social relations between those making truth claims and those affected by them.

Suppose I were to write in my primary record; "Alfred slapped Samuel across the face three times and thrust him back into his seat." Now suppose Alfred and Samuel both object to my account, declaring that this event never occurred. I reply that it did occur and that if they continue to "lie" about it I will see that Alfred is fired and that Samuel is placed in a juvenile detention center. They both quickly acquiesce and give me the validating member check I was after.

This is a ridiculous example, but it is one that illustrates an important point. If power relations are not equal between the observer and the communities of people affected by her truth claims, then these claims can not be validated. Distortions in power relations can be much more subtle than the power of one actor to exercise sanctions on those who will not consent to her claims. Suppose I were to write in my notebook that Alfred stood within one foot of Samuel when arguing about the test. This is a stage one type of validity claim, an objective claim. Later on in my analysis of normative/evaluative and subjective elements (stage two), I make use of this recording to argue that Alfred "violated Samuel's personal space." Here I have employed normative reconstructions to analyze the significance of Alfred's proximity to Samuel. Now suppose that Alfred and Samuel both believe Alfred was standing something like four feet away during this portion of the interaction but, because they foolishly defer to my status as professor and as "expert observer," they doubt their own beliefs and stay silent when reading my account. They therefore do not even learn that they agree with each other, in opposition to my claim. This is another kind of power that equally distorts validity claims. In this case no coercion was used, but differences in social status distorted the situation.

The effects of power on the *objective* claims made by a researcher are not as subtle nor as difficult to control for as are the effects of power on subjective and normative-evaluative claims (see chapters eight and eleven). The following procedures will help reduce the distortions of power for objective claims:

1. Construct your primary record in deference to the participant's perceptions as much as possible.
2. Where conflicting accounts of an event are provided, include all accounts in the primary record. Include all accounts in the final write-up if the event in question becomes important for your analysis.
3. Establish supportive, nonauthoritarian relationships with the participants in your study. Actively encourage them to question your own perceptions. Be sure that participants are protected from any harm that your study could produce and be sure that they know they are protected.

OBJECTIVE VALIDITY CLAIMS AND INFERENCES
Objective Inferences in Quantitative Research

The specialized methods of objective inference developed in statistical science are standardly used in quantitative research and usually not employed in qualitative studies. The basic idea with quantitative inferences is to discover relationships between events open to multiple access. Qualitative research, by contrast, is generally interested in relationships between (1) events open to multiple access, (2) conditions not open to multiple access because of their normative-evaluative nature, and (3) subjective states constituted by the principle of privileged access. Statistical inferences, of no help in a thorough exploration of these relationships, are basically consistent with the principles of objective reference as long as the abstractions involved in constructing objective categories (operational definitions) are carefully defended. Use of operational definitions violates none of our principles, but it greatly limits what can be found in research, and it is highly vulnerable to incorrect mappings of several ontological categories onto one.

Correlations discovered in quantitative research will be theoretically significant only if they are conceived in terms of social action and its conditions, not in terms of "variables" or, worse, "causes." The significance of statistically found relationships, moreover, generally resides in normative-evaluative and subjective factors that are simply assumed in the construction of variables.

Sampling Issues in Qualitative Research

Quantitative researchers must carefully defend their selection of a sample and its relationship to a population in order to make valid inferences. An analogous situation accompanies qualitative research, in which one attempts to discover regularly occurring patterns of action. This means that observations must be taken on appropriately selected "samples" of daily life. While the inferences most important to qualitative analysis involve subjective and normative-evaluative reconstructions, and not correlations between objective categories, reconstructions should be conducted on interactions that seem to recur often within the site of one's study or on interactions that recur rarely but that contrast significantly with other interactions that are frequent. This means that a "sampling procedure" of sorts must be employed when deciding what to observe, how often, and when. Construction of an observation schedule, as discussed in chapter three, is therefore important. One must be in a position to claim that certain kinds of events occur often and other kinds of events rarely.

Objective Claims vs. Objectifications

To claim that a certain event or routine occurs either frequently or rarely is the sort of objective claim a qualitative researcher will have to make in order to reconstruct subjective and normative factors on appropriate portions of the primary record. This requires an objective-like category abstracted from the field notes. "Event" and "type of interaction" are not purely objective categories but are rather objectifications, researcher constructs, that synthesize objective references with normative-evaluative references. For example, one may become interested in interactive conflicts (a type of "event") and construct a set of categories defined in terms of conflict endings. Some conflicts might end only through the use of coercion or influence by one of the parties; others might end through the attainment of a compromise. Yet other conflicts might end through mutual consensus on authority relations (Carspecken 1991: ch. 5).

Here we have something more than purely objective categories. Conflicts may differ very much from each other in terms of precisely where they took place, what was said, who was involved, what issue the participants disagreed over, and other objective characteristics. But despite this diversity the researcher may wish to group some conflicts together according to the norms consented to at their end (for example, an agreement to tolerate each other, to compromise, or to accept a certain authority relation). The researcher has to judge which conflicts fit which categories and must employ criteria that go beyond mere objectivity.

I will say more about this issue in the chapter on coding (chapter nine). One must understand the principles of meaning reconstruction to understand how certain categories, like conflict endings, can be developed. They are developed as codes based partially on meaning reconstruction. Such codes require member checks and peer debriefings to be validated, as well as the use of rigorous reconstructive principles discussed in chapters ahead.

The point to remember is that qualitative researchers have to be able to claim that certain kinds of events occur regularly or infrequently. This means that categories of event have to be developed. Such categories are not purely objective; they are objectifications requiring a synthesis of objective features with their cultural significance. The construction of objectifications will require familiarity with reconstructive analysis: the subject of the next several chapters.

6

Stage Two: Preliminary Reconstructive Analysis

Items covered in chapter 6:

- Initial meaning reconstruction and meaning fields

- The hermeneutic inference

- The concept of "pragmatic horizons"

- Semantic and pragmatic meaning structures

- Validity reconstructions

- Backgrounding and foregrounding

- Settings, negotiations, and setting shifts

- Implicit theories

During stage two, you will begin to make speculations with respect to the meanings of interactions recorded in the primary record, to tease out normative and subjective references, and to articulate normative themes tacitly referenced in consistent ways on your research site. You will also begin analytical work employing second-order concepts like roles and routine modes of interactive power. Coding begins in stage two. All of this is preliminary in that it must be checked, expanded, and probably changed through procedures employed in stage three, when interview data is collected. This sort of analysis is reconstructive because it "reconstructs," into explicit discourse, cultural and subjective factors that are largely tacit in nature.

The analytic procedures employed in stage two will be repeated throughout an entire qualitative study. Many of them may be used on interview data, for example. And often, after completing a number of interviews for stage three, you will wish to return to a brief period of more passive observations, focusing this time on issues raised through preliminary analysis and interviewing. These new observations, of course, will be analyzed with stage two methods as well.

There are a number of procedures that may be followed in stage two, primarily in a cyclical manner. The concepts underlying these procedures mutually inform each other, so researchers should master all the basic ideas I will introduce for stage two and then employ them in any order they wish. I will attempt to introduce the most basic and fundamental conceptual models and analytic techniques of critical social research over the next few chapters. I have had to leave out, for want of space, a number of other models and techniques that I regularly employ in my own work; but I do at least mention some of these other methods at appropriate places in my discussion and cite helpful sources for readers to consult. Most, but not all, of the methods and models I have left out are described in other publications but within different philosophical frameworks. I try to show readers where this missing material fits into critical methodological frameworks.

Once the basic conceptual models and analytic methods I describe are learned, readers are encouraged to employ them in new and creative ways. This and the next few chapters are primarily devoted to the teaching of a conceptual vocabulary from which all sorts of inventions and insights are possible. Reconstructive analysis is at heart a creative endeavor, akin to the creativity involved each time we understand other people in everyday life. A qualitative researcher must acquire a conceptual vocabulary for reconstructive analysis, much as an artist must acquire a set of pigments and brushes for painting. It is also possible, moreover, to increase the number of shades and the range of coarse to fine brushes in your possession. Indeed, one of the most exciting features of qualitative research is the scope it gives the researcher for refining concepts and developing new ones for each study.

INITIAL MEANING RECONSTRUCTION

Preliminary reconstructive analysis ought to begin as a play between low-level coding, initial meaning reconstruction, and "horizon analysis" (explained below). This is because one cannot choose appropriate segments of the primary record for initial meaning reconstruction without at least mentally noting both recurring patterns and unusual, revealing events. But it is dangerous to attempt to note recurring patterns and unusual events without a knowledge of the basic principles of low-level coding. Low-level coding, however, is not going to be fruitful if you are not familiar with meaning reconstruction. And initial meaning reconstructions themselves are ultimately significant primarily because the reconstructions can be subjected to horizon analysis. You must understand the entire conceptual framework involved in the analysis of meaning before you can adequately undertake any particular step.

In a text, however, these things must be introduced sequentially. In this chapter I will first explain and exemplify initial meaning reconstruction, then explain and exemplify horizon analysis. Coding procedures and other analytic concepts will be treated in chapters ahead. Bear in mind, however, that the best sequence in which to introduce these ideas and procedures is not the best sequence in which to *practice* them.

First Steps

Initial meaning reconstruction will, for the most part, take place mentally. That is, before you start, you must be familiar with the general conceptual models involved with meaning and mentally note the possible underlying meanings throughout the primary record. Meaning is first understood in holistic and tacit ways during everyday life, and this holds for getting impressions of meaning from field notes as well. The basic process involved in human understanding is hermeneutic, and hermeneutic processes involve a movement from initial holistic modes of understanding toward more explicit and delineated modes of understanding, which, in turn, modify one's holistic grasp of meaning (Palmer 1969). A circular process is involved: movement from the tacit (intuitive and undifferentiated) toward the explicit (delineated and differentiated) and then back to the holistic.

Thus, you ought to begin meaning reconstruction by reading through the primary record and mentally noting possible underlying meanings. Several such readings will begin to suggest patterns as well as highlight unusual events that may be important to your analysis. Low-level coding procedures can be employed at this point to mark out both routine events and unusual ones. For a discussion of coding procedures consistent with reconstructive analysis see chapter nine.

After reading through the primary record and beginning the coding process, you should next select several segments for explicit, initial meaning reconstruction; the selections must be made in light of your progress with low-level coding. The segments selected ought to be representative of action patterns; some selections should be made of anomalies in the patterns, as these will be quite revealing of the norms underlying more routine events.

The segments selected from the primary record ought to be copied into *new* word processing files, preserving the primary record in its original form. You can use the new files for reconstructions. Then you ought to go through the selected segments line by line and add discursive articulations of tacit modes of meaning you believe may underlie the interactions recorded. All such additions must be made within brackets to clearly distinguish them from the primary record. This is time-consuming work, and you should remember to perform it selectively.

Meaning Fields

The theoretical status of these additions to the primary record must be carefully kept in mind. One is articulating possible meanings: meanings that other people in the setting might themselves infer, either overtly or tacitly. The relevant concept here is that of a *meaning field*. You cannot know for certain what an actor intended with her act, you cannot know for certain what impressions of meaning were received by those witnessing the act or directly addressed by the act, but you can specify possibilities. A meaning field is such a range of possibilities.

The meaning field is not merely an analytic concept, but a substantive concept as well. Subjects interacting within a setting get their impressions of meaning in exactly the same way as the researcher. They are generally cognizant of a range of possible intended meanings for each act, a range of possible interpretations that others in the setting may make of the act, and an awareness that the actor herself is aware of a range of possible interpretations others may make of her act. We could call this the uncertainty principle of meaning: meanings are always experienced as possibilities within a field of other possibilities.

The researcher moves through the same processes as do the subjects of study when getting impressions of meaning. The researcher, however, articulates meaning fields— raises meaning fields from the tacit to the discursive as much as possible. And the researcher must realize that her reconstructed meaning fields may not be the same as the meaning fields experienced by her subjects of study. The reconstructed meanings can use "or" statements, "and" statements, "and/or" statements, to indicate the ambiguities that meaningful acts possess for all parties involved (actors, those addressed by the act, those witnessing the act, and the researcher herself).

As said already, reconstructing meaning fields is no guarantee of articulating the actual fields experienced by each actor. Actors usually experience many portions of a meaning field on totally tacit levels of awareness that may subsequently be forgotten. It is therefore impossible to absolutely validate your reconstruction of meaning fields. But there are definite ways of supporting your articulations. The more familiarity you have with the culture of your subjects, the closer your articulated meaning fields are likely to be to what actors themselves report. Use of member checks and peer debriefers, plus dialogical data generation in stage three, all help to refine articulated meaning fields and to provide your final reconstructions with support.

Initial meaning reconstruction, however, should be viewed as very much preliminary and subject to error. Doing it clarifies issues to be explored through additional reconstructions, continued observations, and interviewing.

Keeping Initial Reconstructions at Low Levels of Inference

Generally, initial meaning reconstructions should be constructed on relatively low levels of inference. You will perceive opportunities for making higher-level meaning inferences but must resist the temptation to articulate them. Higher-level inferences need to be made during the horizon analysis phase, for horizon analysis procedures are more rigorous and help to keep the status of various levels of inference distinct. Horizon analysis, in other words, brings more rigor into the inference process and helps to further check the effects of bias. The difference between low- and high-inference meaning reconstructions will soon become very clear.

The basic idea, for initial meaning reconstruction, is to put more words onto the actions observed, as if the actor had tried to convey the entire meaning of her act verbally rather than through the complexities of vocal tone, posture, gesture, facial expression, timing, prosodic form, and so on. This can be done on levels of low inference (illustrated below) as well as on levels of high inference (as occurs in horizon analysis).

Once several segments have been analyzed in this way, a peer debriefer ought to be asked to read through the reconstructions and to play devil's advocate with them. A "peer debriefer" is a colleague, familiar with qualitative research, who checks your work for signs of bias and partiality. Member checks could be conducted as well, but usually only if the observation stage of the research has been nearly completed.

EXAMPLE OF INITIAL MEANING RECONSTRUCTION

Let us look at some initial meaning reconstructions made on Alfred and Samuel's interaction. Below I present the same segment of field notes used in a previous chapter to illustrate thick description. Meaning fields have been indicated within brackets with the code: "MF" placed in front to distinguish them from "OC" or observer comments. I insert meaning reconstructions for the actions at the beginning section of notes only. Readers can practice articulating their own reconstructions on the subsequent notes.

Field Note Excerpt: Alfred and Samuel with Meaning Reconstructions

[2] A: Alfred looks up in Samuel's direction with placid, smooth facial features [OC: as if bland, nonchalant, "no big deal"].

[3] A: *Samuel let's go now and take that test.* Addresses Samuel in matter-of-fact way, as if "no big deal, time to take the test, as we both know."

[MF: *Alfred conveys social distance in his behavior; no greeting, no smile. He looks at papers first, then mentions the test implying that the test and his relationship with Samuel are just one of many things now on his mind. (OR) Alfred's actions indicate controlled nervousness. He is leery of beginning a conflict with Samuel and delays by looking at the papers*].

[4] S: Samuel frowns. His body tightens in chair. Raises head and chest up. Lips tight.

[5] S: *I'm not taking that test, it's too hard.* Tone implies firm stance but no sharp tones, not loud. [OC: As if: "I'm just not taking it, it's simply too hard, so that's that."]

[6] A: *You've got to take it.* Has moved three steps toward Samuel. Voice firm, not loud, not sharp; calm. As if "you've got to take it and that's that."

[MF: *"We both know you have to take it, let's not play any games, that's the reality." (AND/OR) "There are no negotiable aspects to this, this test must be taken, refusal to take it will only result in consequences unacceptable to you, I want you to know that." (AND/OR) "I am saying that you must take the test, therefore you must take the test."*]

[7] S: *I'm not doing it, it's too hard.* Tone as if becoming angry, or desperate. Eyes have

shifted away from Alfred and toward wall behind him. Body tighter, arms about chest.

[MF: *"I am absolutely frozen with respect to this, I will not take this test, I will not budge physically or mentally on this issue" (AND/OR) "This test is unreasonable, I have my rights here, I refuse to do what is unreasonably asked of me."*]

[8] Silence

[MF: Alfred: *"I'm waiting for you to become more reasonable" (AND/OR) "I'm threatening to come up with some nasty sanction if you don't agree to take the test" (OR) "I'm nonplused, I don't know what to do in the face of such firm resistance.*]

[9] S: *I can't do it. I don't get any help around here!* Loud voice. As if mixture of complaining and anger.

[10] (Silence)

9:44

[11] S: Samuel throws test on the floor. Hums a cheerful song. Arms still about chest but not as tightly drawn. Has turned to a new direction and is looking up toward ceiling/wall intersection.

[12] A: No response from Alfred.

The Hermeneutic Inference

One can see from the example above that meaning reconstructions were produced by putting words on meanings that might be read from the timing, tone, gestures, and postures of each act. Low-inference reconstructions were performed, keeping the articulations close to the more immediate features of the act. Subtle allusions and nuances possible to each act were left out for this stage of analysis in order to reduce the risk of error. You are trying to articulate the meaning fields of the action as the actors themselves would articulate them and as others present to the acts (as second or third persons) would articulate them.

How does the researcher come up with such possible meanings? Epistemologically, there can be no hard and fast rules. What is taking place when one reconstructs meanings in this way is hermeneutic process. The researcher will be able to formulate possible meanings simply because the researcher is a communicative being and can imagine herself within the situation being analyzed as a first-, second- or third-person party to the events. The researcher takes part, mentally, in the intersubjective processes at play. She must become a "virtual participant" in order to articulate the meaning fields.

No definite procedures may be employed in meaning reconstruction, because the distinction between shared access (objectivity) and privileged access (subjectivity) must always be in play for there to be meaning, as must the distinction between tacit/synthetic modes of understanding and explicit/delineated modes. You first gain holistic impressions of meaning through taking the position of the actor and the other people present within the setting. There is no recipe for gaining such holistic impressions of meaning; articulations are developed *from* them.

In everyday social situations, one must constantly infer meaning fields from the actions of other people, note the possible intentions of the actor, note the possible unintended but motivating portions of the actor's impetus to act, note the possible ways in which the actor herself monitors all such features of her act, and note the possible ways in which other actors may understand the act. There is no direct access to most of this. When fully articulated, an understanding of possible meaning appears very complex. Yet this complex feat occurs rapidly and in a holistic manner. Its many parts, delineated in reconstructions, are united at the moment of understanding.

The work that has been done on hermeneutics most clearly objectifies this process of inferring meaning (Palmer 1969). I will here describe features of the hermeneutic inference in some detail so that readers may employ it consciously in their reconstructive work. For our purposes we can note the following features of the "hermeneutic circle."

1. *Its intersubjective quality:* To infer meaning fields you must "take the position" of the actor, the ones addressed by the act, and other people present but unaddressed, in order to note the impressions of meaning possibly experienced by each party. This is intersubjectivity, which consists of taking the subjective position from a variety of perspectives on the act; it is position-taking. To articulate a meaning field into explicit discourse, you move through the various positions in a conscious and explicit manner rather than in the tacit and implicit manner typical of everyday interactions. You must take a performative attitude toward the activity, occupying virtually the positions of the others in the setting, if you are to interpret it.

2. *Recognition of meaning through position-taking employing cultural typifications:* What makes postion-taking possible are tacit generalities typical of a culture. We can gain some idea of what Alfred might intend and how Samuel might interpret him, because their interaction will be recognized by us as a culturally typical one, or as one uniquely constructed from culturally typical interactions. We can position-take because we recognize the situation in certain ways and have been in positions similar to those of Alfred and Samuel ourselves. Cultural typifications and generalities, grasped tacitly, are the broadest structures through which we recognize situations as meaningful.

   Now, our recognition of relevant cultural typifications is contingent upon our familiarity with the culture of our subjects. A citizen of Japan with some fluency in the English language would be able to construct meaning fields after observing the interactions between Samuel and Alfred, but her meaning fields could easily fail to coincide with those experienced by Samuel and Alfred when interacting or those constructed by Samuel and Alfred in an interview situation when asked to reflect upon a video tape or primary record of their interaction. The tacit generalities would differ. The way in which one position-takes depends upon cultural generalities and typifications, and the researcher must try to gain an understanding of the typifications employed by her subjects.

You can gain an understanding of cultural typifications different from those you are accustomed to only through using and modifying typifications with which you are already familiar. This is another feature of the hermeneutic circle. We must position-take initially as best we can through our own typifications and then alter the typifications we first used to conform more closely with those used by our subjects. The way this is done corresponds to the next phase of the hermeneutic inference.

3. *Normative reflection:* First we recognize possible meanings. This recognition occurs, however, through cultural typifications we bring with us to the field, learned earlier in our lives and field work. It can therefore be inaccurate: it can fail to correspond to the meaning recognitions experienced by our subjects. The next step is to reflect upon the conditions of our own recognition of meaning. We must become clear on what tacit typifications were involved in our recognition of possible meaning.

Becoming clear, through reflection, of our own typifications employed in recognizing possible meaning will involve becoming clear on the cultural norms employed. We arrive at norms as soon as we attempt to articulate features of a cultural typification; we are able to get some idea of Alfred's possible intentions and Samuel's interpretations through norms of behavior. Becoming clear about the norms we ourselves employ in understanding another is an important part of the hermeneutic process. I think the following example will get the idea across most effectively and efficiently.

When Samuel refuses to take the test for the second time and Alfred's response is to remain silent (marked as [8] in the notes), my initial impression of the possible meanings is that Alfred is either feeling stymied and uncertain of what to do next, or that he is communicating an expectancy on his part for Samuel to recognize the inappropriateness and impossibility of his refusal, such that Samuel will alter his position. A third possibility coming to mind is that Alfred intends to communicate a threat to Samuel, that a sanction will be forthcoming if he does not alter his position.

These possibilities come to mind immediately. But I next need to examine the reasons why they come to mind: this is normative reflection. In the cultures I am familiar with and that I may well share with Alfred, only a certain period of time may pass before one responds to another person. If that period of time passes without a response, then being silent is probably either deliberate or the result of not knowing how to go on in the interaction. This understanding is constituted by a norm having to do with the timing of responses during an interaction.

When I become clear about the norm I have already depended upon to infer the meanings that quite spontaneously came to mind, I am then in a position to question whether Alfred and Samuel employ this norm. I need to examine a large number of interactions to try to determine whether they do hold to this norm, or need to use interview and/or IPR techniques (as discussed in chapter 10) to gain more clarity on this issue. Does Alfred delay in his response at other times, as recorded in the field notes, in a way suggesting a threat or a feeling of being nonplused? If so, it would seem that my initial impression of meaning is well supported. If not, I shall have to readjust my typification to match those used by Alfred for the timing of responses.

4. *The normative circle:* Getting an impression of meaning will often include a process of

making tacit comparisons between the normative realms you are familiar with and the normative realm that the actor seems to claim as valid. That is, you use your familiarity with normative realms learned in the course of your life history in order to position-take, but doing so often brings out differences in the nature of the act observed compared to the manner in which you would expect members of your culture to act in that situation. Such differences become noted and incorporated within the horizon of your understanding through tacit alterations of your expectations (and thus norms).

This is part of the hermeneutic circle. You use a preunderstanding of an observed act based on your capacity to position-take (i.e., based on cultural typifications you are familiar with) in order to then modify this same preunderstanding to make certain novel features of the act comprehensible. The modified preunderstanding amounts to an altered normative realm of which you possess an internal understanding, better corresponding to normative realms employed by your subjects.

So while we need prior understandings of norms to get any impression of meaning, once we have an impression of meaning we can bring out the norms constituting it for explicit examination. We can then modify them if the actors we study seem to deviate in some way from our initial expectations, and we come closer to an insider's view in the process.

So it is in principle possible that Alfred waits longer than what I take to be the norm in responding to people, at least at times. By repeatedly observing Alfred I may come to this conclusion and begin to understand his activities differently than I initially did. I may discover that Samuel expects these longer periods of time between responses and thus shares the norm with Alfred. The relevant norm could then be a feature of their culture that I initially did not understand. Pauses between interactions are longer in their shared culture than in the cultural contexts I am used to.

5. *Personality factors:* Hermeneutic processes do not simply give you an understanding of normative realms common to a different culture; they also differentiate between culturally routine patterns and individually routine patterns. Over time, a researcher will notice regular but highly individualized mannerisms, vocal tones, facial expressions, and so on that she would tend to attribute to the "personality" of an actor rather than to a "culture." A reconstruction of meaning must be cognizant of the contributions of highly individualized modes of action as well as more shared features. All acts assert some play between the individually particular and the culturally general. As researchers we must be able to spot the lines of differentiation between idiosyncratic and culturally general patterns.

It may be that Samuel interprets Alfred's use of silent periods in the same way that I initially did, as something deliberate. Alfred, however, may not intend anything with these longer-than-expected delays, in which case Samuel would be misunderstanding Alfred in a systematic way. It may be that Alfred is not aware of this consistently occurring misunderstanding. It would be attributable to Alfred's personality: his particular way of understanding certain norms to position-take with others that differs from most other people in his cultural group.

My detailed description of the hermeneutic inference, phase-by-phase, would be intimidating and impractical if readers took it to be a set of procedures they should employ each time they reconstruct meanings. But this is not the case. Reconstructing meaning can never be reduced to a set of procedures. Because it requires learning to position-take as your subjects do, interpretation is ultimately an art (Denzin 1994). But interpretation, meaning reconstruction, makes use of basic processes common to all acts of understanding. Interpretation is hermeneutic.

The purpose of the phase-by-phase description was to raise awareness of an inference process we all employ tacitly in everyday life. Meaning reconstructions in research will often be made quite rapidly, but those who perform them must be mentally aware of the principles involved to produce formulations close to what the actors themselves would consider valid. There will be times when you are puzzled by and unsure of how to reconstruct certain meaningful actions made by one's subjects. In these cases, the phase-by-phase description of hermeneutic inferences given above could be explicitly helpful.

The Purpose of Meaning Reconstruction

One could look at a set of meaning reconstructions of the sort illustrated above and ask, "So what?" What is the purpose of meaning reconstruction? There are several answers.

First: initial meaning reconstructions are performed to help researchers clarify the impressions of meaning they have received from their observations. Impressions of meaning involve large tacit realms. Articulating such tacit realms helps you become more aware of what you might be missing, what biases might be in play, what cultural forms are necessary to understand through further analysis.

Second: initial meaning reconstructions should be given to a peer debriefer to check. A discussion between the researcher and a peer debriefer over meaning reconstructions early on helps to "calibrate" the researcher in making further reconstructions of meaning. It allows an outsider to challenge the researcher on biases and blindnesses in order to increase the researcher's own awareness of them. Later reconstructions need not be so explicitly made as those made early for peer review.

Third: selected meaning reconstructions can be inserted into the final write-up and therefore are not simply backstage operations. They are extremely effective for illustrating general points made in the final research report.

Fourth: meaning reconstructions lay the groundwork for validity reconstructions and horizon analysis.

PRAGMATIC HORIZON ANALYSIS

The Concept of "Pragmatic Horizons"

Understanding meaningful acts takes place holistically and implicitly. In everyday life we gain holistic impressions of meaning from which we act back, or respond, to the original act. When we reconstruct meanings, our response to a holistic impression of meaning is of a specialized variety: it is an effort to articulate portions of our impression linguistically.

With pragmatic horizon analysis meaning reconstruction is carried forth into new levels of precision. I have coined the phrase "pragmatic horizon analysis" by borrowing the term "horizon" from phenomenology and relocating it within the pragmatic theory of meaning associated with Habermas's work.

Classical phenomenologists study perception (both sense perception and the perception of inner states and ideas) in terms of "horizons of intelligibility." An object takes on a distinctive form within perceptual experience only against a background horizon that is apperceived at the same time (apperception means "perceived with"). When we notice an object before us in our visual field, we notice it against many other objects that are out of focus. Implicit contrasts between the focal object and its background bring the focal object out for us. The background is part of our experience, but it is out of focus and plays a barely noticed role in producing object perception.

Gestalt psychology studies this sort of thing in terms of "figure" and "ground" relations. Phenomenologists, however, note the relationship of object and horizon in many diverse experiences, including purely mental ones. We only understand an idea against a horizon from which that idea is brought forth. A structure of background contrasts works to constitute the idea in the foreground. To understand a concept like "finite," for example, there must be an accompanying, but backgrounded, understanding of "infinite." There are several good books on phenomenology and the concept of horizons that readers may wish to consult (one of the best is Caputo 1987).

The idea of pragmatic horizons comes from regarding action, rather than perception, to be most primary in experience. A perceptual horizon is understood to be a special case of a pragmatic horizon, according to this idea, because a perceptual object only becomes fully foregrounded when it is symbolized and therefore located within generalized contexts of possible communication. A perception is knowledge-imparting only when it becomes a possible reference in communicative acts.

The meaning of a meaningful act has a horizon structure constituted by intersubjective assumptions (assumptions about how others in first-, second-, and third-person positions could experience the act). An act of meaning will possess a foreground represented by symbols (usually linguistic symbols) used explicitly by the actor. Symbols are socially constituted; their use assumes their intelligibility to other people in a cultural group. Thus, part of the horizon surrounding a meaningful act consists of a shared understanding of symbol systems. This portion of the horizon is very layered and complex, containing structures productive of semantic units, syntactic structures, grammatical structures, and phonetics.

In addition, all communicative acts take place within social relations. To act communicatively, actors must adopt roles, must employ styles of interaction, must be cognizant of power relations between actors, and so on. Actors must share understandings about the social context of the act for the act to be communicative. This portion of the horizon has to do with pragmatics in the linguistic sense (Gumperz 1982; Seung 1982a, 1982b; Brown and Yule 1983; Carspecken 1992). The basic claim involved with the pragmatic form of the act is that the act is socially legitimate or appropriate. At the level of validity claims as discussed in chapter four, this part of the horizon can be reduced to claims of the normative-evaluative variety.

Meaningful acts also claim and reference certain subjective states on the part of the actor: whether the actor is amused, serious, friendly, hostile, and so on. This part of the horizon consists of subjective claims. Closely associated with subjective claims are claims that the actor is such and such kind of person: a clever person, a competent person, a righteous person, and so on. These claims mix normative-evaluative and subjective claims. I call them identity claims.

Finally, meaningful acts will always refer to an objective state of affairs. If a teacher says to a student, "Michael, it is time to open the books and get going on that assignment," the objective reference is very much backgrounded but clearly includes the claim that teacher and student are in a classroom during school hours. Given this objective state of affairs, certain normative-evaluative conditions are claimed to be in play: that students should obey teachers and that school hours are for doing school work. The reference to an objective state of affairs, within a pragmatic horizon, can be reduced to validity claims of the objective category (see chapters three, four, and five).

All in all there are five main categories of reference and claim within the horizon of meaningful acts:

1. A claim that the act is *intelligible*
2. A claim that the act is socially *legitimate* or *appropriate*
3. A claim that the actor has a certain *subjective state* (feelings and intentions) at the time of acting
4. A claim that the actor has a certain *identity*
5. A claim that a certain *objective state of affairs* exists

Let me illustrate this simply. Suppose you see a stranger waiting for a bus with you on a rainy day. You glance toward the rain and say, "Miserable day, isn't it?" The horizon about your meaningful act includes the use of words, linguistic syntax, and grammar that contribute to the act's intelligibility. You must assume that your utterance is intelligible in order to talk to this other person in this way. You also claim to have benign intentions toward this other person and a desire to engage in light conversation. Closely tied to your subjective references is an identity claim: that you are a good-natured person, amiable and friendly. You simultaneously reference an assumption that this act is socially legitimate: it is an appropriate act in these circumstances. You

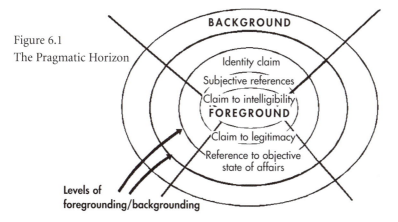

Figure 6.1
The Pragmatic Horizon

are roughly social equals and no major status differences govern your relationship. If you had said, "Give me your umbrella now! I'm getting wet!!" you would also be claiming that your act is socially legitimate, but it is unlikely, in this case, that the other person would agree! Finally, your act obviously claims that something is undesirable with the weather—ultimately, that it is raining (objective claim) and that rain is unpleasant when waiting for buses (normative-evaluative claim).

All of these claims are part of the pragmatic horizon of the act. A pragmatic horizon could be diagrammed as in Figure 6.1. Notice the layered nature of this diagram. It spreads away from an emphasized foreground toward a surrounding set of related but backgrounded assumptions. Each type of claim made can contain elements in the foreground of the act as well as elements moving outwards toward the background. In our example of chitchat at a bus stop, the intention to engage in light conversation and be friendly (subjective claims) are foregrounded. The norm that a comment on the weather is an appropriate way to initiate such conversations is backgrounded.

Structures of the Pragmatic Horizon

Pragmatic horizons are vast and complex. Each possible meaning in a meaning field, as defined earlier on, is intelligible only through its location within a meaning horizon where implicit and remote references work, rather like Gestalt backgrounds, to bring out the emphasized foreground. The categories I mentioned above—claims to intelligibility, appropriateness, subjective states, actor's identity, and objective states of affairs—all fall within a more general feature of the pragmatic horizon that can be named its *paradigmatic axis,* for reasons about to be explained. There is also a temporal axis constituting pragmatic horizons.

Interactive Syntax: The Temporal Axis

To spot the workings of the temporal axis in the meaning horizons of any social act, one must note the location of the act within the participants' awarenesses of prior events and within their expectations of events about to come. Part of the meaning is constituted by assumptions made by each actor of a shared awareness of what has just occurred and thus of what is expected to come next. This is the temporal axis of meaning. All acts of meaning are contextual: the meaning fields associated with them will be constituted by an interactive syntax of past action in relation to expectations of what will come next. The meaning of any particular act will depend in part on its location within a stream of interaction: thus a syntax. If the comment about the weather had occurred in the middle of a discussion about U.S. foreign relations, it would not have had the same meaning as it did as an initiator of conversation.

The constitution of interactive syntax is intersubjective: it works through the assumptions of each actor about a shared awareness of previous acts and their significance plus an assumedly shared set of expectations of what acts could come next. The syntax could therefore be construed differently by different actors, and actors monitor each other's responses partly to gain a more certain understanding of how each interprets what has occurred already and how each expects certain kinds of acts to come next. Qualitative researchers must have an eye to the temporal axis at all times when reconstructing meanings.

Virtual Constituting Structures: The Paradigmatic Axis

The other major axis can be called the paradigmatic axis. This involves the constitution of meaning through structures of similarity, complementarity, contrast, opposition, hierarchical inclusion, and inference that exist "virtually": outside of space and time (see Giddens 1979: ch.1 for a related discussion). Paradigms are implicated all at once, at the instant that a meaning is recognized. Their many parts, and the complex relationship between these parts, are differentiated from each other paradigmatically rather than experientially.

For example, to understand a speech act like, "Gosh, I really hate these macho men!" (said with emphasis on "hate" and a facial grimace), many paradigmatic structures must be grasped all at once. The vocal emphasis on "hate," the grimace, the angry tone of voice, all convey meaning partially through paradigmatic contrasts with alternative ways of saying the same words. This speech act fits into a category of serious, angry, disgusted acts distinguished from acts that mock others, ironic acts, sarcastic acts, reluctant assertions, coerced assertions, light criticisms, and so on. The speaker can be understood by tacitly understanding contrasts between the manner in which she spoke her words and other possible manners. The manner of the act carries a meaning constituted paradigmatically through such contrasts.

On the level of semantics, one must be in possession of paradigmatic structures constituting use of the term "macho." "Macho" probably takes its sense from contrasts with other conceptions of "men" and "masculinity." These are not stated explicitly, however, in the speech act. They paradigmatically constitute the meaning of macho. The semantic category of macho is hierarchically subordinated to the category of men.

It is in contrast with hierarchically equivalent categories like "nice men," "regular guys," "soft males," and so on, depending on the culture.

The validity references implicated in, "Gosh, I really hate these macho men!" also involve a paradigmatic structure. "Macho" seems to be negatively evaluated. Behind the implicated claim, "Being macho is bad," is a more remotely implicated, possible, claim: perhaps "Dominating others is bad" and/or "Social relations should be equal" and/or "Social relations should involve mutual respect." Here the constituting structure is that of implicit inference.

Many such structures work together in the synthetic experience of understanding a meaning horizon. The explicit features of the meaning are brought off through a complexity of constituting structures that are outside of space and time, which means that they are implicated tacitly and holistically rather than explicitly stated. Pragmatic horizon analysis involves the articulation of paradigmatic constituting structures as well as the articulation of an interactive syntax.

Types of Paradigmatic Structures

Just above I have illustrated several paradigmatic constituting structures: those associated with pragmatic and semantic meaning units, and those associated with validity claims. In this short section I will say a bit more about paradigmatic constituting structures, largely to indicate conceptual models and analytic procedures I regretfully must leave out of this book. Readers should note the basic ideas and note my references to other published materials that they may consult to help them with this sort of reconstructive activity. When using materials I reference here, readers should relocate them within the concept of pragmatic meaning horizons to make them consistent with this methodological theory.

Semantic Units

One type of constituting structure is involved with semantic units. The semantic terms employed by an actor take their sense through semantic structures characteristic of a cultural group. If an actor pointedly uses the word "light," for example, part of the horizon of meaning could involve a tacit contrast to dark. Many popular techniques employed by qualitative researchers focus exclusively on semantic structures. Such methods elicit semantic domains, contrast sets and semantic taxonomies (see Spradley 1979, 1980 and Werner and Schoepfle 1987). These methods can be quite powerfully employed within a critical research project. But authors like Spradley conceive of semantic units and their constituting structures as static, fixed features of culture. It seems much closer to the actual state of affairs to consider them, instead, as intersubjectively constituted categories of meaning that are relatively stable, but not absolutely fixed, within cultural life. They are not set, but drift over time as actors innovate uses of them. The meaning of an act is always going to have its unique and particular aspects. Actors draw upon cultural milieu, including semantic categories, to construct their acts of meaning, but actors slightly alter and reconfigure such milieu with each act. Semantic units have relatively stable meanings across a variety of interactive contexts but are always employed in relation to other structures of meaning to bring off the sense of the particular act.

Similarly, the work of structuralist anthropologists on semantic units organized through binary oppositions and homologous relations can be located within the concept of pragmatic horizons (Maybury-Lewis and Almagor 1989; Lévi-Strauss 1967). Once again, however, the concept of "structure" as used by structuralists must be removed from the imagery of fixed structures characterizing a culture to the imagery of claimed pragmatic horizons that can differ and be reconfigured with each act (Carspecken 1992). A structure is a paradigm implicated by meaningful action. A structure does not determine the action, it is rather drawn upon, reproduced, or altered by actors. Paradigmatic structures are fundamentally claims, some of which gain stability and some of which fail to catch on when other people refuse to affirm them.

Pragmatic Meaning Units

Another set of paradigmatic structures involve pragmatic meaning units. I illustrated this above by drawing attention to the meanings conveyed through the manner of speaking. Such nondiscursively conveyed meanings have a singular property within experience, and thus may be called units. People act out roles, claim settings, engage in games, and employ other basically pragmatic structures that others recognize as meaningful in tacit, holistic, and singular ways (Carspecken 1993b, 1993c). Moreover, when recognizing a role or other pragmatic structure employed by an actor, we tacitly understand its significance through contrasts to other possible pragmatic units (roles, setting claims) that the actor has not employed.

An analogy may be drawn from music. Improvisational jazz musicians engage in a sort of conversation with each other, in which one player will introduce what they call an idea and others will expand and develop it. A musical idea has a singular property when it is recognized, but it eludes, absolutely, linguistic articulation. The development of a musical idea always works with intersubjective understandings of possible musical articulations that are not chosen by players. The sense of the musical forms that are expressed depends heavily on references to those left out. Human interaction through roles, rhythms, and sequences is a very similar process.

The idea of pragmatic meaning units has not been much emphasized in the literature on qualitative research to date. Certain types of pragmatic meanings have been studied in sociolinguistics (e.g., Gumperz 1982) and discourse analysis (e.g., Brown and Yule 1983; for philosophical discussions of pragmatics see Seung 1982a, 1982b). But even this literature has not explored the idea of pragmatic meaning units and constituting structures (for beginning explorations of this idea, see Carspecken 1992; Carspecken and Cordeiro 1995).

The basic idea is that actors possess units of understanding that are not semantic in nature and may not even have native terms referring to them. They have a unit characteristic because they are understood in a singular manner, but they are understood on tacit levels rather than on symbolic levels. Many roles common to a cultural group display this characteristic of being units of meaning constituted through contrasts with other such units; so are identity claims. Such things are understood all at once and as bounded units of meaning.

Interpretative Schemes

Finally, one can study a large number of interactions recorded in the primary record as well as conduct many qualitative interviews with the purpose of reconstructing the complex intersections between semantic units, pragmatic units, and generalized validity claims (see below). The results of an analysis like this will include the reconstruction of interpretative schemes specific to certain contexts of life which synthetically unite roles, linguistic patterns, and what is below called "tacit theories." I conducted an analysis like this in my first ethnography and termed the resulting reconstruction intersubjective structure (Carspecken 1991). The reconstructions I conducted on intersubjective structure helped to explain consistent interpersonal conflicts discovered on the research site plus the manner in which these conflicts were eventually resolved. They also displayed both consistencies and inconsistencies between a variety of cultural elements.

Validity Claims and Implicit Inference

I lack the room necessary to include a chapter on meaning units and their constituting structures, so little more will be said about semantic and pragmatic categories, or the idea of intersubjective structure. I will concentrate instead on validity claims implicated within pragmatic horizons. Meaning units, both pragmatic and semantic, generally synthesize validity claims of all three categories. The semantic term "light," for example, might be used in one culture to connote conceptual clarity (subjective reference) that is good, and desirable (normative-evaluative reference) and that underlies identifiable modes of behavior (objective reference). Roles and identity claims also synthesize diverse categories of validity reference. These validity claims can be fully articulated as constituents of a meaning horizon.

It is extremely important to note that the validity claims implicated in a pragmatic horizon are influenced by the semantic terms employed and the roles acted out, but they are not determined by semantic or pragmatic units. To use the term "light" is not necessarily to make reference to a positive evaluation, even if "light" usually carries such evaluations in a particular culture. The situation is just the opposite. The validity references imbibed within semantic units and pragmatic modes of meaning are reproduced, and often slightly altered, by meaningful acts. Every meaningful act uniquely claims a certain configuration of validity claims that are not tied to the pragmatic and semantic units employed but rather reproduce (or slightly change) the sense of such units. This is because validity claims are carried by the entire act, not by the semantic or pragmatic units employed alone.

In the rest of this chapter I will focus on the validity references of the paradigmatic axis and the temporal axis of pragmatic horizons. In what follows, I will first discuss and exemplify validity reconstructions and then the temporal axis of meaning horizons. Remember that implicated validity claims are only one constituting structure within the paradigmatic axis of a meaning horizon. These validity claims, however, are unique to the act in its totality. Reconstructing them is the analytic method closest to this methodological theory, and is simultaneously going to provide the most precise articulation of meaning horizons.

Section Summary

A pragmatic horizon, then, is constituted along a temporal and a paradigmatic axis. The paradigmatic axis includes pragmatic and semantic constituting structures plus validity inferences at various levels of foregrounding. (See Figure 6.2). Everything represented in this figure, and more, is grasped at once, tacitly, each moment one human being understands another.

VALIDITY RECONSTRUCTION IN QUALITATIVE DATA ANALYSIS

Meaningful acts are partially constituted through tacitly referenced validity claims. Meaning reconstructions can focus on these validity claims, dividing them out according to the three categories discussed in chapter four: objective claims, subjective claims, and normative-evaluative claims. One can gain much insight into a culture by paying attention to the validity claims routinely employed in the construction of meaningful action.

I call the articulation of validity claims according to the three categories *horizontal analysis.* It is also important to distinguish between highly foregrounded claims, highly backgrounded claims, and intermediate cases. I call this sort of procedure *vertical analysis.* Another example of vertical analysis should be helpful at this point.

Recently I asked a friend of mine, who works for an engineering firm, how things were going on the job. His answer was, "Morale is down, but we are getting a new executive director soon. With new leadership, or, I really should say with *leadership,* our situation could get a lot better." His second sentence is the most interesting. The most foregrounded claim goes something like this: "Our present director is not a leader." A little less foregrounded is the claim, "Morale is low because there is a lack of leadership." A backgrounded claim, upon which all else depends, is, "Leadership is necessary for good morale," and "A leader is necessary and important for a company like ours," or "Leadership is good," and/or "Leadership depends on personality factors (rather than organizational factors)."

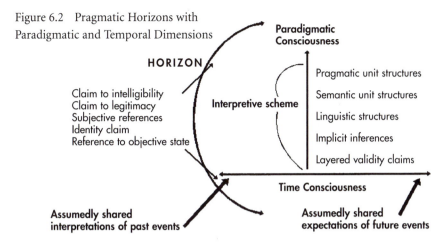

Figure 6.2   Pragmatic Horizons with Paradigmatic and Temporal Dimensions

Paradigmatic Consciousness

HORIZON

Claim to intelligibility
Claim to legitimacy
Subjective references
Identity claim
Reference to objective state

Interpretive scheme

Pragmatic unit structures

Semantic unit structures

Linguistic structures

Implicit inferences

Layered validity claims

Time Consciousness

Assumedly shared interpretations of past events

Assumedly shared expectations of future events

Validity reconstructions are efforts to articulate components of meaning that one normally understands without much explicit awareness. In the case of a disagreement or a misunderstanding, the tacit validity claims underlying meaningful acts will be articulated by the actors themselves to defend their position or to clear up the misunderstanding. When we understand another person, we understand how they would explain themselves to others who either disagree or miss their point. If I had said to my friend, "Well, where I work the rule is that the less leadership, the better!" he might have replied by articulating some of his original validity claims to help me better understand his point. He might have said, for example, "Yes, well, that is because you work in a university. Engineering companies have to be hierarchical. They have to be led." If I instead argued that he had a narrow view of corporate organization, betrayed by his insistence on the need for a leader, he would have had to articulate yet more backgrounded validity claims constituting his original remark in order to defend his views. Whether or not I ultimately agree with him, the more I can anticipate such reasons he would bring to bear in support of his point, the better I understand him.

Thus, understanding meaning includes understanding the reasons an actor could provide to explain expressions. Reasons will generally fall into the three categories of objective, subjective, and normative-evaluative truth claims. Reasons will also differ from each other according to how immediately they are referenced in the original act (foregrounded) or how remotely they are referenced (backgrounded). Validity is internally connected to meaning: one understands validity claims, often tacitly, as soon as one understands meaning (Habermas 1981:116-17).

To demonstrate validity reconstruction that simultaneously employs the horizontal and vertical dimensions of analysis, let us take some of the same speech acts we have been examining in the interaction of Alfred and Samuel. I will pick up the interaction at a point late in the segments already presented and continue with it for a while. When I reach segment [37], I will insert validity reconstructions differentiated according to the three categories of validity claim and according to the level of foregrounding or backgrounding.

Following [37], I will discuss the significance of these validity reconstructions to illustrate their potency in qualitative data analysis generally. Then I will present the next segment of field notes with added validity reconstructions and, immediately after that, continue the field notes for a short while without reconstructions. Readers might wish to try their own validity reconstructions on the last of the notes. To shorten things a bit, I have stripped off some of the commentary added to the actual primary record, which is quite thickly recorded.

Field Note Excerpt: Samuel and Alfred with Horizontal and Vertical Validity Reconstructions

[15] A: *Samuel.* Very calm voice, gentle…

....

[18] A: *Would you come up here please?*

....

[20] S: He comes up with jacket pulled over head, looks at black board.

[21] S: *What?* Sharp and irritable type tone.

[22] A: *We're at a very critical point now, aren't we?* Calm tone....

[23] S: Samuel pulls…jacket down as if angry; a sudden, rapid, crisp movement.

....

[26] S: …*the test and I ain't going to do it.*

[27] A: *We're at a critical point (garbled).* Tone still calm.

[28] S: *WHAT?!* Very loud, irritated, disgusted.

....

[34] S: Samuel sits up as if annoyed at having to do so.

....

[37] A: *Are you upset about home?* Calm and reasonable tone.

Possible subjective claims

Foregrounded, Immediate

"I care about you," "I want to understand you," "I want to help you cope with your problems"

Less Foregrounded, Less Immediate

"I am a kind and caring teacher" (identity claim), "I am sincere"

Possible objective claims

Quite Foregrounded, Quite Immediate

"Events are occurring in your home that many children would report as upsetting"

Highly Backgrounded, Remote, Taken-for-Granted

"You live in a home," "You live with other people—mother and grandmother"

(OR—just possible) "Black families have many domestic problems"

Possible normative-evaluative claims

Quite Foregrounded, Quite Immediate

"It is good to talk about feelings"

Less Foregrounded, Less Immediate

(OR) "Your mother's behavior is bad"

Backgrounded, Remote

"Children have responsibility for their feelings"

(OR) "Mothers have responsibility for the feelings of their children"

(OR—just possible) "Black families (mothers) are often inadequate"

Validity Claims and the Field Property of Meaning

Validity claims are portions of the possible meanings one could read from a social act and as such display the same field characteristic that meaning itself does. Notice my use of (OR) in the reconstructions above. I have placed (OR) in front of especially uncertain claims. Samuel will respond in relation to these tacitly referenced claims and will have to cope with the especially uncertain claims that he is aware of (remember that these may differ from what appears as possible but uncertain to us).

Once validity claims are reconstructed at various levels of backgrounding and foregrounding, many subtle forms of analysis are opened up. Take, for example, the possible remote references I have attributed to Alfred's speech act that have to do with "black families."

The Example of Racial Nuances as Remote, Uncertain Possibilities

The point in articulating possible racial nuances is not initially that Alfred might have such assumptions in the back of his mind when he acts, but that anyone, including Samuel, could be aware of this possibility. If Samuel is aware of these references as a possibility, then he might respond toward Alfred in relation to it, whether Alfred actually has such beliefs or not. Of course, in a field study one will eventually want to find out whether the actors of concern do identify with various beliefs and attitudes, including racist ones. But well before one has accumulated enough information to ascertain such a thing, one needs to be aware of the possibilities, simply because all actors in the setting are going to be aware of such possibilities and act in relation to them.

Here is how Samuel responds to Alfred. I have reconstructed his possible validity claims and references just after giving his response:

[38] S: *No.* Said in new tone, not angry or irritated. Said as if a little defensive, with intonation up by end of word.

Possible Subjective Claims

Quite Foregrounded, Quite Immediate

"I am surprised you could even think I would be upset"

Less Foregrounded, Less Immediate

"You might not believe me, but, honestly, I am not upset"

"I have dignity" (identity claim)

Possible Objective Claims

Quite Foregrounded, Quite Immediate

"No events are taking place in my home that I would call upsetting"

Less Foregrounded, Less Immediate

"My mother is not doing anything that children would report to be upsetting"

Highly Backgrounded, Remote

"I live in a home with other people—my mother and grandmother"

(OR—just possible) "Black families do not have any more problems than white families"

Possible Normative-Evaluative Claims

Quite Foregrounded

"My home is perfectly normal and fine"

Less Foregrounded

(OR) "You do not have the right to question my home"

Backgrounded, Remote

(OR) "It is a sign of weakness or vulnerability to discuss feelings"

(OR) "Children should be loyal to their mothers and not talk badly about them"

(OR) "Mothers do not have responsibility for their children's feelings"

(OR) "Black families are just as good as white families"

As the interaction proceeds, some of what were at first background possibilities move toward the foreground because Alfred and Samuel begin to hone the situation and get clearer ideas of what the other is thinking and intending. See if you can articulate the shift in backgrounding and foregrounding, as well as the introduction of new possible claims:

[39] A: *No? Was mom home last night?*

[40] S: *Yeah.* Same sort of tone: intonation up at end of word.

[41] A: *Yeah?* As if not believing.

[42] S: *Yeah. And then she left.* Samuel's voice has become softer, his shoulders slump forward slightly and he looks down.

....

[51] A: *Why don't you care what she does?*

[52] S: *She can do what she wants.* Emphasis on "she."

[53] A: *Uh umm, but how do you feel about it?* Emphasis on "you."

....

[56] S: *I don't care what I do anymore.* Emphasis on "I."

A little later on in this chapter I will discuss shifts in backgrounding and foregrounding brought off by Alfred and Samuel. First we must understand the temporal axis of meaning horizons in a little more detail.

THE TEMPORAL AXIS

The concept of the temporal horizon is that of an act's references that depend on assumptions concerning shared understandings of what has occurred in the immediate past. The validity reconstructions I conducted above on [37], when Alfred asked whether Samuel is upset about home, would not have occurred to me without some attention to the interactive context in which Alfred's statement took place. Prior to [37], we have seen a series of classroom rule violations on Samuel's part: violations that, as I learned during my long series of observations in this classroom, usually result in sanctions. When Alfred acts in [37], it is reasonable to assume that he has been aware of these classroom rule violations and of Samuel's expectations that a sanction will follow them. Part of the meaning of his act, then, involves his assumption that Samuel has been expecting a sanction of some sort. By not referring explicitly to violated rules and by not imposing a sanction or threatening to do so, Alfred is conveying certain meanings to Samuel. Samuel, for his part, will have an impression of meaning from Alfred's act in [37] that is partially formed by Alfred's failure to mention rules or sanctions. This issue, then, well exemplifies the concept of "temporal axis" or "temporal horizon." Let us analyze the components of this horizon.

37) A: "Are you upset about home?"
Generalized Horizon References from Immediate Past
Students should obey teachers (NORM)
If they do not, sanctions follow (OBJECTIVE)
I am a defiant student (SUBJECTIVE-IDENTITY)
I am a bad student or person (SUBJECTIVE-IDENTITY)
I am fed up (SUBJECTIVE)

Now, one could in principle work up these references in terms of the vertical dimension (backgrounding and foregrounding), but I will not do so here. The main point to be made is that the temporal features of the horizon of an act correspond to tacit assumptions about shared knowledge of past interactions and their references. The assumptions about shared understandings of past interactions amount to generalizations from the paradigmatic horizons of the immediate past. They tell us something of what each actor expects of actions to come, and part of the meaning of the actions that do come involves their similarity to, or contrast with, what is expected.

Alfred's act takes part of its meaning through its lack of explicit reference to the temporal dimension, to what has just occurred. This basically amounts to the suspension of normal expectations in order to claim a different interactive setting, with different norms claimed to be in play. The lack of explicit references to the immediate past, to Samuel's rule violations in this case, produces an implicit reference to them— the rules paradigmatically associated with these past activities are claimed to be out of play by Alfred, which conveys something of his intentions, feelings, and identity.

SPECIAL USES OF HORIZON ANALYSIS

Both attention to the temporal axis of meaning and use of paradigmatic validity reconstructions can be powerfully employed in analyzing strips of interaction. I will illustrate some basic uses of horizon analysis in this chapter's final section.

SETTING NEGOTIATIONS AND SETTING SHIFTS

An interactive setting is a sort of normative infrastructure, tacitly consented to by all parties involved, that helps coordinate activities through giving a tacit specification of the basic purpose of the interaction, its rhythm, and the tacit agreement on associated values, norms, and/or beliefs. A setting negotiation occurs when one actor makes a bid to alter the normative infrastructure. A setting shift occurs when such negotiations succeed and a prior normative infrastructure is replaced by a new one.

The interaction between Alfred and Samuel as presented so far contains several setting negotiations and actual setting shifts, brought about when one actor manages to win the consent of the other on a change in the normative infrastructure.

Looking at this interaction as a whole, it is clear that a key moment occurred right at the beginning, when Alfred tries to get Samuel to take a test and Samuel refuses to take it. Up until [15], the interaction is characterized by conflict over whether Samuel should/will take the test. Samuel employs various methods, bids, and claims in his efforts to refuse taking it, but all this occurs within a sort of umbrella definition of the interaction that foregrounds the issue of whether Samuel is going to take this test. Within this umbrella definition we find an interactive rhythm of Alfred asserting the necessity of taking the test, followed by resistance on Samuel's part, followed by a new assertion on Alfred's part, a new objection from Samuel, and so on.

At [15], when Alfred suddenly says "Samuel" in a calm and firm voice, we have another key moment. Alfred here breaks with the previous rhythm and begins a series of moves to shift the setting definition. He indicates that the test is no longer his principal concern, but he is mysterious about what his central concern now is. Samuel probably does not understand Alfred's intentions and resists Alfred's efforts to redefine the setting.

By [37], when Alfred asks about Samuel's home, Alfred has ceased being mysterious and has explicitly and directly changed the subject by asking about Samuel's situation at home. Samuel agrees to the setting shift but, within the new setting definition, resists Alfred's effort to discuss Samuel's mother. Alfred's outer interactive form is that of asking questions in order to get answers. But Alfred's tone of voice and his persistence on the subject of Samuel's mother carry the not-too-tacit implication that he believes Samuel's mother is a problem and that Samuel knows this himself. Samuel never fully acknowledges this, but contributes to a new interactive rhythm by repeatedly defending himself and his mother from Alfred's challenges. Finally, Samuel tacitly acknowledges that there is a problem but, perhaps because he does not wish to have his mother criticized, offers himself as the target of criticism and discussion at [56] ("I don't care what I do anymore"). This is a complicated movement on Samuel's part, as it both offers himself up as the subject of potential criticism but also makes it possible to receive sympathetic responses from Alfred.

All streams of interaction may be analyzed in this sort of way, by looking at key moments when one or more of the actors begin ultimately successful moves at changing the interactive setting and altering the normative infrastructure. Alterations in the normative infrastructure ("umbrella" or "canopy") are generally accompanied by alterations in interactive rhythm.

Horizon analysis can make the analysis of setting negotiations and shifts much more precise, as the next section will illustrate.

Validity Claims and Setting Shifts

Bringing Background References to the Fore

Particularly interesting, in terms of meaning horizons and setting negotiations, is Samuel's speech act in [42], where he concedes an objective claim that had previously been in tacit dispute: whether his mother left the house the previous night or not. He says, "Yeah. And then she left." This objective claim had been a less immediate sort of reference during [37]–[38] and became a totally foregrounded claim in dispute during [39]–[41]. Once Samuel concedes that his mother did leave the house, the interactive rhythm of a challenge from Alfred followed by a counterclaim from Samuel continues, but with new foregrounds: subjective references (whether Samuel feels upset or not) and normative-evaluative references (whether Samuel's mother behaves appropriately, whether she is "good"). Thus one way of giving precision to the analysis of interactive streams is to look for the way in which backgrounded validity claims are taken, over time, into the foreground by the actors.

Implicit Inferences in Dispute and Negotiation

The dynamics of the interaction between Alfred and Samuel depend not only on the claims and their backgrounded or foregrounded status but also on certain tacit inferences connecting claims. To illustrate this, notice that Samuel appears most concerned with the normative-evaluative implications of Alfred's challenges: he wishes to defend his mother from a negative evaluation. But Samuel has tied his subjective state to certain normative-evaluative implications: if he concedes that he feels upset or unhappy over his mother's behavior, this means (he seems to assume) that his mother appears at fault. A backgrounded inference structuring Samuel's speech acts could therefore be articulated as; "If I feel bad about my mother going out last night this will reflect badly on her" OR "If I acknowledge feeling bad about my mother going out last night, Alfred will infer that my mother is bad."

Tacit inferences are always referenced in leveled or layered ways. Behind this tacit inference is a more general normative-evaluative claim of which the particular inference is a special case: "Mothers are responsible for the feelings of their children." Samuel either assumes that something like this more backgrounded claim is true, or assumes that something like this more backgrounded claim is believed true by Alfred. Unless this more backgrounded general claim is somehow altered, Samuel is likely to continue acting as if it were either true or believed to be true by Alfred. Unless it is altered, the interactive rhythm of challenge and defense will continue until the inter-action itself stops.

Tacit Negotiations of Backgrounded Claims

In [53] Alfred says: "Uh umm, but how do you feel about it?" Here Alfred uses a technique common in counseling psychology: he basically detaches the state of Alfred's feelings from any normative-evaluative implications pertaining to Alfred's mother. Alfred, in other words, offers an alternative way for Samuel to understand the situation. He tacitly suggests that the backgrounded normative claim "Mothers are responsible for their children's feelings" is not valid.

This move works through making new, generalized, and highly backgrounded claims: "One's feelings simply are; they may be discussed without locating responsibility for them with any party," AND "It is good (okay) to discuss feelings." Alfred thus claims the validity of a normative-evaluative perspective that Samuel has not been referencing: one can acknowledge feelings related to significant others without judging these significant others or one's self.

Implicit Theories

A very backgrounded perspective is referenced by Alfred in [53] that could be articulated as an implicit theory of the self. Alfred asks how Samuel feels about the situation, drawing attention to Samuel's self and its autonomy. Implied remotely is the idea that the self is distinct from one's feelings. In other words, the value of one's self, its goodness or badness, is not affected if one acknowledges the feelings one has. Additionally, the goodness or badness of others is not affected when acknowledging one's own feelings, according to these backgrounded claims. The possible theory implicit to these moves is: "The self is distinct from behavior," and possibly "The self is intrinsically valid aside from feelings and behaviors." If Samuel accepts Alfred's offer for a setting shift in [53] and begins to discuss his feelings, he will have tacitly bought into this backgrounded and implicit theory referenced by Alfred. Since this particular interaction is taking place between student and teacher within a classroom, Samuel's tacit acceptance of the backgrounded theory would be evidence of a successful hidden curriculum. Tacit theories, reconstructed through horizon analysis, are a precise way of studying the hidden curriculum (see Apple 1979, 1983 for the concept of hidden curriculum).

Now, in a full qualitative study implicit theories can only be reconstructed in a convincing manner through the analysis of many interactions and through conducting and analyzing interviews. Alfred's move in [53] suggests this implicit theory about the self, but it suggests other possibilities too. One must use evidence from many interactions to be in a position to reconstruct implicit theories. One will find, moreover, that several theories will often underlie the interactions of the same people and these theories can be contradictory, but the number of such implicit theories will generally be small. Once they are reconstructed, streams of interaction taking place over large periods of time will become intelligible in relation to a small number of implicit theories that the actors routinely background in their acts. This is a very powerful way of explaining action routines and patterns.

"Acting As If": Subtleties in Background and Foregrounding

Notice one other thing. Backgrounding and foregrounding can be quite subtle in that one actor can act as if certain references are totally backgrounded and taken for granted when in fact they are foregrounded within this actor's *concerns.* The more backgrounded a reference, the more "assumed" and "taken-for-granted" it is. Actors frequently use this to try to hide their real concerns. One sees some of this in [38] when Samuel says "No" as if the issue of whether he is upset is not a significant issue to him, as if he could not have foreseen that Alfred might think he would be upset at home. He does something similar in [40] with "Yeah"—MF: "yeah, of course my mother was home, I am surprised you would even think she might not have been."

As a rule, backgrounded claims imply that the actor assumes their validity on deep levels and assumes that all reasonable people will also take them for granted. Backgrounding a claim implies taking it to be a feature of common sense. Actors can use this to conceal doubts, fears, and uncertainties or to manipulate other actors in various ways. The social researcher must try to be aware of this when it occurs.

The Inexhaustible Nature of Pragmatic Horizons

Thus, we are in possession of a flexible and powerful interpretative framework with the idea of horizontal and vertical dimensions to validity reconstruction. The horizontal dimension to validity reconstruction, it will be recalled, refers to the distinction between objective, subjective, and normative-evaluative claims. The vertical dimension refers to layers of foregrounding and backgrounding. Remember that horizontal and vertical reconstruction cannot be conducted without attention to interactive syntax: the temporal axis of meaning horizons.

Readers must be sure to understand that there is never a single correct manner of employing this form of analysis because the model of horizontal and vertical analysis concerns nonobjective features of social phenomena. You must interpret events, but in the interpretation of events certain principles must be followed to make your reconstructions probable and supportable. The horizontal categories draw our attention to tacit validity claims made in every meaningful act. They aid us in reconstructing such claims, distinguishing between them, and predicting the course of an interaction for actors to maintain consistently their claims. The vertical dimension aids us in grasping subtle configurations of meaning, meaning negotiations, tacit learning processes, and tacit efforts to hide one's real concerns from other actors. The implications involved in every act of meaning are inexhaustible in nature. You cannot reconstruct every possible reference in a set of data—any effort to try to accomplish this would lead to endless work and a smothering amount of detail. In future chapters it will therefore be necessary to indicate how one may choose representative interactions for detailed reconstruction and how one can work toward the reconstruction of implicit theories capable of explaining general patterns of routine behavior (chapter nine on coding will be most helpful to these ends).

CHAPTER SUMMARY

In this chapter, we have learned how to construct initial meaning reconstructions and perform validity reconstructions both horizontally (by placing validity claims within the three ontological categories) and vertically (by noting the level of foregrounding or backgrounding of a particular claim). Validity reconstructions have special uses: for analyzing setting negotiations, settings, acting-as-if behavior, implicit theories, and the bringing of backgrounded claims into the foreground during sequences of inter-action.

Validity reconstruction is an analytic technique closest to the critical epistemological framework. But I have explained that validity references are but one part of the pragmatic horizon carried by a meaningful act. Pragmatic units, semantic units, and interpretative schemes are all also components of pragmatic horizons. Other texts on qualitative data analysis, like Spradley's well-known books (1979, 1980), focus exclusively on the reconstruction of semantic units characteristic of a culture. Pragmatic meaning units—like roles, types of talk, and sequences—have rarely been studied in terms of constituting structure. I have written some empirical pieces in the area of pragmatic constituting structures (Carspecken 1992; Carspecken and Cordeiro 1995), but this field remains to be fully exploited.

7

More on Reconstructive Analysis: Embodied Meaning, Power, and Secondary Concepts of Interaction

Items covered in chapter 7:

- A model of expressive action and its relation to pragmatic horizons

- The nature of embodied meaning

- Using body postures and gestures in analysis

- A typology of interactive power

- Cultural power

- Analyzing interactive and cultural powers together

- Secondary concepts of interaction

- Roles and role analysis

EXPRESSIVE ACTION, PRAXIS, AND EMBODIED MEANING

In the last chapter I introduced the concept of pragmatic horizon. When humans interact, meanings are recognized through the play of many factors structured paradigmatically and temporally. The components of a horizon, moreover, are layered along a continuum of foreground to background. Typically, one actor will say something while making certain gestures, facial expressions, and eye movements; the tone of voice used as well as the speed of speech will also contribute to the meaning of the act. The foreground of the meaning horizon is what the actor emphasizes, which is not always the same as the linguistic content of the act (in fact, the foreground often is not the linguistic content, or at least not this content alone). The background is a complex set of assumptions made by the actor about knowledge, beliefs, and values she shares with her audience. We learn a lot about people and cultures when we are able to articulate, or reconstruct, frequently employed horizon backgrounds.

In this chapter I will begin a discussion of one particularly interesting feature of the backgrounding/foregrounding qualities of a pragmatic horizon. This concerns both our ability to act meaningfully at all, and our ability to understand another person's act holistically, with all the many complex components of the meaning horizon and all the various structures that constitute these parts synthesized. When we understand another person, for example, we understand, at once, several possible points this person could be trying to make, arrayed in a meaning field. If we then wish to discuss one of these possible meanings—the point we believe most probably intended by the actor—we break that holistic understanding down into some of its components that we articulate explicitly. We differentiate a holistic understanding by either talking back to the person, or by simply thinking about what the person has said, or by writing down what the person said (and how she said it) in a field notebook. We create meaning horizons of our own, with an emphasized foreground and an assumed background. When we act meaningfully ourselves, we also take an initial holistic understanding and differentiate it through our expression: creating a background and a foreground, among other things. Acting meaningfully and understanding the meaning of other people's acts are two sides of the same coin.

Expressivism and Praxis

Not long ago, my eldest son, Sunil, asked me if I knew how to walk. I understood immediately what he was driving at (the point he was making) because I had pondered this same sort of thing when a child. But I thought I would play along with my son to see what ideas he had on this issue. I answered: "Sure, watch me and I will show you." I walked a few steps with a mocking look of pride on my face. "No," he said, "I mean do you know how to walk, not whether you can walk." I was delighted; Sunil is a clever boy whose probing mind makes me quite proud.

We discussed the issue for a while and determined that walking, sitting, catching a ball, and most other things we humans easily do are skills quite beyond our understanding. Each requires an infinitely complex synthesis of many complex movements. We never consciously understand how we bring these activities off: we just start doing them. The bulk of these actions are learned; we are not sort of "wired" to catch a ball but rather must observe other people doing it and practice what we see many times until we acquire the skill. But when we watch others act and learn from them to act that way ourselves, we do it all through holistic, implicit modes of understanding. We understand a countless number of specific movements altogether, whose specificity and relation to each other are an implicit part of our understanding.

The same is true with acting meaningfully. We learn how to act appropriately in social contexts by grasping all at once the many complex components of meaningful action. The right body posture to assume, the right voice, the right gesture, the correct use of eyes: all of these are grasped holistically and become part of a whole of many coordinated parts.

So much for the action involved in meaningful acts. What about the meaning involved in a meaningful act? It, too, is understood holistically. The play of foreground and background, the configuration of pragmatic, semantic, grammatical and phonetic factors, are understood at once, too. It takes other, reflective kinds of acts to differentiate some of these components into explicit expressions (which, of course, must have their own unarticulated backgrounds).

A certain trend in late 18th- and early 19th-century philosophy, called "expressivism" by Charles Taylor (1979), made much of this quality pertaining to meaningful action. Expressivists like Johanne Herder pointed out that when speaking or creating works of art, the actor does not know explicitly beforehand exactly what it is that she wants to express. The act of expression—whether it be speaking, writing, painting, composing—clarifies what is to be expressed. When acting meaningfully, we begin with a subjectively felt impetus to express something that we understand only implicitly. We cannot be sure what it is we want to express until we are actually in the process of expressing it. The meaning of an expressive act does not "exist" prior to the act itself; only an impetus (a complex of desire and preunderstandings) to act meaningfully comes into our experience (Carspecken 1993b, 1993c). Then, during and just after acting, we become clearer with respect to what we wanted to say (or express in other, nonlinguistic ways).

You should be able to recall times when you surprised yourself in a conversation by saying something better than you thought possible and thereby clarifying it more for yourself, just as there are times when we make repeated efforts to express ourselves only to remain frustrated.

Expressivist insights help explain such experiences. Meaningful action begins with subjectively felt impeti that mix the desire to act with holistic, implicit preunderstandings of meaning. The desired meaning becomes clearer during and after the act. The act itself differentiates portions of the impetus, the holistic preunderstanding, into a foreground and background. The act itself also differentiates many components implicit to the holistic impetus: subjective, objective, and normative-evaluative components; semantic and pragmatic components.

The same can be said about understanding the meaning of other people's activity. We first understand the point of another person's act holistically. It takes either action of our own (e.g., responding to the other, taking notes on what the other has done) or reflective thought to explicate and clarify our understanding. We must act to understand others in explicit ways, and our action differentiates features of our initial, holistic and implicit, understanding. Meaningful action is a process of explicating and differentiating. It takes a wholly implicit understanding and gives it another kind of holistic form: a foregrounded region dependent on a complex background—a meaning horizon.

Expressivist themes can be found in many branches of philosophy, linguistics, and social theory. Marx's theory of praxis—that of human life as an expressive, self-producing, process "praxis" (Marx 1977)—owes a lot to the expressivist tradition. Our work is ideally an expressive activity that takes implicitly suspected potentialities and makes them actual through the construction of some product. In capitalist society, however, human work becomes alienated, cut off from the expressive impetus that is fundamental to being a human being. When all the details of work have been planned and directed by someone else and when the production of products becomes fragmented into a series of trivial acts divided among a work force (as in assembly lines), workers can no longer express themselves in their labor. The need for praxis has been denied workers by capitalist work organization.

Recently, David McNeill published the results of a ten-year study of human gesture (1992). McNeill believes that gestures and the linguistic utterances accompanying them originate from a single impetus, which he calls an "idea unit." An act of expression differentiates the idea unit into portions: some that can take a sequential, explicit articulation through language, and some that must be symbolized more holistically with gestures. From the idea unit, meaning evolves into its expression.

In social theory, Anthony Giddens (1979, 1984) points out that humans basically find themselves within a stream of action. An actor becomes aware of the meaning of her act by monitoring the act as it is in progress. The act itself usually just erupts as an impetus evolves into expression. Self-awareness and self-reflection are basically processes of monitoring the eruption of impeti into acts (see also Joas 1993). Monitoring occurs through position-taking, "imagining" the act (usually on holistic and tacit levels of awareness) as others in the second- or third-person position would read them.

In other words, we understand the act of another, as well as our own acts, initially through action impeti arising in relation to it from within our own experience. Such impeti differ by type: some correspond to our ability to try to reproduce the act of another (imitate it from first person-position); some correspond to our ability to act back toward the actor appropriately (from the second-person position); and some correspond to our ability to put the meaning of the act into words (as in a third-person position). Thinking about the meaning of an act is another kind of action: an internalized mode of action.

Thus the distinction between the holistic/tacit portions of a meaning horizon and the explicit/delineated portions in the foreground seems related to the difference between an original impetus to act and the actual act itself, as monitored by the actor and those observing the act. It is a distinction corresponding to the differentiation of a holistic mode of understanding into various parts, only some of which become fully explicit and delineated.

A meaning horizon, however, never fully explicates the impetus of a meaningful action. Large portions of the original impetus remain holistic and tacit. They work within the horizon as its background.

Embodied Meaning

Now, it seems quite clear that the holistic experience of meaning is something felt in one's body. An impetus to act manifests in bodily sensation corresponding to the impulse to move one's body in highly complex ways in order to manifest the act.

Figure 7.1   The Social Act

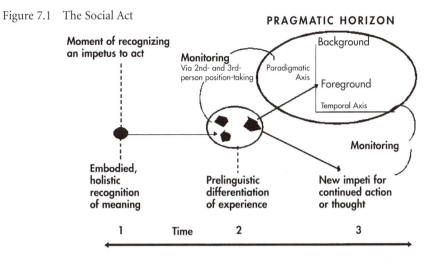

Similarly, understanding the act of another is initially a bodily experience that is only later differentiated into thoughts and actions. Meaning has an embodied quality.

Recently, various social scientists, philosophers, and researchers have begun to study the embodied character of meaning. Mark Johnson has published an exciting theory of meaning, called The Body in the Mind (1987), that seeks to locate universal body sensations as core schema from which concepts and other meaning structures are built up via metaphoric extensions. McNeill believes that the bodily basis of a meaning is given its most immediate, and least differentiated, expression in the gestures and postures that accompany the linguistic portions of an act (McNeill 1992). In critical ethnography, Peter McLaren has pioneered the analysis of bodily postures and gestures as a key to understanding the cultural forms and power relations of a social group (1993).

These insights into the bodily basis of meaning contribute to our theory of pragmatic horizons. Actors manifest an impetus to act that is initially entirely holistic, tacit, and embodied. As an impetus is acted out, actors monitor the act from the second- and third-person positions, differentiating an initially holistic experience into various interconnected parts. Early differentiation is prelinguistic and makes use of imagery and preconceptually understood expectations of how others will respond to one's act. Full differentiation, full monitoring, produces a full-fledged meaning horizon with an emphasized foreground (usually inclusive of an explicit linguistic content) made sensible through a still holistic and tacit background (Carspecken 1993b, 1993c, 1993d). Differentiation gives rise to the various structures discussed in chapter six: pragmatic structures; semantic structures; grammatical, syntactic, and phonetic structures; and identity claims (See diagram in Figure 7.1).

Using Body Postures as Clues for Meaning Reconstruction

Understanding the bodily basis of meaning can greatly aid qualitative data analysis. An excellent critical ethnography, *Schooling as a Ritual Performance* by Peter McLaren (1993), fully exploits this feature of meaning by carefully analyzing the body postures and gestures of students. McLaren generates a theoretical framework for conceptualizing embodied meaning and power that draws upon ritology, postmodern philosophy, and various anthropological theories. It is highly recommended reading for gaining a deeper understanding of what McLaren calls "enfleshed" meaning, power, and culture.

McLaren's work can be located within our theory of expressive action and pragmatic horizons. I will illustrate some of the possibilities by returning to the TRUST study. Some of the interactions we are already familiar with; read them again and this time look for evidence of meaning and power in Samuel's body postures. Remember that a body posture will tell us something about possible action impeti, whether about to be expressed, totally repressed, or only partially expressed. Power will show up when a body posture indicates suppressed or repressed action or indicates an imposed subjective state of some kind.

Field Note Excerpt: Body Language in Alfred and Samuel's Tacit Debate

[37] A: *Are you upset about home?* Calm and reasonable tone.

[38] S: *No.* Said in new tone, not angry or irritated. Said as if a little defensive, with intonation up by end of word.

[39] A: *No? Was mom home last night?*

[40] S: *Yeah.* Same sort of tone: intonation up at end of word.

[41] A: *Yeah?* As if not believing.

[42] S: *Yeah. And then she left.* Samuel's voice has become softer, his shoulders slump forward slightly and he looks down.

[43] A: *And then she left? Where did she go this time?* Alfred has shifted over slightly on table toward Samuel.

[44] S: *She left to work on the car.* Tone implies defensive posture still. Samuel's body has straightened; eyes up but looking away from Alfred.

[45] A: *Left to work on the car?* (pause) *Do you believe that's what she did?*

[46] S: *Umm.* Affirmative tone. Samuel looks at Alfred, puckering lips forward.

[47] A: (*something like, do you like it when she does that?*)

[48] S: *I don't care.* Eyes looking downish and away.

[49] A: *You don't care* (garbled—what she does).

[50] S: *Umm.* Affirmative. Samuel is still looking away, looking up now.

[51] A: *Why don't you care what she does?*

[52] S: *She can do what* she *wants.* Emphasis on "she."

[53] A: *Uh umm, but how do* you *feel about it?* Emphasis on "you."

[54] S: *I don't care.*

[55] A: *You don't care being left with grandma then?* (pause) Another remark that is garbled.

[56] S: *I don't care what I do anymore.* Emphasis on "I." Samuel has taken on more and more of a sort of "hopeless" posture during the last several interactions. He has resumed his slump and his eyes are cast toward the floor.

[57] A: *Why don't you care what you do anymore?*

[58] S: (silence)

[59] A: *Why don't you care?*

These field notes begin providing some details on Samuel's body postures/movements at [39], where Samuel's posture suggests a "defeated" subjective state. Why would he feel defeated? By admitting that his mother left home, Samuel believes that he has supplied a critical suspicion on Alfred's part with some confirmation. Samuel may or may not feel unhappy with his mother's behavior, but either way he does not wish to confirm what he takes to be Alfred's negative views of her. If Samuel is also unhappy about his mother, admission that she left in [39] would allow these feelings to enter his awareness less checked as well. If he does not feel unhappy about her behavior, then his feeling of defeat would mainly be attributable to his failure to defend fully his mother at this point and his lack of power in the setting—his failure to see any way of altering what he takes Alfred's attitude to be.

In [44], Samuel appears less defeated, more energized, and more "hardened" or determined in relation to Alfred. The setting or interactive rhythm taking place at this point is that of a battle over the dignity of Samuel's mother (with possible racial implications).

Now let us jump to [56]. Samuel has here taken on a very defeated posture. Corresponding to this is a bid to change the setting from that of "critical white teacher interrogating minority child" to "disturbed child who has given up on himself being counseled by sympathetic adult." This bid for a new typification, or setting, seems to be a strategy for getting the topic away from Samuel's mother, but at the cost of succumbing to Alfred's direction. Samuel might feel, tacitly, that Alfred is being patronizing. Samuel's body posture here could fully reflect genuine feelings or be an exaggeration of feelings in order to pull off his bid for a shared new typification: it is quite possibly the latter.

Notice that an entire setting, an entire temporally grasped rhythm of interaction—inclusive of expected future behaviors, multiple subjective states on the part of multiple actors, role sets for all parties to play, etc.—is symbolized, offered, and claimed in this single posture when given at just this particular moment. This is precisely what is meant when stating that meaning is experienced in holistic, embodied ways related to typifications. I have called this "the dialogical constitution of the feeling-body" in another publication (Carspecken 1993a).

Tone of voice and gestures will also provide clues to subjective states and holistic forms of meaning. A loud voice with plenty of gestures will correspond to just prior body feelings of freed energy. A soft voice with downcast eyes and few body movements will correspond to just prior body feelings of constraint and implosion.

These sorts of clues should be used only in conjunction with other features of meaning to make supportable reconstructions. McLaren's work provides more precision in analyzing body postures and gestures. But analysis of body postures is necessarily a high-inference process. Support for one's interpretations must come from actual words spoken, either at the time or in interviews later on.

Power and the Body

Noting the connection between meaning and bodily states unavoidably points toward the connection between meaning and power. In the next major section of this chapter I will discuss the concept of power and introduce a number of helpful distinctions and concepts. But for now let us pay attention to the effects of power on bodily states as they are apparent in the section of field notes we just analyzed.

Note that the dynamics of much of the above interaction take place as a series of challenges on Alfred's side and defensive moves on Samuel's side. The situation is a power struggle, at least from Samuel's perspective. It is one in which his recognition needs, needs for dignity, are felt to be under attack. His body shows signs of implosion and constriction when he has to concede points in the battle, signs of extension and mobility when he seems hopeful at winning. The battle for dignity can be analyzed in terms of both interactive and cultural modes of power—especially the latter. Racial nuances may be involved, as may class differences in conceptions of the family and, certainly, culturally constructed age differences. The cultural themes at play work in terms of constructing Samuel's suspicions over Alfred's intentions, of supplying the material through which Samuel attempts to construct a valid identity, and of limiting the material Samuel can use to defend himself. All of this affects Samuel's bodily feelings.

For reasons like these, McLaren calls oppressive cultural conditions a "culture of pain," felt in the bodies of the oppressed (1993: 13). Readers should become aware of the relation of power and meaning to bodily states, seek other publications like McLaren's that treat this subject in more detail, and be creative in their use of the ideas.

Interactively Established Power Relations

Giddens argues, convincingly, that power accompanies all action (1979). All actions "intervene" in the stream of events and therefore "make a difference," no matter how large or small. Moreover, all acts could have been otherwise, in principle, and therefore they express the actor's power of determining one course of action over another. Even situations of extreme coercion, in which an actor is ordered to act in only one way, with the threat of a highly undesirable sanction for doing anything else, do not rob the actor of being able, in principle, to act against the orders and accept the consequences.

So all acts are acts of power. As Giddens puts it, the concept of power is tied analytically to the concept of action (1979, 1984). But action will be considered more or less powerful depending on how successfully it fulfills its motivating impetus and how free of influence and coercion are the conditions of the action. All acts are acts of power, but acts vary in terms of how powerful they are.

Interactive power relations occur when actors are differentiated in terms of who has most say in determining the course of an interaction and whose definition of the interactive setting holds sway. Interactive power is greatest when differentiations of this type are determined without equal communicative inputs from all people involved.

All qualitative studies should examine power relationships closely to determine who has what kind of power and why. A highly effective way of studying interactively constructed power relations is to employ a number of concepts originating in the work of Max Weber (1978: 215–55). These concepts make it quite easy to spot typical forms of authority relations that, in the last analysis, may be more precisely analyzed through the pragmatic horizons model by reducing them to the validity claims they entail.

A Typology of Interactive Power Relations

Weber's famous typology of power relations divides interactive power into coercion and three types of authority: charismatic, legal-rational, and traditional. Readers should already be familiar with this well-known typology, as it is taught in nearly all introductory sociology courses, but the basic ideas underlying this scheme can be broadened. I will use some examples to introduce a broadened typology of interactively established power.

Suppose you are observing a classroom and you see Susan grab the hair of Mary, sitting in front of her, to give it a good tug. Mary cries out, catching the teacher's attention before Susan ceases her aggressive act. Now, consider the following scenarios.

> *First Scenario:* The teacher says: *Stop that immediately!!!* The aggressor (Susan) says: *Why should I!* The teacher replies: *Because I TOLD you so!!!* Susan stops.
>
> *Second Scenario:* The teacher says: *Stop that immediately!!!* The aggressor says: *Why should I!* The teacher replies: *Because IF you don't I will send you to the VICE PRINCIPAL!!!* Susan stops.
>
> *Third Scenario:* The teacher says: *Susan, you are forgetting about our little agreement.* The student says: *What agreement?* The teacher replies: *That you get a candy bar for every day that you manage not to disturb other students.* Susan stops.
>
> *Fourth Scenario:* The teacher says: *Ahh, Susan! I just remembered that I wanted you to share with the class those exciting ideas you developed during science yesterday. They were so original!* She smiles winningly at Susan and moves toward her in a friendly and warm manner. Susan stops pulling hair and stands up in apparent eagerness to speak to the class. The teacher puts her arm around Susan to lead her to the front and says, as they move along together: *Ohh, but I think you forgot about Mary's feelings just now. Could you apologize to her?* Susan turns to Mary and apologizes in apparent sincerity.

In the first scenario, the teacher establishes a relation of power over Susan by claiming her normative rights as a teacher. The corresponding concept of *interactive power* may be termed normative power, similar to Weber's traditional power. The subordinate in the relationship consents to her position and to the power of the superordinate because she consents to a norm according power to a status position. "Do it because I say so!" puts a normative-evaluative claim into foregrounded position. The norm referred to associates power with status alone and without the foregrounding of any reasons. "Students should obey teachers," and that is that.

In the second scenario, the teacher forces obedience through the threat of a sanction. This may be called *coercive power*. It occurs without the consent of the subordinate in the relationship. The subordinate complies not through consent to the teacher's status and rights but in order to avoid an unpleasant sanction.

In the third scenario, the teacher obtains obedience through a sort of contract. "If you comply, then I will reward you." This is an agreement specifying reciprocal obligations between the parties, with one party allowed to determine the course of interaction. The general case may be called *interactively established contracts* and is similar to Weber's "legal-rational authority." The most common case that a researcher will discover is that of the tacit interactive contract: very often, a contract will be negotiated during an interaction on totally tacit levels where it is never actually stated explicitly, but where it is understood by both parties. For instance, if a colleague goes out of her way to support your point of view at a meeting, you might feel obliged to do the same for her in a similar situation. A tacit contract has been established between you.

In the fourth scenario, the teacher obtains obedience through her *charm*. It is her personality rather than her status, or any contract-like agreements, or any threat of sanctions, that wins Susan's consent to her power. Charm is another sort of interactive power similar to Weber's concept of "charisma."

The typology of interactive power described above, then, looks like this:

- *normative power:* subordinate consents to higher social position of superordinate because of cultural norms
- *coercive power:* subordinate acts to avoid sanctions imposed by superordinate
- *interactively established contracts:* subordinate acts for return of favors or rewards from superordinate
- *charm:* subordinate acts out of loyalty to the superordinate because of the latter's personality

Studying Interactive Power

During stage two of a qualitative study, time should be set aside to go through the entire set of field notes looking for interactive power. A list can be drawn up of the types of power employed or claimed by diverse participants. The next step is to analyze more specifically those forms of interactive power common to the site under investigation. If normative power is often claimed and consented to, determine what specific norms were employed. If coercion is used, determine what sanctions are threatened. If contracts are regularly established, determine what values are implicated; for example, what values are taught by a teacher who contracts for good behavior with candy bars? If charm is used, try to work out how: what behaviors are regarded as charming in the setting and why?

POWER AND THE DISTRIBUTION OF CULTURAL MILIEU

The typology of interactive power presented above is best utilized in conjunction with attention to cultural milieu. Every interaction that in some way fits within the typology above will do so because of cultural themes drawn upon by actors. Raw coercion, of course, does not in itself require cultural milieu, but coercion is usually employed within normative frameworks of cultural origin that legitimate it.

In the case of normative authority, it is obvious that the norms consented to will be features of culture. "Students should obey teachers" will work only in cultural contexts where this generally is accepted as a sort of moral rule.

Lack of alternative ways to conceptualize a situation often plays a strong role in solidifying normative modes of authority. Charm is generally the product of people possessing certain skills at using cultural material on hand to win the trust and loyalty of others. People skilled at being "charming" win loyalty from others through the employment of culturally understood identity claims and norms. Finally, interactive contracts are almost always strongly contextualized by normative-evaluative claims (remember the candy bar example).

So the trick is to use the typology of interactive power to spot the general forms of interactive power, but then to further analyze the situation in terms of cultural milieu and its distribution. For example, in Western society today there are cultural themes available to defend equal status and rights for women. Some communities in the West, however, have local cultures devoid of such themes; the members of these communities are not familiar with feminist discourses. If you were studying such a community, you might find women consistently deferring to normative power claims made by men. You would first recognize that normative authority based on gender differentiation is a common feature of your site; you must next ask why. Only an understanding of cultural milieu will give you an answer to this.

Studying Interactive and Cultural Power Together

Let us further illustrate the intersection of interactive power analysis with the analysis of cultural milieu by examining another set of notes from the TRUST study. The following segment of field notes was taken on a day other than the one we have so far devoted our attention to. On this day, Alfred was still trying to get Samuel to take the same test! In the room as well were Jane, an African-American female, and Ricardo, a Hispanic male. You will see how complex actual interactions are with respect to power claims, how the diverse categories of interactive power explained above may work simultaneously through backgrounding and foregrounding.

Field Note Excerpt: Power Plays between Samuel and Alfred

[1] A: *Samuel, you should be taking that test.* Mild voice.

[2] S: Pulls coat over head at his study carrel.

[3] A: (ignores)

[4] S: Kicks carrels and angers Ricardo

[5] A: *Samuel?*

[6] S: *I'm sick.*

[7] A: *Should I check your temperature?*

[8] S: *No!* Throws an object, rips paper

[9] A: *Better see the nurse.* Writes note to see nurse and gives it to Samuel.

[10] S: Takes note, stands up, takes indirect route to door so that Alfred is blocking his way. Comes physically close to Alfred. *Let me by!*

[11] A: *Go this way.* In calm voice, indicating more direct route with arm, and not moving.

[12] S: Goes Alfred's way.

....

[22] S: Returns from nurse, explains that he has no temperature, sits at carrel.

[23] A: *OzK, well you had better take that test then.* Continues to help Ricardo with work.

[24] S: Makes disturbing noises.

[25] A: *Samuel?*

[26] S: *What!!!* Angry voice.

[27] A: *Better work or see the counselor.* Calm tone.

[28] S: *I can't do it, it's too hard, you won't help me!* Very loud at statement's end.

[29] R: *It's a test, you don't get help on tests!*

[30] A: (ignores)

[31] S: Takes out calculator.

[32] A: *No, Samuel, you can't use a calculator, better give it to me.* Walks toward Samuel, putting arm out, palm up, for calculator.

[33] S: (ignores) Continues to use calculator.

[34] A: Starts counting to five. [A classroom procedure is for Alfred to count to five, slowly, when a student refuses to change an "inappropriate behavior." If five is reached without the behavior ceasing, a sanction is administered.]

[35] S: Waits until four is reached, then puts calculator in pocket rather than giving it to Alfred.

[36] A: Accepts compromise by not insisting on having calculator.

[37] S: Sits with very bored, disgusted expression.

[38] A: *Did your mother leave you alone last night?*

[39] S: *I don't want to talk about it!* Loud, angry tone.

[40] At this point Ricardo again expresses frustration with his work, and Alfred goes over to help him with it. It is not a test.

[41] S: *See! You're helping him!* Starts banging carrel.

[42] A: *OK, I guess I'll have to call the counselor.* Starts to count to 5 for counselor.

[43] S: *I don't care!*

[44] A: Sends Jane to get counselor.

[45] S: *You never make Ricardo do anything!*

....

[50] S: Bangs desk, throws lots of paper.

[51] A: *What is it, Samuel? Is this about your grandmother?*

[52] S: *NO!*

DISCUSSION

Interactive Power

This strip is definitely complicated with respect to interactive power. It begins with a claim to normative power on the part of Alfred: "Take your test because your teacher is asking you to." Samuel rejects the claim, indicating his rejection by putting his coat over his head. Later he kicks Ricardo's carrel and angers Ricardo. These are violations of explicit classroom rules indicating Samuel's refusal to accept the normative claim to power and, therefore, rejecting Alfred's claim to a superordinate status.

Alfred does not acknowledge that any challenge to his superordinate status has been made. He uses ignoring tactics and then an expression of concern to redefine challenges to his authoritative position as legitimate occurrences that may take place within his definition of the setting. Samuel then tries a legitimate reason for not being able to work: "I'm sick." Alfred "calls his bluff," and Samuel returns to activities challenging Alfred's status as an authority.

Samuel has basically been trying to undermine any consensual agreements on authority relations to push the power struggle to the level of physical force and coercion. This is accentuated when he moves physically close to Alfred as if ready to come to blows.

Alfred's strategy is to act as if his normative claim to power is never in question, even when Samuel almost physically threatens him. He keeps redefining the setting so that his authoritative status remains in place. When Samuel moves physically close to Alfred on his way to the door, Alfred defines this action as a poor choice of direction: as a "mistake" on Samuel's part.

Underlying Alfred's general strategy of consistently redefining Samuel's activities and "bluff calling," however, is the existence of coercive sanctions, legitimated by classroom rules, that he knows Samuel knows to exist. By calling Samuel's bluff repeatedly, Alfred reduces Samuel's options for challenging his authoritative status progressively. The direction of the interactive sequence is clearly that of a situation in which Samuel could only break a rule in some very overt way so that sanctions will be employed. Alfred will then be able to adopt a role of the "neutral enforcer of rules," a role he often adopts, and give Samuel sanctions, with all the fault falling on Samuel's side.

The configuration of interactive power involved is that of normative power claims (and contractual—see below) in the foreground but coercive power in the background. This works to keep the "responsibility" on Samuel's side. Both Samuel and Alfred are probably aware, tacitly at least, of this fact and both can sense that an interactive rhythm is in progress moving toward a clearly defined end (Samuel going to the counselor). A coercive arrangement is legitimated in this way, by keeping it in the background and keeping it obscured by normative and contractual modes of power in the foreground.

Alfred keeps throwing responsibility for the form of interaction onto Samuel's side. Samuel is not happy with this. He seems to feel that Alfred is at fault for making him take a test he believes he shouldn't have to take. His actions, at any rate, often reference the claim that Alfred is responsible and in the wrong. He never succeeds in winning Alfred's consent to this.

More can be said about the contractual nuances in Alfred's claims to power. Alfred defines the situation repeatedly as one in which students have rights, like the right not to do work if they are sick. He gives Samuel many opportunities to claim a right not to take the test in order to show that in fact Samuel does not meet any of the conditions in a contractual arrangement of power to refuse the test. This too, however, is underlaid with coercive power.

The above interaction displays the workings of cultural power, the distribution of cultural milieu, at more general levels. Samuel's effort to construct a respectable identity is limited in this classroom through a quite tightly constrained student-identity milieu imposed by the school. Alfred will only recognize him in a validating way if Samuel plays the school game to do school work and take tests. Samuel could do his best to play the school game, and he no doubt knows that Alfred would treat him kindly if he did. But Samuel also knows that trying to play the school game would give him a social identity of the "poor student," a "dummy." He would rather resist than assume an identity like that.

Samuel has little to defend himself against the impoverished and truncated identity that conforming to school norms would provide. He wants to feel that he is more than a "dummy," but he lacks familiarity with the cultural milieu that could help him to define the situation in class and racial terms. His plight is common enough. His inability to do well on tests is related to his home culture, which in turn is related to the structural location of the lower class and minorities in American society. But Samuel is not able to interpret the situation in this manner. He interprets it in personal terms and has probably internalized a negative self-image to a large extent. His resistance is rather desperate, not referenced to a counterculture that could affirm him in opposition to the school. (By contrast, Ricardo also resisted classroom activities frequently but used explicit references to his Hispanic identity and the culture of his community in the process, thereby claiming a valid identity through counter school norms. See Carspecken and Apple 1992: 530 for more on Ricardo's resistance. "Ricardo" is "Jorge" in that publication.)

Something of the extent of Samuel's pain was revealed in later portions of his interaction with Alfred on the previous day, the day in which our more commonly used field note segment comes. I will end this section by presenting more of the interaction between Samuel and Alfred on this previous day. The pain you will see expressed there is the product of cultural power. It is pain conditioned by the lack of cultural opportunities provided to Samuel, in years of schooling, for feeling positively recognized and affirmed.

Field Note Excerpt: Samuel and Alfred Discuss Samuel's Feelings

[51] A: *Why don't you care what she* [his mother] *does?*

[52] S: *She can do what she wants.*

[53] A: *Uh umm, but how do* you *feel about it?* Emphasis on "you."

[54] S: *I don't care.*

[55] A: *You don't care being left with grandma then?* [Grandma was very harsh with Samuel]

[56] S: *I don't care what* I *do anymore.* Emphasis on "I."

[57] A: *Why don't you care what you do anymore?*

[58] S: (silence)

....

[63] A: *Don't you think you're good?*

[64] S: *No.* Said softly, barely audible, head down with back and shoulders curved forward.

[65] A: *Do you not like yourself?*

[66] S: *No.*

[67] A: *So do you think you're a good person?*

[68] S: *No.*

....

[86] A: *You come to school every day.*

[87] S: *That's because I have to.*

[88] A: *Would you come to school if you didn't have to?*

[89] S: *No, I wouldn't.*

[90] A: *Why? Why wouldn't you go to school if you didn't have to? What do you think about school?*

[91] S: *I come to school because I want to get smart.* [OC: Very soft voice, body sort of limp and slouched forward, eyes down]

[92] A: *I can't understand what you're saying.*

[93] S: *I come to school because I want to get smart. I come because I'm dumb and I want to get smart but I can't get smart, 'cause I'm dumb.* [OC: This is said in a humble, submissive way and seems to be a genuine revelation of personal feelings. The tape recorder picked the words up but it was hard to hear them in the classroom because it was said in such a low voice]

[94] A: *Would you put your head up?* garbled, like "*I can't hear you with your head down.*" (pause) *Now why, why do you come to school?*

[95] S: *'Cause I'm dumb. And I wanna* garbled but like "*I come because I wanna get*

smart" [OC: He is talking in a hushed voice, reflecting a subdued and defeated type of feeling]

[96] A: *So you come so that you can learn, but you don't think you* can *learn?*

[97] S: *Umm huh, yup.* Very hushed.

[98] A: *Why don't you think you can learn?*

In this sad excerpt, we do not see Alfred making many interactive power claims. Alfred is acting compassionately and attempting to establish a relationship of caring with Samuel. The power we see at work here, evidenced in postures and vocal tones, is that of a whole cultural system that has hurt Samuel since he started school in kindergarten. Cultural power penetrates to the very identity of people, and where it works its effects one will always find pain.

SECONDARY CONCEPTS OF INTERACTION: ROLES

I will end this chapter with a few comments on secondary interactive concepts. The most precise analysis we can ever conduct on human interaction is focused on social acts, located in sequences of interaction and constituted paradigmatically through a variety of structures. In other words, the pragmatic horizon model is our most precise tool for reconstructing action, its meaning, and its cultural conditions.

But sociologists have long used less precise terms to analyze human interaction, and any of these can be employed usefully in a qualitative study. Such terms include "statuses," "roles," "front and back regions," "performance teams," "reference groups," and many others (e.g., Goffman 1974, 1981).

Of this vocabulary of less precise terms, I have found "reference groups" and "roles" to be most useful. I will present only roles in this book, for want of space. Readers should realize, of course, that in their own studies they are free to borrow many interactive concepts from the literature and use them skillfully and creatively in their own analysis. I believe, however, that all such terms can be reduced to the validity claims and other meaning-constituting structures of pragmatic horizons. This is why I call them secondary concepts of interaction.

Role Analysis

The concept of role is particularly useful. A role is a complex mode of activity that actors recognize as having some unity. When recognizing that a role is in play, actors cannot predict exactly what actions will come forth from the role player, but they can predict what basic form actions will take as long as this player is acting out the same role. A role is a pragmatic unit of meaning, understood holistically but only in such a way as to perform congruently with it. Trying to describe roles with words is always risky and will never fully capture what the role is.

I will try to get the idea of roles across only by exemplar by showing what roles I found Alfred to consistently play in the TRUST study. Below I will present the roles I found Alfred to act out consistently in his status as teacher. Of course, he acted out other roles from other statuses he occupied, such as the status of colleague with other teachers and subordinate with the administrators of the school. But I describe each role in terms of how it was used by Alfred to cope with student resistance. This involves noting validity claims associated with each role. The significance of finding and naming roles will always be to understand interactive rhythms and sequences routine to the site of your study, and validity reconstructions are usually important in clarifying the nature of roles.

Alfred's Six Teacher Roles

Alfred exhibited roughly six teacher roles during the research period. Each of these roles communicated a tacit appeal to the students to consent to his authority and definition of the situation. I will list each role observed and mention the claims tacitly made through them. The roles are listed in rough order of their frequency of use:

1. *The friendly guide.* In this role Alfred tacitly claimed goodwill toward the students and a willingness to help them along their program of improvement. The tacit claim was the expectation of a reciprocation of goodwill and cooperation from the students. The role was often used and often with good results.

2. *The teacher who is very busy with other things.* Alfred often kept himself busy with paper work, with making items to put on the walls or board, with the construction of a teaching device for a later lesson, and other such things while he interacted with the students. This occurred often enough to constitute a role in itself. The role carried the implicit message that the teacher, while attending to the students' needs and aware of them, nevertheless had other important things to do and thus was able to devote only limited attention to the students. This generated more distance between teacher and student and was a way of maintaining a degree of control at times. Social distance discourages all forms of intimacy, including disruptive forms and challenges designed to get a quick reaction from the teacher. Keeping busy slowed reactions to the students and thus limited the risk of making a hasty, ill-advised response. Nevertheless, social distance also reduces opportunities for positive forms of intimacy. The tacit appeal to authority in this case involves a reduction of the importance of the pupil to the entire situation and a corresponding increase in the importance of the teacher. The "important" activities carried out by the teacher are not shared with the pupils, who often would not know what Alfred was doing. Thus a subtle assertion of the teacher's greater grasp and control of the TRUST classroom is made.

3. *The self-revealing older peer.* Alfred not infrequently communicated with the students much as an older friend or brother might do and revealed features of his private life and history in doing so. This role is almost the exact opposite of role (2). It enhances intimacy and reduces social space. The tacit claim to authority here has to do with the reciprocation of trust. Alfred trusted the pupils with features of his personal life, communicated goodwill toward them, and, when the role was working, received the same back.

A part of this role involved displaying solidarity with the pupils on various occasions. Alfred was not observed to talk negatively about pupils to other pupils, regardless of whether the pupil in question was present or absent. This is an important practice for maintaining trust. Also, nearly every day during the observation period, Ricardo's mother visited the classroom to hear a report on her son's behavior. Alfred was forced to talk about Ricardo to his mother in Ricardo's presence on these occasions. I several times overheard this conversation after observing long sessions of very disruptive behavior on Ricardo's part, and Alfred usually only said positive things about Ricardo or indicated that there were a few minor problems. In this way he communicated solidarity to Ricardo and to the other students as well. Implicitly he affirmed the role of an older peer or friend who wouldn't rat on his companions.

4. *The neutral enforcer of fixed rules.* In this role, Alfred disassociated himself from the classroom rules and their corresponding sanctions but claimed the role of enforcer with respect to them. This role would be used during many sessions of challenge to the classroom order. The idea was to emphasize the activities of the students and the consequences that follow them. The tacit claim to authority in this case rested on the idea that classroom rules are comprehensible to all, are logical and beyond debate, and that Alfred's role as teacher puts him unavoidably in the position of the enforcer. This role can both be used effectively and abused. It is abused when used in situations where the judgment of the teacher about the classroom violation is clearly contestable, so that the teacher's claim to be neutral will be perceived as false on the part of the student. This role is best used only when real choices exist for the student.

5. *The middle-class progressive parent.* This role is named after a common strategy taken by many middle-class, "progressive" parents. It combines "neutral" rule enforcement with expressions of sympathy for the student, as in "I'm sorry I have to do this, but it is really for your own good." At times, Alfred counted to five as a warning to students that disruption must stop or sanctions would be administered. When doing so he displayed a mixture of sympathy and inevitability toward the students. This role was not used with much frequency, but it was used often enough to mention it. Its tacit appeal to authority was for the student to accept the reasonableness of the teacher and personal responsibility for the sanction, plus the fixed nature of adult-child statuses.

6. *The no-nonsense, traditional parent.* This role was seldom used by Alfred but was observed on several occasions. It consisted of insisting that a pupil "stop the nonsense" and obey the rules. Its tacit claim for authority rested on common definitions of the statuses of "teacher," "pupil," "parent," "child." "You do this because this is the proper thing to do!" "You obey me because you are a pupil and I am a teacher, and you know that is what you are supposed to do!" This role contradicted many of the principles Alfred attempted to employ in his classroom but, as I just wrote, it was seldom used by Alfred and is not a natural interactive style for him.

Through these examples, readers ought to gain the basic idea behind role analysis. One looks for patterned behaviors that consistently reference the same social identity, norms, values, and power claims. By giving such roles names and discussing their significance, researchers can convey much of what occurs within a particular site. Roles should be named in such a way as to get the gist of them across to readers. Often, this will require three or four words strung together into a phrase. As in the examples above, one or more paragraphs should follow a named role to explain its nuances, uses, and frequency.

Some readers may have noticed a difference between the type of role analysis I advocate, and illustrate, and other uses of the role concept in sociological literature. In "pop sociology," for example, family systems are described as having typical roles like "the victim," "the enforcer," "the rescuer," and so on. You should avoid role analyses like these. For one thing, they strip all subtlety from their roles by giving them single names and generalizing them to all social contexts of a particular type (like families, husband-wife relationships, and work organizations.) For another thing, "pop sociology" takes a purely third person perspective on roles, defining them by their *function* in interactive settings as only a detached observer could perceive. The role analysis I advocate prioritizes the first and second person positions, rather than the third, and defines roles according to their meaning, not their function. That is why many subtle nuances emerge with role analysis of this type and why it is necessary to use sentences and paragraphs to characterize them rather than single words.

8

Validity Requirements for Stage Two

Items covered in chapter 8:

• Procedures for supporting normative-evaluative claims

• Power and the hermeneutic inference

• Intersubjective recognition

• Inferring cultural power

Stage two, preliminary reconstructive analysis, is primarily oriented toward the normative-evaluative ontological category. The reconstruction of subjective states, especially as referenced by body postures and tones of voice, is also involved. In this chapter, I will discuss the procedures that researchers may follow to support the validity of normative-evaluative reconstructions. Procedures for supporting subjective reconstructions will be discussed in chapter eleven.

The validity requirements involved in meaning reconstruction are dodgey because researchers will often reconstruct tacit features of a culture for the first time and thus produce formulations that may seem strange even to the people being studied. How can a researcher protect herself from the accusation of simply projecting her own beliefs onto other people? There are procedures that can be followed to greatly lessen your vulnerability to such accusations.

1. *Use stage-three techniques.* Interviews and group discussions (as discussed in chapter ten) basically facilitate subjects in producing their own reconstructive analysis. The most powerful validation of meaning reconstructions available occurs when the subjects themselves reconstruct them when facilitated by the researcher in nonleading ways.

2. *Conduct member checks on reconstructions* to equalize power relations. At some point during a research project it is absolutely essential to share explicitly your own meaning reconstructions with the subjects of study. Explicit member checks can be conducted toward the end of an interview by showing the subject some of your reconstructions and, perhaps, the segments of primary record upon which they are based. The interviewee should be asked to comment on this material.

   If members disagree with your reconstructions, you have to decide whether you are wrong. If you think you have reconstructed accurately but have articulated things outside the subject's awareness and/or vocabulary, you have a moral duty to include their views as alternatives to your own in the final write-up. In this way, readers may compare your interpretations with those of your subjects and decide for themselves.

3. *Use peer debriefing* to check biases or absences in reconstructions. A peer debriefer is indispensable for producing well-supported reconstructions in stage two. Have dialogues with a debriefer about your analysis early on, at the beginning of reconstructive analysis, and again frequently throughout stage two. Keep a record of each debriefing session and include this record in an appendix of your final write-up.

4. *Employ prolonged engagement* to heighten the researcher's capacity to assume the insider's perspective. Specific phases of the hermeneutic inference are outlined in chapter six. There it was obvious that the longer you are in observational and/or interactive contact with the subjects of your study, the more accurate your hermeneutic inferences will be.

5. *Use strip analysis.* The term "strip analysis" comes from Agar's booklet, *Speaking of Ethnography* (1986: 36–38). Reconstructive analysis articulates meanings and cultural themes that one believes to constitute interactions. Reconstructions of most interest are those that seem to be frequently in play and thus that explain many of the social routines and interactions you have observed. Once you have a number of such broadly employed cultural themes reconstructed, you can then take strips of the primary record and check them to see whether they are consistent with the reconstructed themes. If they are not, it will be either because something about your reconstruction is wanting, or because the strip chosen involves alternative cultural themes drawn upon by the actors in that particular instance. Interviews could help clarify the reasons for a poor fit.

6. *Use negative case analysis.* Negative case analysis is very much like strip analysis. If you are pretty certain that actors generally employ certain cultural themes that you have reconstructed but find a few incidents in your notes that do not seem consistent with them, you must come up with an explanation for the lack of fit. Either your reconstructions are faulty or these incidents involved different cultural themes. Actors can always draw upon a variety of cultural material when they act, so a negative case does

not at all necessarily invalidate your reconstructions. But it could, and you should be able to show that negative cases were sought after and explained, one by one.

Be sure to keep a log of peer debriefings, member checks, and negative case/strip analysis to put into an appendix of your final research report.

INFERENCE IN NORMATIVE-EVALUATIVE RECONSTRUCTION

The inference procedure employed to reconstruct normative-evaluative references is hermeneutic in nature; observation and multiple access are not the structuring principles. Hermeneutic inferences require entering the first-, second-, and third-person positions routine to the subjects of study as much as possible so that an insider's perspective is attained. The idea is to learn how to position-take as your subjects do. Once this insider's perspective is attained, normative and evaluative references can be articulated.

Chapter six provided much detail on the nature of the hermeneutic inference, outlining its various stages. Here I will discuss the hermeneutic inference in terms of the pragmatic concept of truth. This will require attention to power and its relationship to truth.

Power and the Hermeneutic Inference

Of course, power can distort the claims made by researchers in the case of normative-evaluative inferences in the same ways that it can affect objective claims. Researchers must take care to have their participants question reconstructions and to get their own views on record. Participant language must be privileged in the analysis and participants made to feel confident of their own views. They should not defer to your status at the expense of their own ideas and experiences.

There is an additional interesting question to be asked about the relationship of power and knowledge when it comes to normative-evaluative reconstructions. Assuming that power relations between researcher and researched are equalized as much as possible so that an "ideal speech situation" (Habermas 1981; McCarthy 1978) to which all may contribute equally is approximated, what conditions structure the processes by which members may or may not consent to the articulations of the researcher? In the case of objective-referenced claims the principle of multiple access answers this question: repeated observations with multiple observers and devices can strengthen the objective-referenced claim, can strengthen consent to the record, if an ideal speech situation—in which all parties have equal input—is approximated.

But multiple access does not give us an answer with respect to normative-evaluative claims. No number of repeated observations or of group discussions on the meaning of object-terms is going to support a normative-evaluative referenced claim and thus a hermeneutic reconstruction. What does structure the consent, if power relations are equalized? If no one coerces you into agreeing to a value or a norm, what factors would lead you to agree?

Intersubjective Recognition

Remember that normative-evaluative claims are claims about what is good, bad, right, wrong, and proper. Actors agree on normative-evaluative truth claims when they recognize a personal interest within them. (The concept of interests is explored in chapters twelve and thirteen.) There are three different kinds of interests: strategic, material, and social-psychological interests. Strategic and material interests are supported by values and norms that allow each participant to meet experienced needs (e.g., "People should allow others to pursue jobs of their choice"). Social-psychological interests usually concern human needs for valid identities and a sense of dignity. These are usually met through group support of values and norms used by each member to construct the person's sense of who she is.

Consensus to values and norms will occur most deeply when a single set of normative-evaluative claims wins the recognition of all parties involved, without influence or coercion, because each member "finds herself" as a valid human being through them. The ideas of what are good and right held by the group correspond to the ways each member seeks to make herself "right" and "good": make herself a valid human being in possession of dignity. If this occurs without influence or coercion, the normative-evaluative claims can be nothing other than shared by the group of consenters—to be universal within this group. The claims about what is right, wrong, good, bad, and proper are consented to in an "all for one and one for all" manner. They are acknowledged as part of our "world" when recognized as such by members of the group. They are in "our" interests.

It is possible to propose a small number of fundamental human interests universal to all people if one examines noncoercive, rationalized discussions of value issues between people of diverse cultural origins. Once such discussions are established, some normative-evaluative infrastructure must be established simultaneously: it is a communicative requirement. Liberals who agree to differ with other people basically reference a universalized normative-evaluative claim of human rights and tolerance that all people (from any culture) should consent to. Religious groups who explicitly advocate intolerance of any who do not accept their beliefs also make a universalized claim: that all humans should believe as they do.

Universalized normative-evaluative claims are inevitable in any cross-cultural communication process. Whether actual agreements can ever be fully established between diverse cultural groups is an empirical question, with as-yet-unanswered implications for a theory of universal human interests. People disagree (almost violently) on this question. However, readers should note that universalized normative-evaluative claims are inevitable, and that any cross-cultural communication process must, simply because communication occurs, successfully establish some normative-infrastructures to which the parties agree (e.g., an agreement to communicate and a positive evaluation of communication itself; plus, usually, a norm of mutual respect).

Where normative-evaluative claims are understood, we have intersubjective recognition. Such recognition is intersubjective because it is a process of framing the normative-evaluative claim from the position of others. One can do this, can recognize a possible self and associated set of values and beliefs, without feeling compelled to identify with it.

But what is the nature of intersubjective recognition? It is not like perception as this is usually conceived, for it involves the spark of familiarity, of "seeing" something clearly that one has already known in an unclear or implicit way.

Recognition Is at the Root of the Hermeneutic Inference

When recognition occurs, an intersubjectively noted value or norm is experienced in match with a subjective state grasped holistically and tacitly. One finds one's self (or a possible self) affirmed within a normative articulation that by nature is claimed for an entire group—for "our" world. This idea of a match will be further discussed in chapter eleven when the validity of subjective-referenced claims is explored. Recognition involves both the normative-evaluative and subjective categories simultaneously. Thus, we must wait for a more elaborate discussion of subjective truth claims before we can take our understanding of hermeneutic recognition much further.

We do understand here, however, that the hermeneutic inference is based on recognition, not perception. The researcher is in a position to articulate the normative-evaluative claims of others only when she can recognize them as her subjects do. This means that her own cultural horizons must be altered through contact with the cultural horizons of those she studies: the "hermeneutic circle" (Palmer 1969) must be entered and employed repeatedly to bring about the insider's view (see chapter six).

An Application: Inferring Cultural Power

Once an insider's view is attained, tacit normative-evaluative claims will be recognizable to the researcher as they are to her subjects. Not infrequently they will appear as distortions: as reflective of unequal power relations that her subjects of study are caught up in, perhaps unconsciously or semiconsciously. To spot the distortions, the researcher must be able to recognize the claim to universality, to "our" world indefinitely expanded, referenced by each particular normative claim considered. Then she must note the failure of the norm or value she recognizes to meet its own claim to represent mutual interests of an entire group.

Thus one way in which power becomes associated with the category of normative-evaluative research claims is that it is part of what one must find in the setting under study. Cultural power cannot be observed objectively but must be found within the normative-evaluative horizons of the culture being studied. Cultural power is discovered through hermeneutic inferences (position-taking) as something internal to the intersubjective realms of one's subjects. It is discovered in this way when the reference to universality carried necessarily by all normative-evaluative claims is spotted as a sham. Normative-evaluative claims necessarily claim validity through their capacity to win the recognition of all members of a group, which means their capacity to fulfill an interest universal to a group. When this limit claim of universality is experienced as falling short, cultural power is at play. When one cannot fully recognize one's self, one's own interests, within an articulated norm or value, then one would only consent to this norm or value because of the play of power.

Researchers are often in a good position to spot and then describe the workings of cultural power because they are able to juxtapose more than one cultural realm: the realm(s) they are familiar with outside of contact with the community being studied, and that of the community studied. Subjects often lack familiarity with multiple cultural milieu. Familiarity with several cultures, from an insider's position, is the best way to gain an internal assessment of universalized claims, because it is the best way to check the breadth of "our" world such claims reference. Thus, familiarity with several cultures is the best way to spot cultural power: the falseness of claims to universality.

Summary

Thus, in summary, normative-evaluative inferences are based on recognition, rather than observation. The hermeneutic process is basically a process of recognizing meaning in new contexts and configurations.

Cultural power can be spotted when the researcher has attained enough of an insider's position to understand the claims to universality inherent in the horizons of a cultural group. If the researcher discovers these claims to universality as falling short, cultural power is at play. Cultural power masks the partial manner in which beliefs and values support human interests by making it difficult to challenge their claims to universality or to see where these claims fail. Insider familiarity with several cultures is the best way to assess universalizing claims and thus to spot the workings of cultural power.

9

Coding Procedures Congruent with Reconstructive Analysis

Items covered in chapter 9:

- Low-level codes

- High-level codes

- Procedures for developing codes and subcodes

- Themes and the reorganization of codes

- Choosing emphases for extended analysis and the final report

Nearly every book you can find on qualitative research will discuss coding. I believe, however, that the coding procedures appropriate for reconstructive analysis differ somewhat from those used in other forms of qualitative data analysis, and I will accordingly describe some procedures I have found to be effective.

Coding may begin as soon as one's primary record has been completed or nearly completed. It does not end until one has moved through at least stage three of the research process. I have not yet presented stage three, but since coding should begin before one starts to generate data dialogically, it seems appropriate to discuss coding procedures at this point in the book.

LOW-LEVEL CODING

Begin with low level-coding, which is coding that falls close to the primary record and requires little abstraction. Since every social act is unique, any category you construct to name a type of interaction will involve some abstractions. But low level codes abstract very little and aim to reference mainly objective features of the primary record.

Examples of Low-Level Codes

Here are some examples of low-level codes I used in the TRUST study:

1. *Reasons for not doing classwork*
(a) Sick
(b) "Having a bad day"
(c) "It's too hard"
(...)
2. *Resolutions and controls attempted by Alfred to end conflicts*
(a) Changing discourse from immediate situation to family
(b) Talking about feelings
(c) Appealing to coping mechanism taught in class
(d) Having students take the attitude of others
(e) Abstracting from feelings
(f) Focusing on the response rather than the provocation
(g) Coercive threats
(h) Polite requests
(i) Keeping busy
(j) Alteration of seating arrangement
(k) "It doesn't concern you," "we aren't talking about that"
(...)

Low-level codes are sometimes going to be primarily objective in nature. In my examples above, very objective codes include: *alteration of seating arrangement, keeping busy,* and codes that use participant speech acts of repeated use: *"Having a bad day," "It's too hard," "It doesn't concern you."* Each of these codes refers to activities that are open to multiple access.

Other low-level codes introduce some interpretations supportable through horizon analysis. Examples from above include: *by polite request, focusing on the response rather than the provocation;* and the more general code headings: *Reasons for not doing classwork, Resolutions and controls attempted by Alfred to end conflict.* These are still "low" in terms of the abstractions and inferences involved, but are more than purely objective categories.

Use peer debriefers early on to check the inference level in the codes and to question your choice of codes. Member checks can also be used after a large set of field notes has been compiled. In this case, participants are asked to read selected portions of your field notes and to comment on them, without access to your coding scheme. Their comments may well reveal possible new codes that you otherwise would not have considered. After this sort of process, it is possible to show participants your actual coding scheme and invite their comments.

HIGH-LEVEL CODING

High-level codes are dependent on greater amounts of abstraction. The higher the level of abstraction, the greater the need to base the code on something other than the primary record alone. Low-level coding is needed to begin meaning reconstructions and other forms of analysis at appropriate places in the primary record, higher-level codes are generally based on explicit meaning reconstructions and horizon analysis. Thus high-level coding should take place after one has developed low-level codes and used these codes to select segments of field notes for intensive analysis. High-level coding is needed to generalize findings that emerge from various forms of qualitative data analysis, particularly meaning and validity reconstruction, horizon analysis, and the analysis of interactive power.

Examples of High-Level Codes

High-level codes will usually be placed alongside low-level codes sharing the same general coding category. In the example below, I will put a star (*) next to high-level codes and two stars (**) next to codes constructed at especially high-levels of inference. The unstarred codes are low-level.

   3. *Student conflicts*
   (a) Student reprimanding other student
   (1) For causing a disturbance
   *(2) For not understanding/following a class or school norm
**(3) Triggered through use of other in battle with Alfred
   (b) "Your mama"
   (...)
   4. *Resistance*
   (a) Challenging a teacher's rule with behavior
   *(b) Displays of autonomy
   (1) Singing, humming
   *(2) Delays

   (....)

High-level codes are extremely useful for picking analytic emphases to be employed in the final write-up. They must be used with caution, however. Each high-level code should be backed up with an exemplary horizon analysis. Peer debriefers should be invited to go over your high-level codes very carefully. Ideally, high-level codes will match statements made by participants during the interviews and group discussions of stage three.

SUGGESTIONS FOR CODING PROCEDURES

There are no doubt many ways to construct codes for a qualitative data set. I will briefly describe my own preferred manner here, to give readers some ideas, but of course you are free to use a method of your choice.

More and more qualitative researchers are using software programs to help in coding these days. I find these programs dangerous. Software programs that cut a primary record up into sentences and segments risk obscuring the effects of temporal horizons and the existence of interactive rhythms and syntax. When coding, it is important to be as immersed as one can in the context of the interactions. This means reading through the primary record, slowly and repeatedly. I prefer to use word processor programs capable of bringing several files up at the same time and of splitting the screen to display two or more files at once.

Coding methods

My coding method consists of the following:

Step One: Open up the first word processing file containing a portion of the primary record.

Step Two: Open up a new, blank file and split the screen so that one can see both the data file and the blank file.

Step Three: Begin reading through the data file on the screen. Whenever something in the primary record strikes you as worthy of a code, toggle to the blank screen and type the code out in as explicit detail as you think necessary. Give the code a number or a letter, and in an indented section below the code write the file number, the page number, and the lines on which the first occurrence of this category has appeared.

Step Four: As one continues to read, one will continue to construct new codes but will many times spot important distinctions occurring within an already established code. When this occurs, return to the relevant code (using the "search" feature of the word processor), type in the subcodes suggested by the new section of primary record, and arrange file, page, and line references appropriately. This is how a coding scheme begins to take on a hierarchical structure of categories.

Step Five: Continue reading through the primary record, generating new codes and subcodes where appropriate, and going back to already established codes and subcodes to add file, page, and line references for each additional occurrence of an established code. Use of the "search" command makes it easy to find already established codes when a new section of the record matches them.

Step Six: Employ reconstructive analysis on segments of the primary record to which coding has drawn your attention. From the results of this analysis, formulate possible high-level codes and go back through the primary record, using the lower-level codes as an index, to find instances of these higher-level codes. You will need to consider carefully and analyze instances that seem to fit your higher-level code, both to strengthen the rationale of the code and to determine whether these instances fit.

Higher-level codes are based on a horizon analysis of one possibility within a meaning field, and therefore require support from other sections of the primary record. Keep a record of your horizon analyses, and be sure to have peer debriefers give special attention to high-level codes.

RAW CODES

As coding proceeds, one develops a long list of raw codes. They are "raw" because no effort has yet been made to organize them into a tight hierarchical scheme. They will intersect with each other and be filled with redundancies. A single event recorded in the field notes will often be listed under many different codes. Codes should be developed very close to the data and should be redundant and intersecting. If your codes do not display redundancy and intersection, then something is wrong. One must not use a priori codes, and only a priori codes would lead to nonredundant categories.

Below I present more examples of codes I developed for the TRUST study. Notice their intersecting and redundant nature. Notice the amount of detail given to each code and to the specification of instances. With word processing technology, it is not necessary to have a scheme of briefly worded codes. I include the name of the person involved in the incident as well. Finally, note the specification of instances below each code. "F" refers to file number and "p" refers to the page number of that file where an incidence of the code occurs.

Example of Raw Codes for TRUST Study

12. Teacher's comments directly referenced to self of student
(a) Positive, but tied to effort at behavior shaping
Ricardo: F2, p3—called "good" but within argument to change behavior around
Ricardo: F2, p4—"good handwriting"
13. Students' comments directly referenced to their own selves
(a) Tied to behavior or school work
Ricardo: F2, p3—Ricardo says he's "not good" because of points
Will: F6, p9—picture of airplane no good. Alfred says it is good
Will: F6, p10—this picture is stupid and ugly. Ricardo says his picture is the same
Samuel: F5, p7—compares himself with Alfred when Alfred was a kid
Will: F6, p9—says he doesn't want other kids in school to think he is in trouble
(b) Generalized
Jane: F3, p7—says she shouldn't be around sharp things, would use them to attack others
Samuel: F4, p3–7—Samuel says he doesn't think he is good, and a string of comments following
Jane: F7, p7—says she can't stop herself fighting when she is angry. Alfred says she does in fact stop herself
Jane: F10, p5—capable of being loved

PULLING CODES TOGETHER: THEMES AND THE REORGANIZATION OF CODES

Producing your low- and high-level codes will automatically result in a hierarchical scheme, with some codes subsuming others. In the TRUST study I ended up with 123 raw codes and subcodes, including both low and high-level. They were organized quite organically through emergent code headings, as my examples illustrate.

Once you have a thick set of these codes you will be in a position to decide how to focus your analysis. I will here explain what is involved in reorganizing one's codes into a hierarchical scheme, but readers must bear in mind the fact that *codes should not be reorganized until one has completed at least stage three of the research*. Interview and group discussion material must also be coded, and must be used in support of the horizon analyses employed to produce high-level codes.

This being said, code reorganization goes roughly as follows. Certain codes will group together into a few large categories. These large categories will be suggested from the codes you have already developed, but one must choose from many possibilities at this point: make a decision on how you are going to focus your study, and group codes according to that.

In the TRUST study, I grouped codes together to produce seven large categories. I present these below:

1. Taught Culture and the Social-Psychological Pedagogy
2. Student Negotiations and Power
3. Critical Situations
4. Control
5. Harmonious Student-Initiated Interactions
6. Interactions Relevant to Student Profiles
7. Teacher Culture and the Trust Classroom

Most of my 123 raw codes and subcodes fell into these seven categories. I also developed 35 intermediate categories during my efforts to come up with these seven. Many raw codes fell into more than one large category and more than one intermediate category.

Choosing Emphases for the Final Analysis and Write-Up

It is impossible to provide any recipes for choosing analytical emphases to be employed in one's final project narrative since many possible criteria can be chosen. All that can be said in general terms is that coding should begin well before emphases are chosen, peer debriefers should be used many times during coding and reconstructive analysis, and peer debriefers ought to be consulted when you do pick your emphases.

Exemplars are always helpful, so I will explain my own decisions in the TRUST study. The seven categories listed above were chosen for organizing my codes hierarchically because they matched certain analytic angles I decided to develop in the final report. The analytic angles were close to the data and close to the coding scheme I developed prior to considering emphases.

But the angles I chose also matched the interests of the school and funding agency, which wanted to know whether TRUST was working. Their goal was to teach disruptive students the idea of having choices every time one acts. They believed that if students learned to think about possible consequences before acting, they would begin acting in less disruptive ways. Therefore, the "choice" concept was a natural angle for my final analysis, particularly since it was a word used repeatedly by Alfred during classroom interactions.

I decided to use the material I had on student-teacher conflicts to work out what covert lessons students learned with each type of conflict resolution. The basic idea here corresponds to the theory of meaning employed throughout this book, and to the concept of pragmatic horizons in particular. Conflicts occur with large tacit references in the backgrounds of each meaningful act. In Project TRUST when conflicts were resolved noncoercively, students and teacher reached tacit consensus on back-grounded references: they shared a horizon. I was particularly interested in tacit theories referenced in uses of the "choice" concept(s). By reconstructing many instances in which "choice" was used explicitly, or fairly immediately foregrounded, I found diverse tacit theories of the self consistently referenced within the same horizons employing some form of "choice." My analysis displayed two distinctive tacit conceptions of choice repeatedly referenced and consented to; only one of these two matched the formal goals of TRUST. I also found five distinctive tacit conceptions of "self" repeatedly referenced; only three of these were congruent with the formal goals of TRUST. Different resolutions of conflict resulted in an emphasis on different configurations of "choice" and "self," different normative horizons and implicit theories associated with their different uses.

My next effort was to understand which actions on Alfred's part seemed to contribute to which kind of conflict resolution. I had to use various codes to arrive at an answer—especially codes having to do with interactive power, with interactive rhythm and syntax, and with forms of setting negotiation. I found consistent relationships between kinds of teacher actions and kinds of conflict resolution. Role analysis was used to support this exploration.

I then examined the horizons involved in various student-student interactions and in nonconflictual student-teacher interactions to see whether students had actually internalized covert messages about self and choice and, if so, which ones. Observations of these same students in a park after school and in their homes were also examined to this end. I did find evidence of internalization—particularly strong evidence when students used expressions in nonclassroom contexts that I had seen Alfred teach them.

Last, I examined the tacit theories repeatedly referenced by Alfred's actions in light of system constraints within which Project TRUST operated. This involved noting cultural and institutional conditions shaping Alfred's activities and looking at the home environments of each TRUST student and the cultural milieu that seemed to exist there. It meant taking account of the racial and ethnic backgrounds of Alfred and his students. Many of Alfred's routine actions and strategies were strongly conditioned by system factors; but I have reserved chapter thirteen for a discussion of the procedures involved in systems analysis.

The final narrative described effects of both the explicit and the hidden curriculum on student interactions; particularly conflictual interactions. It suggested teacher strategies for bringing about desired covert lessons on conflict resolution, emphasizing the backgrounded conceptions of self, choice, and other horizon components that necessarily accompany all such lessons. Through an analysis of system relations, I attempted to indicate the amount of freedom teachers in a classroom like TRUST actually have for pedagogical change by displaying constraints in operation that teachers could do little to alter.

In summary, good coding will almost deliver your final analysis, particularly when reaching the stage of code reorganization. This last stage of coding, however, should not be attempted until stage three has been completed.

10

Stage Three: Dialogical Data Generation through Interviews, Group Discussions, and IPR

Items covered in chapter 10:

- The role of facilitator

- Qualitative interview questions

- Constructing an interview protocol

- Six types of interviewer responses

- Analysis of interviews

- Other ways to generate dialogical data

- Interpersonal Process Recall (IPR)

Interviews and researcher-facilitated group discussions stimulate the production of a distinctive type of data: "dialogical data." Dialogical data is generated through dialogues between researcher and researched that are rarely naturalistic. Subjects will often talk during interviews in ways they seldom talk in everyday life. Why? Because very often people are not listened to as intently as the researcher listens to them, taken as seriously as the researcher takes them, and supported in the exploration of their feelings and life as much as a skilled researcher will support them.

You should wait until a thick record of observations has been compiled before beginning interviews and group discussions. As soon as interviews and facilitated group discussions are introduced into the research process, the routine activities you are interested in may well change. This is particularly true when you are studying people who are not accustomed to being intensely listened to and taken seriously.

A central purpose of stage three is to democratize the research process. Stage three gives participants a voice in the research process and a chance to challenge material produced by the researcher. But you will not democratize the research process by immediately treating the subjects of study as your colleagues and sharing all of your ideas with them for comment. Researchers are steeped in a technical vocabulary and are familiar with theories of human interaction and the social system that are usually outside the experience of people studied. This vocabulary and familiarity with theories will necessarily play a role in your inferences and reconstructions. To dump them on the subjects of study immediately will definitely distort communicative contexts and very often it will make subjects feel incompetent to comment on their lives and experiences. You do not want to encourage subjects to try to "talk shop" with you, which would result in statements that do not genuinely reflect their experiences and ideas.

Therefore, the best role to play in beginning stage three is that of a facilitator rather than that of a colleague or peer. As a facilitator, you construct a supportive and safe normative environment with your subjects and help them explore issues with their own vocabulary, their own metaphors, and their own ideas. You should not initially get into debates with the subjects of study nor should you initially share many of your own ideas with them. Later on during a research project it is perfectly appropriate to engage in debates, to share all your own ideas, to explain the meaning of researcher vocabulary and social theories, and sometimes to actively help your subjects in various ways. In fact, to fully make the research process democratic with power relations equalized as much as is feasible, these sorts of peer discussions must take place in some form and to some degree. But they should take place after extensive stage three work has been completed, through the role of facilitator.

THE QUALITATIVE INTERVIEW

The qualitative interview can be conceptualized in three distinctive ways: in terms of the *types of questions* the interviewer will ask, in terms of ideal *interviewer responses* provided throughout the interview, and in terms of *data analysis* to be conducted on interview transcripts. I will discuss each of these areas, but concentrate on interviewer responses.

There is a lot of literature on qualitative interviewing that suggests appropriate questions and explains methods of analysis. There is little in methodological literature on interviewer responses. Yet during a skillfully conducted interview the researcher will spend most of her time responding to things said by her subjects rather than asking questions.

Qualitative Interview Questions

The ideal qualitative interview will be semistructured. To prepare for an interview one should construct an interview protocol that allows for maximum flexibility during the interview process. I have found that formulating two to five lead-off questions before an interview is generally sufficient.

Lead-off questions are designed to open up a topic domain that one wishes a subject to address. They should be formulated very concretely; avoid abstract questions. To get at abstract issues, think of a way to have your subject describe a concrete event that took place as if she were making a video recording of it. As she describes the event from her memory, use appropriate interviewer responses (discussed below) to slowly elicit the background beliefs, values, and feelings involved with her depiction of it. Then, with appropriate interviewer responses, attempt to move the subject toward generalizing some of the background issues to other contexts of life.

For example, if I want to hear what Alfred has to say about his students' problems, his beliefs about their causes, and his ideas on how to help students, I will not ask: "Tell me about your students' problems," or "What do you think are the best ways to help your students?" If I ask abstract questions like these, I risk putting Alfred into a very different mind-set than he typically has in the classroom. I want to hear about the implicit theories constituting his actions, not about the way he theorizes with colleagues. Often people act according to one implicit theory, and talk out theories that are very different.

Instead, I will get Alfred into a concrete mind-set and use appropriate interviewer responses to his talk to elicit the implicit views I am interested in. A good lead-off question would be, "Yesterday I saw you and Samuel in dispute over a test. Can you pretend I wasn't even there and just tell me everything that happened? Pretend you are making a video of what occurred and run it by me."

I have always found it best to lead off with a concrete question about an event you recently observed the subject take part in. This gives you the added benefit of comparing what the subject says in interview with what you have in your primary record of observations.

However, you cannot always ask this sort of question. Sometimes you are conducting an interview-only study. Sometimes the date of the interview is too long after you have observed the subject to ask a question about what occurred. In cases like these, you can ask questions well described and discussed by Spradley as descriptive questions (Spradley 1979). You can ask a "typical day" question, or a question about an actual event that took place but that you did not observe, or a "tour" question. Examples of such questions are:

1. "Tell me about a typical day in the classroom. Start from when you first enter the school, and then take me through all your activities, one by one. Don't be afraid of giving too much detail: I am interested in everything."

2. "Can you think of a recent time when you had a dispute with a student about something? You can? Good! Now please tell me everything that happened. Describe it as if you were making a movie about it."

3. "Here is a diagram of your classroom with the desks and other things drawn in. I'm not a very good artist, am I? Anyway, could you give me a tour through the diagram and

explain everything about each item? You can add items important to your work that I have missed."

The Interview Protocol

Before an interview, then, one will wish to formulate several lead-off questions, each designed to open up a topic domain. In addition, I recommend jotting down a list of items for each topic domain that you wish your subject to address during her talk but that you do not want to ask explicitly about because that could lead the interview too much. These items may be called *covert categories*. By jotting them down, you basically set them in your mind as well as produce something to refer to during the interview so as not to forget anything important. Once a topic domain is opened up, the interviewer must respond skillfully to what the subject is saying in order to guide, without leading, across all the covert categories.

Finally, it is a good idea to write down possible follow-up questions for each topic domain. When writing these down, try to anticipate possible directions the conversation could go and then formulate possible questions that could be asked if responses are not enough. Follow-up questions should often be concrete, but not always. You may effectively use material provided by the subject in her talk to ask a follow-up question. If the subject has become abstract in her talk, an abstract follow-up question is perfectly appropriate as long as it is close to what the subject herself has been saying.

Thus, four items make up the interview protocol, according to my recommended method: two to five topic domains, one lead-off question for each domain, a list of covert categories for each domain, and a set of possible follow-up questions for each domain. Here is an example of an interview protocol for interviewing Alfred on TRUST.

Topic Domain One: Social-Psychological Issues

Lead-off question

"Yesterday I noticed that Samuel was reluctant to take an examination. Can you tell me about the whole event, as you recall it? Pretend I wasn't there and describe what happened as if you were trying to give me as vivid a picture as possible."

[Covert categories: Alfred's perceptions of Samuel; his strategies for handling student resistance; his beliefs on what causes resistance; whether or not he consciously tries to teach messages through the way in which he handles conflicts; whether he felt he was using coercive strategies in any way; his views on Samuel's mother and grandmother; his implicit psychological, social-psychological, and sociological theories]

Possible follow-up questions

1. "Okay, so Samuel pulled his coat over his head. Can you tell me more about that?"

2. "You say Samuel is lazy. What other things do you remember Samuel doing that were lazy?"

3. "Do you have other students who are not lazy? Tell me about them."

4. "If you had asked Ricardo to take the test, what would he probably have done?"

5. "Well, so you tried to be patient with Samuel through all of this! But he still wouldn't cooperate. What happened at the end again? Can you describe that in more detail?"

6. "So, it sounds like Samuel's home environment is not the most desirable! What else do you know about his home?"

7. "Did you describe this conflict to another teacher afterward? You did? Oh, could you tell me what you said and what the teacher said, as best you remember it?"

Topic Domain Two: Institutional and Political Issues

Lead-off question

"Now, I'm interested in these standardized tests. Do you remember a time when you discussed these tests with the principal? Yes? Tell me what you remember of that conversation: who introduced the topic? Who said what?"

[Covert categories: Does Alfred think these tests are valid? Does he take them for granted? Does he object to them in any way? What is his relationship with the administration of this school? Does he feel pressured to get good results from his students on these tests? What does he think would happen if he did not make his students take the tests? How conscious is he of the political origins of these tests? Does Alfred have any views on the nature of student intelligence?]

Possible follow-up questions

1. "I see. The principal told you that you would have to give the students the tests, because of the state laws. Now, do you remember what you said back to her?"

2. "How would you imagine the principal describing the test scores of your students to the vice principal, if you weren't there?"

3. "You seem to be saying that of all the things you do in this classroom, some are 'essential' and some are 'playing the game,' as you put it. Can you tell me some other things that are 'essential'?"

4. "You are 'forced' to give these tests. Say more about that."

5. "You said that these tests are state mandated. Can you tell me more about that?"

INTERVIEWER RESPONSES

I do not mind repeating the important point that the way one responds to the interviewee is much more important than the wording of your questions. This is true, at least, if your actual questions are concrete, nonleading, and domain opening. It will be helpful to categorize interviewer responses into types and then to recommend emphasizing certain types of responses over others during certain stages of the interview process.

Following is a typology of interviewer responses organized according to how frequently they ought to be employed. I have been strongly influenced by Norman Kagan's work on psychological counseling, and my typology is based on one constructed by Kagan for clinical counselors. I have made changes to adapt his highly effective scheme to qualitative interviewing (see Kagan 1980, 1984; Kagan and Kagan 1991; Kagan and Schneider 1987).

A Typology of Interviewer Responses

1. Bland Encouragements

Characterization and purpose: Usually one-word utterances and/or facial expressions that show attention, interest, and acceptance. These are excellent for establishing rapport and encouraging the interviewee to keep talking.

Examples: "Right"; "humm"; "Oh, that's interesting"; plus smiles, nodding of head, opening eyes wide to indicate attention, interest, and acceptance.

When to use: All the way through an interview, but heavily during the beginning portions of a topic.

How often to use: Very often.

2. Low-Inference Paraphrasing

Characterization and purpose: Restatements of information the subject has provided in new words but without adding content to what the subject has supplied. The purpose of low-inference paraphrasing is to encourage the subject to keep talking on a topic of interest without leading her and to indicate that you have understood what she has said so far. Low-inference paraphrasing is a good way to keep a subject on the topic you are interested in rather than going off on tangents without betraying your interests or suspicions.

Examples: "I see, you sort of got the job by accident." "So, you went back to college after your divorce." "You don't look at the clock when working the line because that makes the time go faster."

When to use: Use low-inference paraphrasing when you sense that your subject expects you to say something and when you have been using bland encouragements for a time. Pepper these responses in according to the rhythm of your interview. Some subjects like to talk a lot and need little encouragement, while others need frequent responses to keep going. The frequency of use will depend a lot on the subject and the flow of a particular interview. Use this type of response when your subject covers a number of topics in one gush of talk, and you wish to hear more about only one of the topics she mentions. In general, use most frequently at the beginning of a topic discussion and less frequently toward the end.

How often to use: Use quite often during the beginning portions of a topic discussion.

3. Nonleading Leads

Characterization and purpose: These are modes of questioning, without leading, that offer a nice variation from low-inference paraphrasing. Their purpose is to elicit more material on a certain topic and to indicate interest and attention.

Examples: "Oh, tell me more about that!" "Umm, could you keep talking about that?" "This is interesting! Keep telling me about it!"

When to use: These can be used frequently and are particularly appropriate during the beginning portions of a topic discussion. Use them as an alternative to low-inference paraphrasing.

How often to use: Use quite frequently during the beginning of a topic discussion, but make sure you do not sound mechanical. Alternate between questions like these and low-inference paraphrasing. Use when you wish a subject to hone in on a mentioned area.

4. Active Listening

Characterization and purpose: With active listening responses, we put words on feelings we suspect a subject has about some item of the interview but which the subject did not explicitly articulate. Active listening responses are excellent for establishing good rapport and helping a subject to open up about certain things. The responses must be used with caution, however. Interviewers must not open up modes of self-disclosure they cannot then handle!

Examples: "Sounds like you're angry with him." "I'm hearing frustration; seems like you feel frustrated with this situation." "You seem proud of what you've done."

When to use: Use active listening responses when you suspect that a subject is foregrounding feelings in her communications to you without being explicit. It is fairly safe to use this type of response when a subject basically seems to be telling you what her feelings are, but in tones and gestures rather than words. You can also use this form of response when you suspect a feeling that the subject is not fully aware of nor intending to communicate to you. But this is more risky. It can result in material of invaluable worth, but it can also threaten subjects or encourage them to discuss feelings with you that you are not prepared to cope with. Be careful. Use this sort of response toward the middle of a topic discussion, not right at the beginning.

How often to use: Definitely use this response less often than the others mentioned so far. Frequency of use will vary from situation to situation, depending on the extent to which you are interested in learning about your subject's feelings, the extent to which you are prepared to aid subjects in working through difficult feelings, and the extent to which getting clear on feelings will facilitate further information disclosure on a topic of interest.

5. Medium-Inference Paraphrasing

Characterization and purpose: This type of response involves articulating some of your speculations about the meaning or implications of material provided by a subject. Its purpose is to check out ideas you have that might become important features of your analysis. Unlike active listening responses, medium-inference paraphrasing articulates the implicit beliefs and theories (rather than feelings) you suspect your subject holds. To make this response appropriately you must stay very close, in your wording, to what your subject has said but push things just a little further.

Examples: Suppose a subject says, during an interview: *So I suppose I just try my best, you know. If you think you've got to be perfect you're always going to be down.* A medium-inference paraphrase would be: "It's impossible to be perfect?" Notice that it is close to what the subject said, but articulates an apparent background reference. The apparent reference concerns beliefs rather than feelings.

Here is another example. A subject once said to me: *Sure, we've got some discontent around here. The secretaries seem to think we're made of money and could give them a raise at the blink of an eye. I mean I'd like nothing better than to give out raises all the time. But this is reality.* Like many streams of talk elicited during interviews, this one implies many things. Your paraphrase will have to focus on one of several implications. Possibilities include: "You have no control over the situation"; "The secretaries don't have a realistic perception of their position." A *high*-inference paraphrase could be: "It's *reality* that secretaries get lower salaries than their employers." An active listening response could be: "You seem irritated by the secretaries."

When to use: If you make sure that your medium-inference paraphrase is genuinely medium-inference and not high inference, it can be used quite frequently from the middle portion of a topic discussion to the end. Of course, you will want to vary the kinds of responses you are using so as to not sound mechanical. Do not respond with several paraphrases in succession, just pepper them into the conversational flow with plenty of other types of responses in between. Use these when subjects seem close to articulating background beliefs of interest to you.

How often to use: Limit use to the middle to end of a topic discussion.

6. High-Inference Paraphrases

Characterization and purpose: High-inference paraphrases are articulations of suspected background beliefs that have not been explicitly stated by a subject. At the very end of an interview they can be very effective for checking out some of your speculations about general beliefs held by the client.

Examples: "What I think I've heard you saying over the last ten minutes or so is that these minority students can't learn: it's too late for them by the time they get to your classroom." "Does all this boil down to the idea that children are basically unruly and will turn out bad unless they are disciplined repeatedly?" "I've heard you describe your life and compare it to the lives of others. The picture I get is that life is a sort of ladder that must be climbed, and some people can climb it, and others get stuck at the lower rungs."

When to use: Hardly ever use this sort of paraphrase. This type is very dangerous in that it can lead the subject being interviewed into agreeing to things she does not really believe or denying things she really does believe. These paraphrases can also seem offensive or threatening. Ideally, other sorts of responses and questioning strategies will facilitate full articulation of beliefs without your having to use a high-inference paraphrase. At the very end of an interview, however, and, even more appropriately, at the very end of a series of interviews with a single subject, high-inference paraphrases can be extremely effective. Use them when you have enough other interview material already recorded so that if the paraphrases go wrong you will not have jeopardized your entire interview.

How often to use: Use very rarely. Many interviews will not require this sort of response at all. If used, use it once or twice at the very end of an interview.

INTERVIEW ANALYSIS

I will not take up much space writing about the analysis of interview data because one generally performs reconstructive modes of analysis identical to those discussed for stage two. Interview data has the additional purpose of checking suppositions developed during stage two. If we think, for example, that Alfred's acts in the classroom are partially constituted through references to backgrounded lay theories on child psychology, then we will want our interviews to give Alfred plenty of opportunity to articulate these theories for us without leading. If he does and if they match our reconstructions, then we have excellent support for our previous analysis. If he articulates something different, then we will have to look back over our preliminary reconstructions carefully: we could have been completely wrong. Or perhaps he acts one way and talks another way. Only careful comparisons between the interviews and the fieldnotes will give us an answer.

Interview material, of course, will have many unarticulated but referenced meanings associated with it. To uncover them we need only go through the steps discussed in earlier chapters: meaning reconstruction, validity reconstruction, and horizon analysis.

Horizon analysis of interview transcripts will require attention to the contextual nature of any particular statement made by the subject. Because the context in this case is that of lengthy talk, use of narrative-analytical techniques may be employed. One reads through a transcript looking for its narrative structure. Does the subject use a scheme of hero vs. villain? Does she speak in a humorous style or a serious style? Does her talk emphasize people, things, emotions, ideas, or events? When events are described do they appear to be the products of natural or social powers beyond the control of the subject or the products of her own decisions? Does she repeatedly employ the same metaphors to express ideas? All of these sorts of things will tell you much about the interpretative schemes used by the subject.

Use of horizon analysis on interview transcripts is new and open to all sorts of creative exploration. I have coauthored a paper exploring new techniques and conceptual frameworks in this area (Carspecken and Cordeiro 1995). This paper develops theoretical linkages between interview conversations and cultural milieu employed routinely by the subjects in their daily social activities. A theory of the relationship between pragmatic categories and semantic categories is presented to this end. The paper also employs the "text" metaphor to examine backgrounded references to binary oppositions of racial categories, tacit metaphors of the social system, and three tacit concepts of time. In this respect, the analysis developed synthesizes methods similar to Spradley's work on semantic categories, taxonomies, and contrast sets with the distinction between foregrounding and backgrounding, plus some ideas developed within structuralist anthropology (e.g., the idea of binary oppositions and the homology in the paradigmatic axis of meaning).

The final analysis developed in a qualitative study will draw upon strips of field notes and associated segments of interview transcripts. Coding, particularly high-level codes, should be rooted in matches between interview material and observation records. The final project report ought to defend cultural reconstructions with references to both interview and observation material. You may emphasize items in the final write-up that were tacit in both the primary record and interviews, but the most strongly supported conclusions you can make will show consistency with primary records of observed interaction and explicit formulations elicited from subjects in interviews.

OTHER WAYS OF GENERATING DIALOGICAL DATA

The interview is not the only way to produce dialogical data. One can bring groups of subjects together and facilitate a group discussion. If recorded and well facilitated, such discussions can be extremely revealing. A single subject may have difficulty artic-ulating a particular cultural theme that she understands tacitly. Or she may formulate it in a way that she really feels somewhat uncertain about if simply discussing things with an interviewer. In a group of peers, this same individual may be able to produce more potent formulations through bouncing ideas back and forth with those who also live within her culture.

Group discussions should be facilitated and not led. Topic domains can be opened up following the same principles described above for qualitative interviewing. As members of the group begin to talk, you should help quiet people get a voice in the discussion, keep the conversation on track with paraphrasing, and point out areas of apparent disagreement to stimulate more in-depth explorations of issues. Interventions can become more abstract as a topic discussion reaches maturity. To this end the you may articulate issues you believe to be in the background and not yet fully articulated. All interventions in the discussion should make references to what someone in the group has said and should emphasize vocabulary used by the partici-pants.

Interpersonal Process Recall

A particularly excellent method for generating dialogical data has been developed by the psychologist Norman Kagan, whom I have already mentioned with respect to interviewer responses. In addition to developing widely recognized and practiced methods of clinical counseling, Kagan has explored the therapeutic and educational possibilities of playing video tapes of interaction back to the actors and allowing them to comment on any portion of the events they choose. The method is called Interpersonal Process Recall or IPR (Kagan 1980, 1984). It is unbelievably potent for eliciting articulations of tacit cultural material as well as for stimulating the expression of subjective material.

The basic idea is to video tape interactions or a group discussion. Then group the actors together to view the video tape and invite them to stop the tape at any point they choose to express how they were feeling at that time, what they were thinking, or what tacit norms they believe to have been at play. Other members may comment on the remarks of the one who stopped the tape. Keep a tape recorder running to get a record of what is said. The researcher can also ask questions about what the members are expressing. Kagan has specific recommendations for facilitating the talk of subjects about the events they have selected, and his publications are strongly recommended reading (see Kagan 1980, 1984; Kagan and Kagan 1991; Kagan and Schneider 1987).

You can try to video tape naturalistic interactions for IPR purposes, but the presence of a video camera really does affect the way people act. I recommend using IPR after constructing a primary record and conducting interviews. Stage a discussion of some issue relevant to your research interests and derived from observations and interviewing. The subjects know they are being taped but need not know, initially, that they will be asked to comment on the tape themselves afterward.

11

Validity Requirements for Stage Three

Items covered in Chapter 11:

- Procedures to support subjective validity claims

- Getting "wounded" through field work

- Inference procedures and subjective-referenced claims

- The distinction between subjectivity and intersubjectivity

- Power and subjective truth claims

- Self-recognition and "cathartic validity"

Interviews and group discussions produce many subjective truth claims: claims that people believe, feel, intend, value, and experience various things within a realm closed off to others. Subjectivity is the realm of privileged access. We depend on honest and accurate self-reports to learn about the subjective states of others. There are procedures that will strengthen stage three claims:

1. *Use consistency checks on recorded interviews.* A tape-recorded interview will generally be objectively sound. The objective features of these data concern only what was said, and a tape recorder usually captures that perfectly well. To analyze an interview transcript adequately, however, one must have some idea of whether the subject was being honest and accurate. One way of checking for honesty and accuracy is to determine whether or not the subject is consistent. If she says early on in the interview, "I hated my brother," and then says much later on, "I admire my brother more than any other man I've ever met," you may have problems in taking both statements at face value.

The first part of conducting a consistency check is to look for any apparent discrepancies like this. If found, the next step is to go back to the subject and explain that you are confused about a couple of things she said. Show her the passages you have difficulty putting together and see how she explains them. She may acknowledge not being fully honest or clear at one point, or she may explain to you how the several sections in apparent disharmony are in fact consistent. One can both hate and admire someone, for example.

2. *If the research design allows, interview the same subjects repeatedly.* Repeatedly interviewing the same subject is likely to produce richer and more self-disclosing information than that produced in a single interview. You also build up a larger data set for conducting consistency checks.

3. *Conduct consistency checks between observed activity and what is said in interviews.* Frequently, your interviews will encourage a subject to talk about events you have observed or about matters related to what you have observed. You can then check the consistency between what the subject says and what you have in your primary record. When the subject talks about objective events, inconsistencies will reveal either a misperception on her part (assuming you used multiple recording devices and have a sound record of the events), a memory problem, or a lack of veracity. You can go back to the subject if you suspect a lack of veracity and see what she has to say about the two conflicting accounts. Misperceptions, on the other hand, will tell you something about the interpretative schemes employed by the subject.

4. *Use nonleading interview techniques.* Leading can be very subtle. Simply asking a question that is too abstract, like "What are your views on standardized tests?" can be leading. I used a good deal of space in chapter ten on how to interview in nonleading ways.

5. *Use peer debriefers for checks on possible leading.* Peer debriefers ought to be invited to look through some of your interview transcripts early on, to pay close attention to what you said and asked. A good debriefer will be able to spot instances of leading on your part.

6. *Use member checks.* Member checking ought to be part of the interview process. Toward the end of an interview, show your subject some of the reconstructions you have conducted on field notes and invite commentary. You should also summarize the results of the interview, as you understand it, toward its end and invite challenges from the subject. With repeated interviewing of the same subject, it is possible to facilitate discussion of your analyses of previous interview material.

7. *Encourage subjects to use and explain the terms they employ in naturalistic contexts.* Subjects often will try to please the interviewer by adopting terms they think the interviewer favors. Discourage them from doing so. Ask them questions with terms you have learned from them and paraphrase what they say from time to time with their own terminology.

SUBJECTIVITY AND RESEARCH METHODOLOGY

Subjective-referenced truth claims crop up methodologically for the social researcher in two distinctive ways. The researcher must be able to reconstruct subjective-referenced claims as her subjects of study themselves make them, and the researcher must be cognizant of the fact that her own act of doing research and writing it up will carry references to herself—her intentions, qualities, capacities, and identity.

Regarding the latter, researchers must be prepared to become hurt through their work; to allow their contact with others to threaten and perhaps alter their usual ways of conceiving of themselves. The researcher must strive for personal honesty at the deepest levels, and frequently this will induce states of anxiety, anomie, and self-doubt.

Why is this so? Because of the hermeneutic inference. Researchers have to be able to enter into the typifications of their subjects of study and understand the normative-evaluative claims made there through the recognition process. This can be an existentially threatening experience if the researcher studies people whose cultural world is fundamentally different from the worlds in which the researcher normally constructs herself, i.e., develops her own identity and evaluates it. Intersubjective recognition can undermine habitual ways of understanding your self. Some of the core issues involved are discussed below.

Inference Procedures and Subjective-Referenced Claims

The inference procedure involved in subjective research claims, like normative-evaluative claims, rests upon recognition. By definition, there is no multiple access to subjective states. The manner in which a subject refers to her intentions, states of awareness, desires, feelings, and so on, becomes communicative only if those who pick up the references can take the position of the one talking or acting. As soon as subjectivity is represented in any way, linguistically or through mental imagery, it becomes intersubjective. One gets an idea of what another person intends or feels by implicitly taking the position of that other person; in other words, by implicitly sensing what one would feel or intend oneself when talking in a similar manner. Subjective references carried by the acts of others must be recognized as subjective states one could feel oneself.

The implications of this are profound. We ourselves can only become aware of our own subjective states through reflection and thus through representing our subjectivity to ourselves via cultural symbols. This means that subjectivity becomes something to discuss, something to infer, something in any way to note, only through intersubjectivity—position-taking. As is the case in sense perception (see the discussion of Derrida in chapter one), our own awareness of how we feel, what we think, what we intend, and so on comes after the moment of experience. Our awareness, our "privileged access," is once-removed from moments of experience always-already gone.

Privileged access to experience occurs only through internalized monologues (or "premonologues," if differentiation in thought does not reach linguistic levels, see chapter seven). Such monologues are really dialogues between ourselves and an abstract audience, an internalized reference group or generalized other (Mead 1934). Subjectivity is tied to cultural symbols as soon as it is something about which one can be aware, as soon as it becomes knowledge-imparting for us.

But subjectivity is not solely a social construction. Symbolically represented subjectivity is the product of expressive action, as discussed in chapter seven. As such, it involves the distinction between an undifferentiated, felt impetus and the expressive act itself. When we represent our own subjective states, we move from holistic understandings to more explicit symbolic representations such that we can position-take on our own expressive act. Our "subjectivity" then appears as a reference carried by our own act or thought. But this reference carried by action and thought can be experienced as either matching or falling short of our holistic understanding of the action impetus, experienced prior to and during the act. There is an internal standard by which we judge the adequacy of our self-expressive acts. This is why we sometimes surprise ourselves by expressing a subtle idea better than we had imagined. A successful expressive act clarifies its impetus for the actor, including references to the actor's identity that all expressive acts carry. This is also why we sometimes feel that our expressions fall short of our ideas.

Thus, some manners of displaying subjective states performatively are going to work better than others. Similarly, some manners of naming the feelings we *just* had will seem better than others. This is why recognition is at play. We must be able to recognize our subjective experiences, which are always already past as soon as we become aware of them, *through* the names and images that arise to structure our awareness of them. Self-awareness is culturally mediated.

The distinction between subjectivity and intersubjectivity (position-taking) is absolutely crucial to subjective-referenced claims. Subjectivity is not the immediate effect of social relations, cultural forms, languages, and discourses. It is rather given through a play between such intersubjectively constituted symbols and raw, unmediated subjective experience that is always referenced but that is always already removed from experience when we represent it. Time has always moved between our privileged experience and our representations of it.

Pure subjectivity is always already gone when symbolized. But the act of symbolizing subjectivity involves a series of representations that move through very vague, holistic, and bodily felt forms outward toward delineated and explicit symbols (chapter seven; see also Carspecken 1993b, 1993d). When we recognize our own acts as successful expressions, we experience a match between holistic, embodied forms of awareness and our symbolic expression of them. Similarly, we know when the final stage of an expressive act has failed to express what we wanted it to.

When interviewing others it is important to be aware of any indicators of how successful they feel their own expressions to be. Good interviewing must be aimed at facilitating good self-expression, self-expression that the subject feels is in match with her preconceptual, intuitive experiences.

Power, Subjective Claims, and Truth

The match between a subjective state and its intersubjective representation brought about by expressive action feels good. It is empowering. Human beings desire it. It is a step toward knowing who we are, becoming more certain of our potentialities and capacities. This is why many people enjoy talking about themselves.

In communicative settings there is very often a desire to be truly recognized by other people so that we may be more sure of our selves. The desire for recognition underlies the human need to construct and maintain a positive self. There is a desire to make an intersubjectively framed representation of your self affirmed by others.

Hence the very inference procedure fundamental to normative-evaluative and subjective truth claims—recognition—is a motivated one, is a feature of desire. We have recognition needs, desires for self-affirmation. Power becomes intertwined with subjective truth claims in a wholly internal way because the desire to affirm the self is a desire for self-empowerment.

In day-to-day life, people create meaning and gain impressions of meaning from others through exemplars. One acts meaningfully and claims an entire order of values and norms, plus an identity, plus a structure of "kinds of identities" into which one locates the self, plus an implicit theory of society, all at once. Meaningful acts claim the existence and validity of entire worlds within which an identity is defined and located. Meaningful acts are instantiations of worlds claimed valid by the acts themselves. They are exemplars. When others position-take to understand an act, they tacitly grasp the world it claims.

Other people understand our meaningful acts by recognizing the vast order of claims they implicitly carry. They find a position for themselves within our claimed worlds and either reject it or affirm it or modify it when acting back. People communicate and learn through exemplars of the most universal implications. Every meaningful act is an exemplar of what an entire world is like: a claim to the validity of a vast order.

So, one invests one's self, stakes one's self, in one's acts of meaning and the world of claims they carry. One reacts to the normative and identity claims of another in relation to the manner in which one recognizes the self there. Recognition desires are the motor behind learning and communicating through exemplars.

It is no different for the critical researcher. What you see in the field is going to effect you existentially. To honor the three categories of validity claims involved in producing meaning and knowledge, the researcher will have to be open to feeling threatened by what she learns. If she is not open in this way, power may act through her privileged position as the one who writes about others, as the professor or the professional, to distort the representation of what is there at the expense of those studied. If the worlds claimed by other people seem to offer only limited or truncated identities for the researcher, gut-level responses will be defensive and negating.

To avoid this, you must be prepared to be threatened and to change through your field work. Peter McLaren expresses this beautifully when he says that the ethnographer must be prepared to be wounded in the field (1992). You sense a place for your self in the meaningful acts of other people that might threaten the habitual ways in which you construct your self. If you are not prepared to be wounded, you will not make inferences true to the validity requirements of normative, intersubjective, and thus subjective, reconstruction.

Therefore, power plays an important internal role when it comes to hermeneutics and intersubjective recognition. We have seen that truth must be kept separate from power in the sense that equal social relations are required for well-supported truth claims and for genuine recognition. Equal power relations corresponding to different social locations and statuses must be checked for as an external threat to valid research claims. An "ideal speech situation" in which all parties have equal say must be approximated for all three forms of validity claim.

But at the same time power is the spring from which all claims to truth flow forth. Truth claims, even about the most mundane "objective" sorts of things, are always made within complex social contexts and always carry identity claims pertinent to such contexts. Truth claims will always implicate recognition needs on some level of foregrounding or backgrounding. Internally, all researchers seek some form of self-empowerment through their work, just as all people in everyday settings seek recognition and dignity. This is basically the insight given to us from praxis theory (see chapter seven). Research is a kind of praxis.

The more we reduce those modes of power that prevent all people from having an equal voice, the more open we must be to existential threats. But being "wounded" through conducting research with integrity is ultimately going to be more empowering for us because it will change us, broaden our horizons, help us grow as human beings. This is a point related to Patti Lather's concept of cathartic validity (1986). Cathartic validity basically refers to the degree to which a researcher allows herself to change and grow through field work, change and grow in ways that often challenge oppressive cultural forms.

Thus, paradoxically, the more we conduct research with a universal community of equals in sight (and thereby reduce the play of external power), the more empowered we all will be. Society at present structures too many identity claims on comparisons with other groups of people: "I am a worthy human being because I am not one of them." Researchers carry this baggage as much as anyone. But any identity that depends on negating the worth of others is ultimately limited and ultimately falls short of human potentiality.

This is finally why social research is inevitably political. Not because critical researchers "choose" politically relevant "values," but because all truth claims, including those made by social researchers, are complexly intertwined with the power issues tied to recognition needs. Self-empowerment is, at the end of the day, an experience of self-affirmation only attainable intersubjectively. Equal social and cultural relations for all are presupposed, usually at remote and tacit levels of reference, by every individual effort to gain a sense of dignity and affirm the self to the fullest extent possible.

The pragmatic theory of truth upon which most of this book is based implicates a high standard for social researchers of all colors and stripes. At this time in human history, few people fully recognize their necessary connection to all others. Most people gain a sense of worth through cultural systems that pit them against other groups of humans. This is why many people enjoying a privileged position in society feel threatened by the plight of the poor. They do not want to know too many of the details. They want to explain social inequality by blaming the victims or in any other way that leaves their accustomed identities intact. They are afraid of being wounded. But the social researcher of integrity must be better. She will always be a criticalist whether she knows this or not. She will make her work a praxis through which her own ideas about who she is constantly changes. Research as praxis means both personal growth and social commitment. The pursuit of truth in social science cannot be followed without becoming open to wounding, without caring about those who are impoverished and oppressed. It will be painful at times, but it will develop and empower those who follow it with integrity.

12

Conceptualizing the Social System

Items covered in chapter 12:

- The importance of systems analysis
- The base-superstructure model
- The correspondence principle
- The cultural reproduction model
- Cultural circuits
- Epistemological issues in systems analysis
- System integration
- Cultural, political, and economic power

Stages one through three of this methodological scheme are generally focused on one social site or one cultural group. Stages four and five concern the complex relationships existing between the social site (or group) of focal interest and various other social sites (groups). These relationships have to do with system factors. In stage four the idea is to discover specific system relationships, such as relationships between a school and its surrounding community, or a youth culture and the popular media. In stage five the idea is to consider one's findings in relation to general theories of society, both to help explain what has been discovered in stages one through four and to alter, challenge, and refine macrosociological theories themselves.

Therefore, stages four and five require a conceptual framework giving useful sense to the term "social system." The conceptual framework I shall introduce in this chapter flows forth consistently from the models of action and meaning introduced earlier. But there are special epistemological difficulties entailed with system analysis, or "structural analysis," as it is sometimes called.

In the early days of critical qualitative research (the 1970s and early to mid-1980s), models of social structure were developed and refined from empirical findings. Epistemological issues were largely ignored. Insights into the nature of social structure that are found in the empirical studies of Willis (1975, 1976, 1977, 1981), McRobbie (1978) and Everhart (1983) influenced social theorists, like Michael Apple, who drew upon such findings to formulate theories of the social whole—what is wrong with it and how it might be changed (Apple 1979, 1983, 1986, 1993). The concept of social structure was a subject of extensive debate. But the theory of knowledge implied by any analysis of social structure was not problematized enough.

By the late 1980s and early 1990s, critical researchers were treating the issue of social structure much more cautiously. This is because epistemological issues had been brought to the fore by postmodern and neopragmatist intellectual trends, and the very possibility of developing a social theory had been challenged. Confidence in the viability of any macrotheoretical models eroded in many quarters.

As a consequence, some criticalists now simply ignore the issue of social structure. Others pop sweeping statements into their writings that disclaim the validity of any effort to produce a theory of society. These same authors frequently then go on to make other statements implying a theory of social structure and never bother to reconcile what appears to be contradictory assertions.

The problem does not lie with postmodernism or neopragmatism per se; the problem is rather that postmodernism and neopragmatism have taken a watered-down form in many methodological works (Carspecken 1993d). The original writings of Jacques Derrida, Michel Foucault, and Richard Rorty bear important insights that must be taken into account. But, unfortunately, there is a secondary postmodern literature that thrives on mere "buzz words" and style. Today, all one need do to impress certain audiences is to pop in sweeping epistemological disclaimers like "reality is ambiguous and contradictory," "all efforts to represent reality silence other possible views," "all analysis is the product of a researcher's personal interests and limited by the historical period in which she lives." Statements like these will identify you as one of the "in crowd." Once made, you are free to go ahead and make your statements against oppression by gender and oppression by race, statements that presuppose some theory of social reality. You need only let a tacit wink absolve you from contradicting yourself. To take a stand against oppression is to implicate a theory of oppression, a systems theory. But since reality itself is supposed to be nothing but a play of unstable meanings, contradicting yourself can even seem profound these days.

For my part, the influence of postmodernism and neopragmatism are welcome, but only if used with the same sort of rigor that their founding authors (e.g., Derrida and Rorty) display. I have little tolerance for sweeping statements and glib disclaimers. My view is that systems analysis must accompany good research and that such analysis is possible without ignoring postmodern insights. In this chapter I will briefly look at the history of how social structure has been treated by criticalists since the 1970s and then present a conceptual framework to aid structural analysis today. Some of the epistemological issues begged will be touched upon during my discussion. Recommended procedures for conducting stages four and five, based on the conceptual frameworks of this chapter, will be outlined in chapter thirteen.

CRITICAL RESEARCH AND THE CONCEPT OF SOCIAL STRUCTURE

It is possible to divide the short intellectual history of critical qualitative research into a number of phases distinguishable through how the question of social structure was framed and handled. Critical qualitative research was basically born in the 1970s with studies of education. Since educational institutions play a major role in system integration across time, across the live cycle, they are prime sites for system analysis. These early studies were taken, by readers, as an entree to raging 1970s' debates between Marxist-functionalists, Marxist-culturalists, and Marxist-structuralists, each having its own models for understanding society.

Aiming for a broad readership, I have decided to review the theoretical models in dispute during the 1970s to help readers unfamiliar with the social theory from which criticalism has emerged. The conceptual frameworks I myself advocate for studying the social system owe much to these earlier models, so readers will understand stages four and five all the more through an understanding of the base-superstructure model, the cultural reproduction model, and the cultural circuits model.

The Base-Superstructure Metaphor

Traditional Marxism, the Marxism of many communist parties, held to a basically mechanistic view of social structure. Influenced by certain passages in *A Contribution to the Critique of Political Economy* (Marx 1970: 20–21), this was a view of society that would have all its cultural, social, and legal/political forms determined by economic "structures."

Marx's analysis of capitalist society emphasized the social organization society employs to produce useful products. Because meeting the basic biological needs of life is absolutely fundamental to any social system (without meeting such basic human needs, society could not exist), Marx argued that economic arrangements are the key to all other features of society. Cultural products, beliefs, political institutions, family structures, religions, laws, educational institutions, and so on, must all support the economic structures of society, or society will not be able to exist. People must first have food, shelter, and other, more culturally defined, material needs met before they can enjoy a cultural and political life, which in turn must not threaten the system of economic cooperation, or else basic needs would not be met and society would immediately crumble.

In *A Contribution to the Critique of Political Economy,* Marx referred to the economic organization of society as "the base" and virtually everything else as "the superstructure." The base was supposed to determine the superstructure. "Base" and "superstructure" caught on. Base-superstructure models of society became rampant in traditional Marxism.

By economic "base," Marx meant two things: the technology by which society harnesses energy and produces products, and the social organization employed to manufacture needed goods. Economic social organization was termed "the social relations of production"—the way people cooperate to produce the goods that all must use in daily life.

Systematic Economic Exploitation

In capitalism the social relations of production are inherently exploitative. One class of people, the proletariat, sell their labor to produce goods. Another, much smaller, class of people, the capitalists, own the material means of production (factories, energy sources, and raw materials). They employ workers to make products which they then sell for a profit. The social relations of production in capitalism involve two main groups, according to Marx: the relations between those who own and those who work for wages drive the economy and give rise to a supportive superstructure.

Capitalists live by profits; workers by wages. What is the basis of profits according to Marx? It is the labor put into the manufacturing process by the proletariat. People need and use air, but because no labor is required to produce and distribute air it is "free." People need and use shelters, but these cost money because many other people had to work in order for houses and other shelters to be built. Money values are (complexly) related to the amount of human labor put into a product. Capitalists make a profit because they sell products produced by human labor. But capitalists do not themselves work, they rather employ other people to do so. Thus, capitalists make a profit only by paying workers less than what the workers actually produce. Profits are nothing but a system of robbery; the result of paying workers less than they have contributed to social production.

If you are not familiar with Marxist theory your gut reaction to this view may be one of skepticism. After all, do not corporate managers and directors perform a type of labor when they plan production and keep all the various parts of making, advertising, and selling well organized? Is not this activity work? Well, managers and directors do perform labor, but according to Marxist theory they are not pure capitalists. They are simply a higher tier of employee.

Pure capitalists in contemporary society are people who do not need to work at all because they own enough stock in corporations to have a good living. Think about these people; I have met some of them, and you probably have too. They live in houses built by other people; wear clothing made by other people; drive cars and enjoy products like televisions, swimming pools, computers, and so on that other people worked hard to produce. Yet they do nothing in return for enjoying these products; they do nothing with their labor that "returns the favor" to the people who made their trousers, telephones, and TV sets. Moreover, they enjoy many more such socially produced goods than do people who must work for their wages.

The exploitative features of a system that allows this sort of thing to occur should be obvious to you. A basic idea in Marxism is that economic products are the result of human cooperation; we should enjoy the use of such products but should also do our share of the work of producing them or our share of the work in providing services that others may benefit from. The cooperative nature of production ought to be explicit so that inequalities may be easily seen and eliminated.

Though the specifics of Marxism as an economic theory are problematical (how, for example, could you determine the comparable worth of management labor and factory labor?), the values carried by the theory are easily understood and perfectly congruent with the ideals of freedom and democracy that are advocated by capitalist societies themselves. The inequalities of capitalist production should not be so hard to spot and should raise objections from most people living in western societies.

But in the capitalist system the cooperative nature of production is not explicit; it is hidden behind laws allowing certain forms of private property to exist, and behind the use of money itself. As Michael Apple points out, human rights are masked behind property rights (1993). Money itself plays a large role in obscuring the cooperative nature of economic activity.

What is money? Money basically symbolizes human labor, the value of products and services. Ideally, money exchange would work as a shorthand for an exchange of labor, a cooperation among human beings. But money appears in popular culture to be economic value itself. The inherently symbolic nature of money is reified, such that economic value becomes equated with money instead of with work.

In the capitalist system the people who have most access to social products are those who contribute the least, and this is absolutely exploitative. Managers and directors are a class of people in between the pure capitalist and the pure worker. They do perform socially necessary work, though their power over the production process could be made much more democratic than it presently is. They get paid for the work they do. But they get paid more than their contribution to social production could actually justify. Thus they enjoy a share of the robbed spoils of an exploitative system. In addition, many people in these higher tiers of the job structure have extensive investments that pay large sums of money for simply owning, for doing nothing.

Marx and Engels argued that the exploitative social relations of capitalist production are reproduced and maintained by virtually everything else in society, by the "superstructure." The cultural understanding of money is an example of this. Money is a sort of shorthand for labor, but this is hidden in a culture that regards money to have intrinsic value, to be economic value.

Many other cultural beliefs play similar roles in hiding exploitation. People in American society typically believe that they are free and that they live in an egalitarian nation. This is a theme in widely distributed cultural milieu. Moreover, in many ways this belief is true. Political rights are more equal in this country than they are in many other countries, though they are not as equal as many people believe. Moreover, people are technically speaking free to seek jobs of their own choosing and to quit a job if they do not like it, which makes wage rates seem all the more fair (workers agree to them when they sign up for a job).

But it is often the partial truths of such cultural beliefs that make them all the more effective for hiding just-as-true forms of inequality. Michael Apple has said that the best way to understand how an ideology works is to first see what is correct about it; then, look at how it simultaneously distorts a truth in the interests of a powerful group. In capitalist society, those born to the lower classes have far fewer chances of ending up with large incomes and enjoying extensive political influence than do those born to higher classes. The education system and other complicated cultural systems ensure that this is so. We have (imperfect) forms of political democracy in our society, but we do not have economic democracy.

Moreover, what is "equal" and "free" about a society that requires a lower class of underpaid workers to exist? The social relations of capitalist production necessitate the existence of a lower class. Even if jobs were awarded purely on merit alone, which has never been the case, would we call a society "free" that puts those who get the lowest test scores, or otherwise end up lowest on some "merit scale," into jobs that are demeaning, boring, unhealthy, and low paid? In Ursula LeGuin's novel *The Dispossessed* (1974), a visitor from another planet becomes shocked when learning that an entire class of people do nothing but the most menial and stultifying work in a society that is like Western nations on Earth. He expresses his shock and then asks whether this class of people at least receives higher pay and prestige for performing these services. His shock deepens when he learns that they receive the lowest pay and have the least prestige! We, too, ought to be shocked. The very cultural themes that are prominent in Western societies—themes of justice, equality, humanism, and fairness—should convince most people that our class system is undesirable. Yet this is the system we live in. It has never been questioned loudly and clearly enough to change it. It is disguised, masked, hidden by dominant cultural beliefs.

Marx believed that the superstructure of society—its cultural, political, and legal realms—hide the reality of exploitation so that the base may be supported. Without such masking, the entire system would collapse. These superstructural realms also reproduce the base from one generation to the next. Children learn not to question the reality of exploitation and learn the skills and values necessary to move into positions of the base when reaching adulthood. For the majority, this means learning how to perform alienating labor for low wages without going insane or becoming rebellious. It means learning to blame one's self for failing to get a higher position, to assume an impoverished social identity.

Critique of the Base-Superstructure Model

The base-superstructure model of society seems to explain many features of capitalism. For this reason, and for the fact that it is easy to understand, it was popular among traditional Marxists. Figure 12.1 gives a graphic illustration of it. Despite its popularity in traditional forms of Marxism, there are obvious problems with this model. Accordingly, it came under attack by Marxists themselves during the 1960s.

It is a mechanistic model, for one thing. It is a metaphor suggesting that society

Figure 12.1 The Base-Superstructure Model

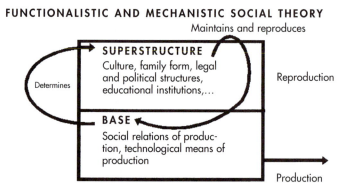

operates rather like a machine. We can visualize a "base," consisting of two classes, that somehow "cranks out" a superstructure made to order. This contributes to several reifications that theorists of the 1960s attacked. One is the reification of society itself. The model suggests that society is a single thing, when in fact the word "society" is an abstraction from the complexities, enormous complexities, of ongoing social life.

Another reification concerns the term "class." With the base-superstructure model, we are tempted to imagine two (or perhaps three) social groups whose membership is defined in a hard and fast manner. Lines between the groupings are unambiguous. Classes are special kinds of "things" that interact mechanically with each other. In actual fact, class membership is tricky and complex. Today we have a majority of workers who do not actually make things but rather who work in service industries. Always we have had large numbers of women who work without wages in homes; this was never easily taken into account by the base-superstructure model. Gender and race are as important as class for understanding social inequalities, but neither is well captured in the base-superstructure image.

Mechanism, Structuralism, Culturalism

An alternative was proposed in the 1960s by Louis Althusser (Althusser 1969; Althusser and Balibar 1970), who developed a theory of society by using structuralist metaphors in opposition to mechanistic ones. Structuralism is an intellectual tradition with origins in the structural linguistics of Saussure (1960), who wrote at the very beginning of the 20th century. Saussure's basic idea was that every element within a linguistic system owes its identity to an entire structure of contrasts and differences. In language, both sounds and semantic units are understood only through a simultaneous understanding of other sounds and semantic units: they take their particular form only within a system of differences. When we hear the consonant "r" in English, we simultaneously contrast it with "l" and other sounds. Oriental languages do not employ this particular structural contrast. When we understand a semantic term like "masculine," we simultaneously contrast it with "feminine." "Masculine" owes its meaning not to an immediate perception of men but to a structure of contrasts. This sort of analysis applies to pragmatics as well. As briefly indicated in chapter six, when we recognize a certain role in play during social interaction, we simultaneously contrast this role with a whole set of roles possible within a cultural setting. The phoneme, the semantic unit, the pragmatic unit are constituted by structure.

In the 1950s, Lévi-Strauss applied to culture this basic metaphor, the metaphor of a simultaneous structure of contrasts implicated by each particular unit in the system. He invented structural anthropology, and argued that all individual cultural practices and beliefs are what they are only through their place within a structural whole. Rituals, mythical themes, kinship rules, and agricultural practices express a single structure. Cultural life is the manifestation of cultural structures (Lévi-Strauss 1967).

With the advent of structuralism, social theory developed two main camps: theories that thought of society through the imagery of machines and theories that thought of society through the imagery of grammatical systems. Mechanistic models of society, like the base-superstructure model, basically viewed all social institutions and practices as connected cogs within a large mechanism: when one cog turns all the others must turn in a coordinated way. All the parts function to maintain a smoothly working device. The "motor," for base-superstructure theory, is the economic base: the social relations of production. Capitalists strive for profits and must win over their competitors. Workers strive to get jobs paying a decent salary. In such socially constructed strivings lies the energy that turns all the gears.

Structuralist models of society, on the other hand, basically viewed social phenomena as the outward manifestation of grammar-like rules that actors articulate in their daily lives. Each social act comes forth in a way determined by the structural whole.

Mechanistic models viewed the basic units of society to be like real things existing in space and time but connected to each other with feedback loops and other empirically identifiable linkages. Structuralist models viewed the basic units of society to be like the core elements of a language system which do not exist in space and time but that are rather holistic structures operative in something like a mental sphere. Each social act is a particular instantiation of the whole structure. The structure has a virtual existence, implicated holistically in every social act. Structures must be inferred; they cannot be observed. They do not have a spatial or temporal existence.

Louis Althusser rejected mechanistic forms of Marxism, like base-superstructure models, and produced a Marxist-structuralist theory. His work was extremely influential for a period of time. His improvements over the base-superstructure model included his insistence that political and cultural institutions have relative autonomy from the economic sphere. That is, not everything that happens in what was called the superstructure is totally determined by the base. His work was particularly influential in the study of capitalist governments—"the state," in capitalist society. Theorists of the capitalist state published work that is still important (Offe 1974, 1984). Some educational sociologists have made good use of this work as well (Dale 1982, Shapiro 1990).

Marxist *culturalists*, whose most visible member was E. P. Thompson (1963; 1978) objected very strongly to both mechanistic and structural social theory because neither properly accorded a place for human choice and free will—human volition. Mechanists, we have seen, viewed culture as a determined product, and thus human agency became reduced to the result of underlying economic organization and its functional requirements. Structuralists tended to reduce human agency to the manifestation of grammar-like structures. Louis Althusser, for example, sometimes wrote of human beings as mere "support agents" for underlying structures. No emphasis was given to human choice or volition. Structures constitute human agency, produce the subject, and not the other way around. Culturalists like E. P. Thompson wrote virulent attacks on these views, using historical studies as support, and pressed for the primacy of human culture and agency.

The Birth of Critical Ethnography

System Relations and the Correspondence Principle

When Paul Willis published *Learning to Labor* (1977)—arguably the classic work in critical ethnography—it was at a time that agency and structure debates raged. Culturalists advocated a theory of agency and volition. Mechanists implicitly reduced agency to the turning of cogs in a grand machine. Structuralists saw agency as constituted by structures and explicitly called for an end to humanism, to theories that put individual human choice and experience in primary position. Willis's study offered something new.

Before discussing Willis, however, it will be important to review another classic of the 1970s. Just prior to the appearance of *Learning to Labor*, Bowles and Gintis published a study of education called *Schooling in Capitalist America* (1976) that made use of the mechanistic base-superstructure model. This book, and the challenge posed to it by *Learning to Labor*, are so important as to warrant a review of Bowles and Gintis here.

Employing an extensive review of quantitative studies and historical data, Bowles and Gintis presented an influential theory of education that placed it firmly within the superstructure of a base-superstructure model. Perhaps the most influential idea in their book is what they called the "correspondence principle," which can be simply explained as follows: schools teach different hidden curricula to children of different social classes. The hidden curriculum is the set of beliefs, coping strategies, personal identities, and tacit theories (see chapter six) that children acquire indirectly through their schooling experience. The hidden curriculum can be transmitted through what is absent in textbooks (e.g., images of minorities and women in professional occupations; contributions of African-Americans to the history of the United States); it can be transmitted through what is implied in textbook illustrations (e.g., girls passively watching, with happy and admiring facial expressions, while boys climb trees or do other daring sorts of things); it can be transmitted through the way that teachers

Figure 12.2   The Correspondence Principle

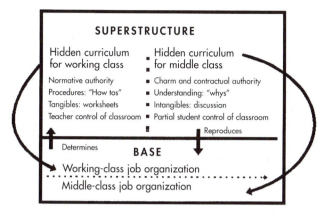

establish authority in the classroom, organize school work, reward and punish, and the extent to which they either encourage or discourage classroom creativity.

Bowles and Gintis argued that working-class children receive a hidden curriculum corresponding to the values and beliefs necessary to perform alienated labor. Teachers of the working-class emphasize procedures ("how tos") rather than understanding ("whys"). Working-class kids get a hidden curriculum that teaches them to produce tangible products (e.g., worksheets) by following the rules established by their teachers. Authority relations are purely normative (see chapter seven): "Do it because your teacher tells you to."

In a nutshell, the correspondence principle argues that working-class children indirectly learn the skills required of alienated labor; labor controlled and planned by other people. This prepares them for an adult life in working-class jobs. Middle-class children, on the other hand, learn skills and attitudes that will help them occupy professional and semiprofessional jobs. Why is this so? Because the social relations of capitalist production require it. Figure 12.2 illustrates the correspondence principle as a particular articulation of the base-superstructure model.

The existence of the correspondence principle actually has good empirical support, even from studies that did not seek to test this principle nor refer to it in any way (McDermott 1977; Metz 1978; Eder 1981; Anyon 1980, 1988; Carspecken 1991; McLaren 1993). Many schools service primarily one socioeconomic class (because of de facto segregation), and the pedagogy in these schools consistently reflects the hidden curriculum indicated by Bowles and Gintis: a hidden curriculum corresponding to the socioeconomic status of the students. Other schools service students from mixed socioeconomic backgrounds but employ tracking systems to segregate students by "ability." Tracking has consistently put a majority of low S.E.S. children into lower tracks, a majority of high S.E.S. students into upper tracks. The pedagogies one finds in tracked classes often correspond, in the way Bowles and Gintis indicate, to the dominant S.E.S. of their students.

The correspondence principle is a systems theory because it relates what goes on in some social sites (schools) to what goes on in others (work sites). But Bowles and Gintis did not give a good explanation of the principle. It is dependent, in their original treatment, on a base-superstructure model of society that cannot really tell us how and why it occurs. The basic explanation is completely functionalistic: because the social relations of capitalist production require it, children of different social classes receive a different hidden curriculum.

Moreover, there are substantive problems with the correspondence principle as originally formulated. It puts too much emphasis on what teachers do, whereas school children play a large role of their own in establishing classroom interactions and the hidden curriculum associated with them. Metz found, for example, that teachers trying to teach "progressively" to low-track students soon found themselves forced, through subtle classroom interactions, to adopt normative authority relations and emphasize worksheets (1978). Offers to have a classroom discussion with lower-track kids were met with complaints: "Just give us some worksheets and show us what to do." Empirically, the correspondence principle is well supported but such empirical regularities were not well explained with the base-superstructure model.

The Intervention of Critical Qualitative Research

This is when critical qualitative research entered the scene, through Willis's classic study. Willis did qualitative research on a small group of anti-school males in a working-class English school. These boys, who called themselves "the lads," actively rejected school by refusing to do school work and continuously playing up teachers. They "resisted" the authority of the school by creating their own culture; an anti-school culture. Willis reconstructed this culture, examining the implicit theories and values implicated in the lads' activities, including their humor, their sexism, their views of work and fun, their emphasis on fighting and "macho" forms of behavior.

From Willis's reconstructions we find another sort of "correspondence principle." On the remote levels of meaning horizons, constructed by the lads, are views of life, desired identities, and beliefs about society that correspond to working-class shopfloor culture. These cultural themes are not imposed through a hidden curriculum but rather constructed by working-class students, their parents, and their cultural ancestors, in order to cope with alienated and underpaid labor. It is by resisting school, and thus throwing away their one chance to escape working-class jobs, that the lads prepare themselves for a working-class future. Willis argues, for example, that other boys in this working-class school, boys who took their teachers seriously, still wound up with working-class jobs when they got out but were less prepared to handle the conditions of alienated work.

The model of society suggested by Willis's study still implies the fundamental importance of the social relations of production. The lads' culture is the product, ultimately, of people trying to retain positive identities and a sense of dignity in alienating conditions of work. But because we find the lads constructing this culture themselves, rather than a school imposing it upon them, the distinction between base and super-

Figure 12.3   Cultural Reproduction Model

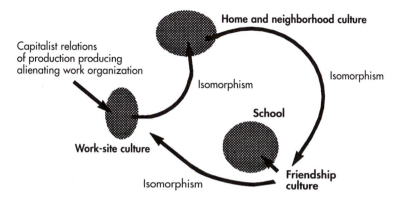

structure begins to vanish. The social relations of production are reproduced, not mechanistically, but through human agency itself, including the agency of those who have most to lose from these relations of production.

Willis's analysis nicely mixes mechanistic themes with cultural themes. The relations of production are both outside and inside working-class people (all people). They are outside because we are born into situations not of our choosing and quite beyond our full understanding. We must cope with these situations whether we want to or not. But they are inside because the social relations of production are themselves the products of cultural activity, reproduced through the production of culture that all people take part in.

Willis's theory has been called "cultural reproduction" because it emphasizes the development of culture through the volition of social actors. Culture, however, is produced when people draw upon cultural themes they are already familiar with. They draw upon such themes in response to institutional settings and the constraints these settings exert upon them. The lads drew upon themes learned in their homes and communities that produced an anti-school culture. Although this culture was in many ways unique, it made use of the same remote references as can be found in the cultures of their parents and neighbors. These home and neighborhood cultures, furthermore, are related to work-site cultures, cultures produced by working-class people in alienating conditions of work.

Thus, Willis described a series of isomorphisms between the cultural realms of a number of related social sites: the home, the friendship group at school, and shop-floor culture. Such isomorphisms basically "locked" these sites together into a reproductive loop such that children from the working class ensured their own movement into working-class jobs upon the completion of school. His model of the social system is roughly diagrammed in Figure 12.3.

Although the production of culture through human volition is central to Willis's model, his explanation for why the lads produced their particular culture centers on capitalist work relations and their alienating quality. Willis assumed, with good reason, that the drive for dignity and positive social identities has led working-class people to produce a resistance culture when faced with alienated work. Dominant culture offers only the lowest forms of prestige and dignity to the working class: working-class people have little control over their work; they are subordinates in hierarchical work organizations; their work is demeaning, underpaid, and looked down upon. But the drive for a positive identity and self-respect is strong in all human beings. Workers cannot meet this drive through their actual work so they have developed ways of meeting it socially. They have developed cultures that reverse many values of dominant culture, and they earn respect from each other by resisting authority, sabotaging the work process on a small scale, and looking down upon those who have mastered "book learning" and who live lives of the "posh."

Willis also tacitly used structuralist themes in his analysis. The culture of the lads, as he reconstructed it, is a system of similarities and differences implicated holistically in each social act. The identity of the lads was constantly claimed through fighting, joking, and bantering. Each act emphasizing an identity claim implicated a system of contrasts: maleness against femaleness, nonconformity against conformity, fluency in street knowledge against fluency in school knowledge. All these terms were part of a single cultural structure.

But Willis, unlike hard-core structuralists, emphasized the continuous creation of cultural structure rather than the determination of action from structures. Each act can innovate on cultural themes. Cultural structures are iterated through human volition; they are never referenced in exactly identical ways from social act to social act. This relocation of structuralist insights into a theory of action has been expanded upon in other qualitative studies. McLaren also reconstructs a structure of binary oppositions and homologies, but relates them to bodily feeling states (1993). I have reconstructed binary structures on pragmatic, rather than semantic levels and related them to non-binary cultural themes (Carspecken 1992).

Post-Willis Advances

After *Learning to Labor,* many other studies appeared to show how oppressed people create a culture of opposition that simultaneously ensures their continued oppression. Some post-Willis studies sought intersections between a hidden curriculum and student-created cultures (Carspecken 1991). McLaren's ethnographic study introduced new conceptual insights into the basic picture of cultural reproduction by including attention to body states and the multivocal feature of cultural symbols (1993). My own first ethnography introduced the concept of "intersubjective structure" and the relationship of prerational identity claims to rationalized beliefs (Carspecken 1991).

The Cultural Circuits Model

Richard Johnson, of the Centre for Contemporary Cultural Studies, expanded the cultural reproduction model to take into account system relations that are not dependent on the movement of people from site to site. Cultural commodities—produced by advertising companies; music, television, movie, and video corporations; governments; and many other institutions—influence the cultures of many sites without any movement of people between them. Their influence is spread through economic and political relations rather than physical movements of people.

Johnson offers a simple but powerful model for analyzing cultural products of almost any type, including those that are not commodified or formalized in policy documents. He published his model in a widely influential paper, titled "What is Cultural Studies Anyway?" (1983). In this paper, Johnson suggested that cultural products display a "circuit" quality when carefully analyzed. He called it the "circuit of cultural production."

Cultural "products" include everything that results from a meaningful act. The act itself could be viewed as a product that can be "read" in various ways (multiple possible meanings) and that affects other actors through their readings of it. But cultural products are also such tangible things as songs, books, soda cans, billboards, and cars. All human products are cultural in that they carry meaning fields.

Johnson's circuit model has four main points along its course. I have slightly reinterpreted these main points to include: (1) the conditions of production, (2) the autonomous possible meanings of the product, (3) interpretations given the product by various cultural groups, and (4) the effect of the product on routine activities of various cultural groups (see Carspecken and Apple 1992).

A circuit is completed when the effects of the product come back to influence its further production. In the case of routine activities, actors will monitor the effects of their action on both conscious and semiconscious levels. They will note how others respond to their activities. Such monitoring will influence how they act again under similar circumstances. This is a circuit, but a small one that may only help to integrate a few social sites.

In the case of tangible, commodified cultural products, producers will monitor sales, and this will influence whether and in what way they produce them again.

Cultural products, like social policy documents, will be monitored more broadly in terms of how they affect people's lives, if formulated by idealistic agencies hoping to better society. If formulated by more opportunistic politicians, policy documents will be monitored according to voting behaviors.

To understand everything involved with a cultural product of any type, Johnson recommended studying it in terms of each of these four points. First, look at how the product was produced. You need to examine who the producers were, what their interests were in producing the product, and the cultural traditions that influenced their product.

Next, look at the product itself. What possible meanings could it convey? Which meanings are overt and which covert? During this phase, you examine the product as if it were a literary text. Any possible meaning that occurs can be articulated and recorded. But you must remember that you are dealing only with possible meanings during this stage. There is no guarantee that the product will be read by significantly large numbers of people in ways similar to your analysis. More empirical work has to be conducted to find out exactly how people read the product. That will be the third point on the circuit. Initial analysis of the product's possible meanings paves the way for an investigation of how actual people interpret it.

The third phase of analysis requires an interest in a specific group of people exposed in some way to the product. Observations and interviews must be used to determine how the group interprets a film, textbook, television show, popular music, etc. One of the several possible meanings derived during the second phase of circuit analysis may be found to be the reading most frequent to a group. On the other hand, studies of the group may reveal readings you had not thought of before.

The fourth and last phase of cultural circuit analysis involves noting routine activities of the group in relation to their reading of the product. People can talk about a cultural product in one way but act in another. Their interpretation of the meaning of a product is no guarantee, in itself, that their behavior will be affected.

An excellent example of scholarly work employing the cultural circuit model is Michael Apple's *Teachers and Texts* (1986). Apple analyzes school books and policy reports through all four phases of the cultural circuit. He is able to show how complex intersections of economic, political, and patriarchal power have led to the production and distribution of school books and educational policy documents in the United States. He also carefully examines the meaning fields of these products, especially in the case of policy documents, and he predicts how various populations of people will read and be affected by them. This book is an outstanding piece of systems analysis, employing conceptual models reviewed in this chapter.

Another, smaller-scale example of using the cultural circuits model is given in my paper with Apple ("Critical Qualitative Research" [1992]). Here, the way in which school children interpreted a television show is examined and compared to the actual social routines of these same children (points [3] and [4] in the circuit).

Generalizing from the cultural circuits model we find an extension of Willis's theory of cultural reproduction, as diagrammed in Figure 12.4.

The basic elements of this model can be summarized as follows:

1. "Society" is not regarded as a single entity, like a machine or an organism, but rather as a complex set of intersecting factors.
2. Thus, there is no social system but rather many system relations that bring about varying degrees of integration between social groups and social sites. Monitoring activities will put into place one type of system relation.
3. The factors that integrate social action between groups and sites may be regarded as conditions of social action. Actors act with volition, with agency. But actors act only within specific contexts; all action is conditioned. The distribution of action conditions will be a series of system relations.
4. Conditions of action vary in nature. Some operate internally to the volition of actors as systems of values, beliefs, and desired identities; these are cultural. Others operate externally to the volition of actors; they are resources and constraints that will face

Figure 12.4   Social Sites within the Social System

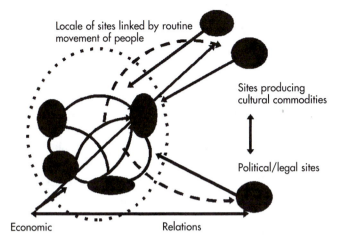

Locale of sites linked by routine
movement of people

Sites producing
cultural commodities

Political/legal sites

Economic   Relations

any actor, with any set of beliefs, given a certain social location. These are not strictly cultural in nature but are rather economic and political.

5. People themselves produce and reproduce system relations, but under the influence of conditions. To describe social systems, then, is to describe both typical social routines and their connection with other typical social routines through the distribution of action conditions.

These points will inform my own framework for studying social "structure." Before clarifying some of the terms used above, however, I want to return to the question of epistemology as it is begged by systems analysis.

Studying Social Systems; Epistemological Problems

Cultural reproduction improved over the base-superstructure model and encouraged new qualitative research and qualitative data analysis to produce ever-refined conceptual frameworks for understanding the social system. However, by the late 1980s the epistemology of structural analysis was put into doubt by postmodern slogans. As I said earlier in this chapter, some critical researchers now either ignore the question of social structure or address it with so many caveats as to greatly reduce the impact of their work.

A number of recent authors point out that even cultural reproduction theory and its refinements boil down to a machine model of society (e.g., Wexler 1992). Cultural production is still conceived to be driven by fixed, coglike, economic relations of production. The "age of the machine," industrial society, is the age of modernism. The "age of information," of symbolic orders, is "postmodernism." Mechanistic metaphors had their place in history but are now surpassed by social change. It is time for social theory to catch up with the postmodern age.

The same may be said for epistemology. If society is argued to be like a machine, one must assume the epistemological stance of a "floating observer" who views this machine in a detached and uninvolved way. The descriptions of this floating observer are based on what can be "seen"; they "mirror" society.

But critical epistemology, as I have developed it so far in this book, does not use perceptual metaphors at its core. Moreover, many critical analyses of qualitative data performed at the systems level are not guilty of mechanistic imagery nor of mirror epistemology. Willis's study does not depend on a mechanistic view of society, a sort of device that tricks people into reproducing itself; only a shallow reading of Willis would leave one with this impression. McLaren's study (1993), as another example, manages to employ postmodern insights, avoid the epistemology of the "mirror," and deliver a systems analysis. Many criticalists of recent years who still dare to study social structure are neither mechanists nor naive realists, but we do lack a sound critical epistemology with explicit discussions of the problematical issues. How might these issues be addressed?

This book has so far shown how holistic, preconceptual, and communicatively structured experience may replace the perception metaphor in epistemology. Epistemological principles have been developed for reconstructive analysis based on this alternative scenery. Now we must examine what epistemological principles are required in the analysis of social structure.

First let us review how critical epistemology works for reconstructive analysis—the analysis employed in stages two and three. Reconstructive analysis emphasizes insiders' views and meaning fields. We perform stages one through three very well when we articulate the perceptions of objectivity, the allegiances to norms and values, and the representation of subjective states, that participants routinely employ. This requires attention to meaning fields and validity claims. Thus it brings attention to ambiguities, cultural drifts and shifts, and even to contradictory claims made in everyday life. We do not end up with a single reality but a field of reality claims consistently made by the participants of study. In most studies, however, one will find that such fields are limited in number and display bounded qualities: we do not discover an infinite number of possible realities. This is an empirical claim on my part; if you do not believe it, test it out in field work. People live with conflicting and sometimes contradictory conceptions of reality but there is a tendency towards unification in cultural processes. Perhaps the reason for this lies in something like Giddens's belief that people have ontological needs for security (Giddens 1979).

Thus, reconstructive analysis avoids mirror epistemology by being as inside the object of inquiry as possible. Hermeneutic inferences require taking an insider's stance as much as possible. Such inferences reconstruct reality claims, ontological claims, made by others. Those who criticize the mirror metaphor of traditional epistemology often do so by declaring the impossibility of a totally outside perspective. Trying to attain one produces distortions, renders other people's cultures to objects constructed within the culture of the researcher.

Thus, *inside vs. outside* is a sort of theme in many critiques of traditional epistemology. Reconstructive analysis seeks the insider's view. But there is, of course, a dialectical play between insider and outsider views. There is never a totally inside view, just as there is never a totally outside one. The people one studies will themselves constantly make outsider claims, third-person claims, about events. This is a communicative imperative. We are "inside" a culture when we understand how our subjects themselves distinguish between outsider positions (multiple access) and insider positions (privileged access and the shared insider's position of the normative-evaluative realm).

So, understanding other people necessitates a movement between the claim to a floating third-person position, and the claim to totally immersed insider positions. Understanding occurs not through occupying one position or the other but rather in learning the cultural movement between them. Understanding is intersubjective, not subjective or objective.

In addition, communicative acts always contain some universalizing claims: claims that all people, regardless of who they are or where they stand, will consent to them. People claim entire worlds in their meaning horizons and claim them as valid. Researchers who aim for the objective, floating view of another culture are rightly criticized for making their own cultural constructions appear universal. But to move inside another culture is to find that these people make their own, everyday, universalizing claims. Constructivists and relativists rarely criticize those they study for their ethnocentrism; they simply reserve that sort of critique for other methodologists.

So the point is this: when pursuing forms of analysis that extend beyond the cultural horizons of the group you study, do so in a way that incorporates your subjects' own insights and terminology. Pit their universalizing claims with your own and let the two engage in dialogue. Invite those you study to participate in your specialized forms of analysis. There is nothing wrong with universalizing outsider claims, as long as efforts to see through the universalizing implications of these claims are sought. This means getting the actual contribution of others to your formulations with the aim of winning broad consent.

Systems analysis necessarily goes beyond reconstructive analysis because it tries to explain cultural formations in terms that may go beyond the culture of a specific group. Epistemologically, systems analysis foregrounds universalizing claims to multiple access. These claims approach the "total outsider," but in our epistemological theory a total outsider is not really a floating observer. A total outsider is a position that any anonymous person could occupy: it is a claim to multiple access taken with respect to as universal an audience as possible.

Thus, according to critical epistemology, the outsider position is still inside and therefore still fallible (chapter one). But it aims for the limit case of being inside human cultures at this particular historical period. It aims to meet standards such that any human being living today would agree with the claims made from this position if uncoerced and if in agreement with the terms employed.

Systems analysis must therefore be open to as many cultural contributions as are practically possible in a study. Given cultural differences and the limited distribution of sociological terminology—the very terminology one employs when developing a systems analysis—the safest way to proceed is to begin with the participants' experiences and life situation as this becomes understood by the end of stage three. Their understanding and consent ought to be your first priority for both epistemological and moral reasons. It is their lives that we are trying to understand and explain, and it is their lives that are likely to be most effected by your analysis. In the next chapter, I will give guidelines for prioritizing participant experiences and terms when conducting stages four and five. The last section of this chapter will clarify some systems concepts.

CONDITIONS OF ACTION AND THE SOCIAL SYSTEM

Stages one through three emphasize social integration, stages four and five emphasize system integration and the relationship between social and system integration.

> *Social integration* refers to the coordination of action on one site through face-to-face interactions. (Giddens 1979: 74)

> *System integration* refers to the coordination of action between social sites separated in space and time. (Giddens 1979: 74)

In studies of system integration, we become interested in how and why routines that take place on one social site during one period of time are coordinated with events and routines on other sites at other times. This sort of coordination is what makes a society. The base-superstructure model, the cultural reproduction model, the correspondence principle, and the cultural circuits model are all efforts to explain system integration.

Diverse factors are involved in system integration, but most of them can be spotted through attention to the conditions of action operating on each site. Three general categories cover most conditions of action:

- the distribution of cultural milieu
- economic relations
- political relations

Cultural Conditions of Action

Cultural conditions of action are those that resource and constrain through the volition of the actor. "Volition" is something like "free will": volition is "an act of will preceding a physical movement" (Flew 1979: 370). The concept of free will is tricky and contentious. According to our theory, however, actors are capable of monitoring their actions and altering them during their course. Actors are also capable of thoroughly thinking through possible actions and action consequences in order to choose how to act. In the course of everyday life we rarely think, explicitly, before acting, but we do monitor our stream of action on preconceptual levels of awareness and continuously adjust our behavior. This is how we should understand volition. It has to do with monitoring actions according to our values, norms, and desired identities.

Volition itself depends on cultural structures to exist, because monitoring action impeti requires internalized position-taking. But actors can innovate upon the cultural structures of which they are aware as well as choose among alternative cultural themes. Culture does not determine action. Each meaningful act made by any one of us will usually reconstitute cultural structures and be a new creation to a certain extent.

Culture is a fundamental and necessary resource for social action. But culture is simultaneously a constraint because actors can only be innovative to the extent that available culture allows. The distribution of cultural themes across various social sites will act as a constraint on action. One cannot act in ways that would require themes to which the actor has no access.

In addition, the frequency with which certain themes are reproduced in the activities of a cultural group will constrain or resource social action. Actors are less likely to draw upon themes seldom used by others than upon themes frequently modeled.

Finally, the currency of cultural themes will resource and constrain social acts. Actors are less likely to employ themes of small currency or of negative currency—themes that are understood and available but somehow frowned upon by most members of their cultural group. Actors are more likely to employ themes enjoying wide recognition by members of their group. This is how affirmed identities are constructed.

Cultural Power and the Social System

What makes some themes available, others absent, others present but of low or negative currency? Features of the social system do. The distribution of cultural themes and their normative-evaluative weight is a system phenomenon. Many themes are widespread throughout society, helping to coordinate activities on diverse social sites through influencing the beliefs, values, and norms of vast groupings of people. Similarly, the consistent discouragement of certain kinds of cultural productions from gaining wide distribution and currency is a feature of the social system.

The extent to which one has control over, or benefits from, the distribution and currency of cultural themes is cultural power at the system's level. Clearly, some groups have greater amounts of this power than others, have much greater say in which forms of culture are to be taken seriously and employed widely and which forms are not. When examined carefully, one will see that cultural power intersects in complex ways with what will soon be introduced as economic and political power. Groups enjoying extensive cultural power will also usually enjoy economic and political power.

Advertisers, for example, have a good deal of influence over widely distributed cultural themes: they express cultural power in their activities. So do Hollywood filmmakers. These occupational groups deliberately affect culture, but do so primarily in order to make profits. The full effect of their advertising and entertainment products on mass culture is not their primary concern. Many side effects on cultural realms accompany the distribution of advertising and entertainment products.

Advertisers and filmmakers are economically powerful occupational groups. They express cultural power in their efforts to expand or maintain the economic power they enjoy. They wish to attract people's attentions and desires in order to sell products, and they use their influence over culture to this end. Economic structures underlie the cultural power these groups employ.

Class societies also selectively distribute certain forms of culture so that dominant groups remain in dominance. Accents, attitudes about ethnic groups, the currency of certain cultural forms in terms of their prestige, and the privileging of certain types of knowledge over others (Apple 1993) are all part of this sort of cultural power, related to class structure. For example, elite private schools reserve highly prestigious forms of learning for the wealthy, while cultural themes distributed to all groups support a general perception of this elite knowledge as prestigious.

Here, cultural power is expressed in many cases with less awareness on the part of the powerful group than is the case with advertisers and film producers. Most members of the British upper class, for example, really believe that the knowledge taught in their expensive private schools, that their accents, that their norms of polite behavior, and so on, are "the best." They do not conspire to make all the rest of society agree with them on this, but their privileges in the realms of economic and political activity result quite naturally in giving their forms of culture high visibility and currency. Power arrangements can thus work systematically to privilege a certain form of culture over others without this being exactly intentional. Activities in one sphere of society become linked to activities in other spheres such that each sphere helps to maintain the patterns occurring within the other.

As a last example of cultural power, consider totalitarian states like those that existed under Hitler and Stalin. The powerful groups in these societies maintained their positions through political and coercive modes of power. Once in power, very deliberate efforts were made to influence mass culture in favor of the ruling group. Pictures of the dictators were placed everywhere; the press and media were tightly controlled to provide only the views of the dominant group, as were school curricula. Cultural power was expressed in these cases in association with political, police, and military power. The effects produced on mass culture were monitored very thoroughly and intentionally.

Thus cultural power is the extent to which one has control over, or benefits from, the distribution of cultural milieu. This sort of power can be the result of:

- *Fully intended* efforts on the part of one group to influence the culture of society as a whole (e.g., totalitarian states)
- *Partially intended* efforts to influence mass opinion in order to sell products (e.g., advertising and entertainment industries, which affect gender themes, beliefs about success and happiness, beliefs about what is socially "natural," and so on)

- *Unintended* effects of a system that gives more visibility and opportunity to one group than it does to others

In addition, cultural power is often resident in the cultural productions of subordinate groups themselves, who must cope with lower class status and harsh living conditions. Willis, as described already, showed how working-class boys in England produced a culture to resist school and all forms of authority in order to heighten their sense of personal dignity and worth within the harsh conditions of lower class life (1977). This culture benefited these boys in many ways, but it also ensured their movement from school into the lowest paid and most alienated forms of work available. Ogbu has argued that African-American culture transmits "competencies" to its youth that help them survive a racist society and race-based "job ceiling" (1979). These cultural competencies are helpful in retaining dignity and surviving economically within a racist culture, but these competencies also make it difficult for African-American children to succeed in American schools. These are examples of unintended modes of cultural power, produced in this case by subordinate populations rather than superordinate. The economic, political, and cultural conditions into which subordinate populations are born are ultimately responsible for forms of culture like these.

Political Conditions of Action

Political conditions of action involve formalized relations of authority that are distributed widely throughout a society. Our laws, produced by our political system and maintained by our system of justice, are exactly formalized relations of authority.

Where consent to politically distributed authority relations breaks down, political power is backed by the coercive power of police. Laws put political conditions of action into place; the police back such conditions with coercion. Political conditions of action will always be colored by cultural themes, but they appear within an actor's experience as something external to their volition. To break a law is to incur a sanction. This is true regardless of one's particular values and beliefs.

The existence of police, the national guard, and prisons reinforce political conditions of action with coercion in those cases where people do not consent to the authority relations involved. But many people who do not live in totalitarian police states generally will follow political rules because they consent in principle to the legitimacy of the law and the consequences incurred if the law is not obeyed. Culture legitimizes political relations to make the laws widely regarded as fair, or democratically produced, or simply to give currency to the law-abiding citizen identity.

Political Power and the Social System

Political power on the system level is the extent to which one has control over and access to authoritative resources and their distribution (Giddens 1979). In a democratic society, all people have some political power. People are free to vote, to lobby, and (sometimes) to demonstrate. But it is obvious that some groups enjoy much more political power than others. In Western democracies, people with wealth can influence the political system much more easily than can people lacking it. In addition, people are aware of their political rights and act on them only through cultural themes. Not infrequently, the culture of an underprivileged group obscures the political rights each member in fact has. Culture will either encourage or discourage people from acting politically.

ECONOMIC CONDITIONS OF ACTION

Economic conditions of action will be experienced as very much external to one's volition. The way in which people can meet their basic needs for food, clothing, housing, and medical care is economically conditioned in the United States. Some welfare state systems in Europe have government housing and medical care that is politically guaranteed rather than economically conditioned. In the United States, political arrangements do provide some support for economically disadvantaged groups, but it is not much. Economic arrangements are the main way in which the material resources needed for life are distributed among various groups of people.

Economic Power and the Social System

Economic power at the system's level may be regarded as the extent to which people have control over or access to material resources (Giddens 1979). Once again, it is obvious that some groups control material resources much more than other groups. The distribution of private property and stocks in large corporations is what most differentiates groups economically in Western societies. The system of income differentials between occupations is another important factor.

CHAPTER SUMMARY

In this chapter I have argued that the analysis of systems relations is both epistemologically possible and absolutely crucial to gain a full understanding of qualitative research findings. I have reviewed models used in the analysis of social structure: the base-superstructure, cultural reproduction, and cultural circuits models, as well as the correspondence principle. Each of these is flawed, but each has played an important role in understanding systems analysis.

I have also reviewed some major concepts to employ in systems analysis, including: system integration, conditions of action; and cultural, political, and economic power. The next chapter of the book will present procedures for conducting stages four and five of this methodological scheme.

13

Stages Four and Five:
Conducting Systems Analysis

Items covered in chapter 13:

- Illustrating the difference between stages four and five

- Stage four: concepts and procedures

- Validity requirements for stage four

- Stage five: concepts and procedures

In stage four, the idea is to discover particular system relations by examining several related sites. In stage five, the idea is to seek explanations of your findings through social-theoretical models. In stage five, additionally, existing system theories (like the correspondence principle and the cultural circuits model) will often be altered or refined in light of your findings.

The Willis study *Learning to Labor* (1977) exemplifies the difference between stages four and five. Willis carefully reconstructed features of his subjects' culture, which is a stage one through three activity. Then he presented some additional cultural reconstructions based on his observations of factory life (where his subjects' fathers worked) and of the homes in which his subjects lived. By displaying isomorphic relationships between the cultures of these three sites (school friendship group, factory, and home), Willis engaged in stage four analysis, which is based on empirical findings from several sites. Willis argued that his subjects, "the lads," produced a culture congruent with shop-floor cultures, thereby rejecting chances for social mobility. At the same time, they taught themselves coping skills for performing alienated work.

Willis then speculated about the general significance of his findings. He noted that capitalist relations of production have produced alienated working conditions for many generations now, and posited that working-class culture must have developed and transmitted themes related to these conditions. Some of these themes, such as the heavy emphasis on physically demanding work and associated "masculine" (macho) values, are now out of sync with contemporary production technology but have been retained as a tradition, exhibiting a sort of cultural lag. This comprises stage five analysis, because it goes well beyond Willis's field findings and it makes use of established social theories (e.g., the theory of alienated labor) while also contributing to these theories (e.g., rejection of the base-superstructure model).

Willis also claimed, and this is important, that the lads' culture contained certain implicit insights into the nature of capitalist production, into the stage five model Willis himself used. The lads, using cultural themes bearing a long tradition in working-class culture, seemed tacitly aware of what has happened to labor under capitalism. Labor has become abstract—separated from the full praxis of conceiving and creating products. Under capitalism, workers do not plan their activities; they carry out procedures planned by superordinates. Labor is therefore abstract in the sense that jobs are fragmented, with individual workers contributing only small mundane forms of work to the entire process (as in assembly lines). It is abstract in the sense that workers are paid for labor, measured in time, rather than for the products that actually embody labor. The lads seemed to be subconsciously aware of this feature of capitalist work, because they regarded all jobs as basically the same and showed no interest in the emphasis given to career choices and types of jobs by their school careers counselor.

Here we find stage five forms of analysis that connect the social theory Willis employed to the experiences and perceptions of his subjects. This is epistemologically important, for it takes a culturally constructed meaning horizon of the subjects studied and broadens it, extends it, to a theory outside the cultural horizons of the group. Rather than a machine model of society, conceived from the floating position of an uninvolved observer, we have an expansion and fusion of meaning horizons between subjects' culture and researcher culture.

Of course, Willis did not do a perfect job in this area: he did not actually involve the lads in the specifics of his theory other than have them read his book and invite discussion. The lads did not share enough of Willis's specialized vocabulary to contribute fully to the theoretical portions of the book, which is often a problem in qualitative research. With some populations of people, only extended periods of "teach-ins" and sociological workshops can help subjects gain an insider's view of the researcher's culture. Some groups will not be motivated to participate in teaching sessions, others will lack time. Still, we can understand the ideal case and strive to approximate it. Good stage five analysis comes not only from the researcher's gaining an insider's position in the culture she studies but also from the subject's gaining an insider's position in the researcher's culture.

STAGE FOUR: DISCOVERING SYSTEM RELATIONS

In stage four, then, we look for relationships between specific social sites, studied empirically. The site and cultural group, rather than noncultural social groupings like "class," will usually be the main units of analysis in stage four. This is because the concepts of site and cultural group are empirically immediate. Concepts like class, on the other hand, are not empirically immediate, involving greater abstractions from ongoing social life. They can be operationalized (e.g., "class" as a type of job) but such operationalizations abstract from particular social contexts and particular cultural groups to a great extent and therefore ought to be reserved for stage five forms of analysis.

Class, race, and gender are often referred to in the same breath as broadly distributed social categories. Kinchloe and McLaren, for example, refer to these as "the holy trinity" (1994). But analytically these are different types of construct. Gender groupings and racial groupings are primarily cultural as experienced by individuals and will take on very specific cultural articulations within particular sites. Thus gender and race can be important to stage four. They become important in stage five, too, because the cultural themes associated with gender and race have been strongly tied to class relations, producing very broad patterns. Class itself is not always experienced in a cultural manner, however, except in societies that culturally label people in interactions as being from one class or another (e.g., British society labels you by class in typical interactions as soon as your dialect is heard). In general, the noncultural dimensions of class are best studied in stage five.

Site relationships may include those based on the actual physical movement of people or on cultural commodities and political documents. They may be those fully intended (e.g., legislated social policy programs), partially intended (e.g., advertising), or totally unintended (e.g., unmonitored cultural loops of the sort Willis discovered).

Looking for Cultural Isomorphisms between Sites

The sort of analysis Willis performed in *Learning to Labor* (1977) is focused in the first instance on site-specific cultures and their relationships through the physical movement of people. The system relations he found are of the unintended variety, which are among the most subtle of system relationships. Here are some pointers for discovering them.

A qualitative researcher should examine her full cultural reconstructions, as worked out in stages one through three, to seek system relations. The question to ask, for stage four, concerns the origins of these cultural themes. If you suspect an origin in other sites frequented by the people you study, then you will need to conduct some additional field work on these sites. Studies of classroom interaction, for example, will usually require the examination of home and neighborhood cultures as well as teacher cultures (evidenced in the teachers lounge and faculty meetings).

A number of field procedures will be helpful to this end, as will be the use of key informants. Interviews with parents and community members; observations in parks, apartment complexes, lounges, meetings, and malls; observations and interviews at parents' work sites; and so on will all help in the discovery of unmonitored system loops. These observations can be recorded in the field journal without an effort at intensive thick description (see chapter three); time constraints usually (but not always) rule out thick records for multiple sites.

One should perform reconstructive analysis on the new data and then compare it with the reconstructions already produced. What one must look for is a similarity in form between the two sets of reconstructions. Cultural themes need not be identical to show up a system relation of this kind; they simply need to be isomorphic with each other, congruent in form. People will adapt themes they routinely employ on one site when acting on another, such that remote references will remain untouched across sites even when foregrounds, roles, and interactive styles differ.

To complete the analysis, you should build up some kind of evidence to support your claim that a system has been found, that routine activities discovered on one site influence those on another. In the case of a reproductive loop entailed in schooling, you would have to make strong arguments that the culture constructed by children predicts career choices later in life. A longitudinal study is best for generating this sort of evidence; interviews probing into future plans is another method.

Cultural Isomorphisms in the TRUST Study

In the TRUST study I discovered a number of isomorphic relations. Samuel, an African-American living with a white mother and grandmother, frequently employed themes learned from home to defend himself from feelings of low self-respect in school. He would try to change academic topics introduced by Alfred by talking about his "Auntie Sweetie" or about meals he cooked at home (Samuel loved food and was very interested in anything having to do with it).

When attempting to renegotiate classroom settings that were stressful for him (like teacher efforts to explain academic concepts), Samuel would often bid for a session of chit-chat on themes that were rewarding for him at home. He was basically trying to change the interactive infrastructure to a homelike setting, where the rules for a positive identity were under his control. This sort of activity remotely referenced a distinction between home culture and school culture that would not be so marked for a middle-class child. The particulars of the home/school distinction Samuel repeatedly bid for during school interactions constituted the isomorphism—a distinction Samuel learned from his home that he sought to reproduce within the school.

The isomorphism is a complex one involving a higher regard for home culture than for school culture, with the difference between them strongly marked. It was a tactic to maintain dignity by separating the self from school definitions of possible selves, none of which suited Samuel's need for dignity. Visits to Samuel's home led me to believe that school was basically seen as a foreign institution there. Neither his mother or grandmother had attended school for long, and they saw school as something one had to bear until old enough for work. Samuel's bids for alternative interactive settings basically, tacitly drew upon the same theme and reproduced it as a remote reference to his identity claims.

Samuel was very sensitive about his race, African-American, and sometimes claimed that he was white. His strategy in the classroom was to appeal to home values he thought Alfred might share. He wanted Alfred's positive regard but felt this could not be gained through school culture.

Ricardo, another student in the TRUST classroom who displayed slightly different isomorphic patterns, was very different. He was proud of his ethnicity and claimed his identity through it. He used the Hispanic identity to oppose, actively, school culture. Ricardo frequently engaged Alfred in conflicts that took a nearly violent form. When such conflicts worked against him, as nearly always happened because of the sanctions Alfred had at hand, Ricardo would often start speaking and singing in Spanish—the language of his home and neighborhood. This sort of behavior referenced an opposition between "us" and "them" that was lacking for Samuel. Ricardo's counter-school identification was not just based on his home but also on an entire group of people in American society: lower-class Hispanics. He did not try to appeal to Alfred's positive regard through a cultural setting he and Alfred might share (as Samuel did), but rather appealed to the reference group of his neighborhood. It was not Alfred's regard but rather the regard of Ricardo's community that he was after.

In both these examples, we see culturally constructed views of school and society learned in the homes and neighborhoods of students. Students drew upon these themes in highly specific instances of classroom interaction to protect their identities. In drawing upon such themes, these students reproduced them at the same time that they claimed an identity for themselves. The identities claimed were constituted by strong home/school contrasts claimed valid and solid in the social action. Undoubtedly, these identity strategies of Samuel and Ricardo worked against their school careers and will play a role in reproducing class and ethnic stratification if these two boys continue in this vein.

Behavior Setting Surveys and Stage Four

Another, as yet largely unexplored, method for conducting stage four analysis involves the appropriation of Barker's Behavior Setting Survey (Barker 1963, 1968; Schoggen 1989). The Behavior Setting Survey (BSS) was developed by Barker during the 1960s as an alternative to traditional psychological theory. It emphasizes the contexts in which human behaviors occur and provides a rigorous set of methods for characterizing molar human behavior (goal-rational, purposive behavior) in relation to environments. A BSS reveals typical molar behaviors in various settings, the frequency of such behaviors, and the relationships between the behaviors taking place in one site ("behavior setting") to those taking place in other sites that are geographically and temporally close. System concepts, like "goal circuits," "maintenance circuits," and "veto circuits," have been developed by Barker (and those who have carried his work forward) that can be extremely helpful for a stage four analysis.

To bring the BSS within a critical qualitative methodology like the one outlined in this book requires some conceptual modification, including a movement from the concept of "behavior" to the concept of "social action" and an integrated perspective linking molar acts (predominantly goal-rational acts) to dramaturgical and normative acts. Work in this area has just begun, with one of my students, Doris Georgiou, leading the way (Georgiou 1994). I mention the BSS here in order to draw readers' attention to it and encourage explorations of linking this approach with critical methodology. The BSS could turn out to be a powerful method for conducting stage four analysis if certain conceptual modifications are introduced (Georgiou 1994).

Examining Cultural Commodities and Circuits

In terms of qualitative research, one must notice cultural products that seem to impact the subjects of your study. Studies of elementary school children will undoubtedly encounter video games like Nintendo and Sega Genesis. Textbooks, comic books, TV shows, popular music, and movies also influence young children. Many teenagers listen to and talk about heavy metal and rap music. They borrow terms and phrases learned from this music in their interactions with friends. Cultural commodities are a resource (and a constraint) in the construction of identity.

Here we find a situation where culture produced on sites far removed from the site of direct study is influencing the routine behaviors and culture found on the field site. These are important system relations. People who produce cultural commodities do so to make money. They deliberately try to effect at least one type of behavior routinely taking place on many other social sites: consumer behavior. Less deliberately, these products influence many other sorts of behaviors and routines on sites far removed from music studios and television companies, the sites where they were produced. Many areas are affected, including relations between men and women, relations between racial groups, ideas of success, and career choices.

To study the influence of such products, one may use the cultural circuits model discussed in chapter twelve. The first step is to make a list of cultural commodities important to your subjects. In the case of the TRUST study students clearly spent a lot of time in front of the television and playing Nintendo. Next, you ought to examine these items carefully and consider their possible symbolic and cultural meanings. Then, special interviews and group discussions can be conducted that focus on the items of interest. A television program or a piece of popular music could be played for a group, followed by a discussion. Next, you can compare what is said in the interviews and discussions with what you have learned about these subjects' culture and social routines. Last, if time permits, you can either research the production of the products or consult other studies, like Apple's study of textbook production (1986), that have done so. Putting things together will suggest important system relations.

I did not conduct this sort of analysis for the TRUST study due to time constraints. I did notice, however, that television shows depicting violence, race relations, and gender stereotypes were quite influential on the TRUST students. Violence was quite popular with them. Many days I heard the students discussing a show seen the previous night in terms of the violent acts depicted. Ricardo often got up from his desk to imitate violent behaviors he had seen. In teacher-guided discussions about social conflicts, many of the TRUST students said they would "kill," "rip apart," "shoot," and "destroy" those they were in conflict with. Racial themes also emerged not infrequently. Television programs about "black gangs" were referred to by Hispanic students to criticize blacks. Samuel and other African Americans in the classroom strongly objected on these occasions, although at times, and this is terribly sad, Samuel would respond by saying that he was white, not black.

These days, the influence of cultural commodities is extensive and penetrating. If you notice the importance of some such commodities to the group you are studying (e.g., students frequently listening to "rap" on boom boxes), you should consider examining the situation in depth. Get the people you study to talk about the product. Note how possible messages carried by the product are aligned and configured with other cultural themes in the group. The violence on television shows, for example, often shows "good guys" winning over "bad guys" and often has the heros or heroines speaking against violence. Do young people read such programs according to these explicit moral messages? Often it is the reverse. Ricardo, for example, seemed to identify with the gang members he saw on television, not the "good guys." He ignored the explicit moral lessons of TV programs and acted out the exciting violence he had seen. Ricardo, like everyone else, read such programs through his own set of life concerns and cultural milieu.

Validity Requirements for Stage Four

Stage four involves the comparative analysis of cultural reconstructions performed on more than one social site. The purpose of stage four is to discover and describe system relations between social sites that are brought about primarily through cultural forms. The behavior of children in a school, for example, is going to be related to the cultural forms they have learned in their homes and communities. The validity requirements of stage four are roughly the same as those in stages two and three. Cultural forms must be reconstructed appropriately for several sites, following the criteria for stages one through three, and then compared. Special interviews and group discussions should also be conducted for a stage four analysis, and in this case the validity requirements pertaining to stage three must be observed.

Techniques for Meeting Validation Requirements of Stage Four

There are four primary conditions required to successfully validate your stage four analysis:

1. *Prior fidelity to the validity requirements of stages 1–3.* Little needs to be said on this. Stage four takes completed reconstructions developed through following stages one through three and looks for matches between them and those pertaining to other social sites. The reconstructions analyzed must be sound before you begin stage four.

2. *Match between researcher's comparative analysis and subject's commentary.* Stage four involves finding relationships between different social sites within a social system. The connection between sites will correspond to certain experiences routine to your subjects of study. Interviews and group discussions may be designed to encourage talk about experiences involving the connections between social sites. Sometimes this will be about subjects' experiences in one setting compared to subjects' experiences in another setting. In these cases, the researcher is looking for relationships between social sites that subjects physically travel between. At other times, one will be interested in how subjects experience cultural products made on sites the subject never visits. Movies, videos, popular music, and so on are produced far from the majority of sites on which they are consumed. Interviews can focus on the way a subject experiences and interprets such cultural products. What the subject has to say ought to be consistent with the researcher's ideas on system relationships.

3. *Match between researcher's reconstructions and those produced and published by other researchers.* Because stage four is an attempt to discover the relationship between the site on which one has conducted field work and other sites in society, existing literature may be consulted to aid in the analysis. If popular music seemed to be an important part of Samuel's life, for example, and seemed to be a partial explanation of why he interpreted his schooling experience as he did, then studies on the production of such music (who produces it, why, how it is distributed, and so on) could be fruitfully employed to deepen your analysis. If textbooks become an important piece of your analysis, then studies like that of Apple (1986) can be consulted.

4. *Use of peer debriefers and member checks.* As always, it is highly recommended that you have colleagues examine your analysis during stage four and provide you with feedback. Group discussions should also be held for member checks of your analysis.

STAGE FIVE: USING SYSTEM RELATIONS TO EXPLAIN YOUR FINDINGS

Stage five goes beyond stage four by looking at your findings in light of existing macrolevel social theories. You can be very creative when doing this sort of analysis; there is definitely no single way to perform it. You will need to avoid social theories that are mechanistic in form, however, and those that depict society as a single entity rather than as a complex field of coordinated action that crosses spatial and temporal regions.

The principal inference involved in stage five is that of a "fit" or a match between the highly specific reconstructions built up over stages one through four and an existing social theory. But matching alone is not quite enough to produce a convincing argument. As indicated above, you must build abstractions off of your empirical data to the point where a fit can be recognized. You must strive for a fusion of cultural horizons between the group studied and the culture of the research community. Being cognizant of different kinds of conditions of action, as discussed in chapter twelve, will help to this end. In addition, several other ideas will aid you in your efforts to build up such abstractions and then display a fit.

Culture and Environmental Conditions

First of all, you can note the relationship between cultural reconstructions and the physical environments in which your subjects live, learn, and work. People produce culture to cope with daily conditions of life. Environmental conditions such as crowded living areas, overpacked school rooms, the availability of utilities to meet basic needs, odors, noises, and so on will affect cultural themes.

Once in possession of a set of relationships between routines, cultural forms, and physical properties of the environment, the next step is to ask why the environment is like it is and why these particular people live parts of their lives in an environment like this. Answers to this question will quickly move into the area of economic and political conditions of action. People live and work where they can afford to. The amount of economic and political power your group has will emerge as an explanatory factor.

You will need, however, a macrosociological theory of some sort to make the link between environmental factors and economic/political arrangements. Why do the poor have to live in decrepit housing and crowded neighborhoods? Who builds, rents, and sells such housing and why? Why do working-class people have to take jobs that are boring, demeaning, and low paid? Who are the employers, and why do they structure work organization in this way?

Macrotheories are indispensable for understanding such things, and it is up to you to choose one that you think best fits your findings and that you think has earned good support to date on its own. It could be a theory of capitalism, of patriarchy, of race relations, of the state, of the role played by information technology and the media in postindustrial society, or a synthesis of these. Researchers will differ according to which macrosociological theories they believe are well supported in the literature. Use a theory you are convinced of, and present scholarly arguments in your research narrative to display support for the theory. A "good fit" means that certain cultural themes have been well traced to environmental conditions and that these conditions, in turn, have been explained economically and politically.

The Concept of Interests

The other key social-theoretical concept to aid one in building abstractions off of empirical data toward macrosociological theories is that of interests. An interest is a socially constructed means for fulfilling a need or desire (Giddens 1979: 189). Needs and desires may be categorized as material or social-psychological in nature. Needs for dignity, self-esteem, self-expression, and personal growth are social-psychological rather than material. The satisfaction of either a material or a social-psychological need will involve interests: socially structured means for meeting needs and desires.

Diverse social groups have diverse interests but similar needs and desires. Your interests are partially determined by the amount of access you have to economic and political resources. To discover the interests your subjects have, ask yourself how they meet basic material needs and how they meet needs for dignity, respect, and recognition. Most people meet material needs through securing an income. What incomes are within the reach of your group? What jobs are they able to get? Are government benefits the main way in which they can satisfy material needs? When you get answers to these questions, you will simultaneously gather information by which to locate your group occupationally and in terms of its social class.

Most people meet their needs for dignity, respect, and recognition by constructing and reproducing cultural forms that make their way of life a respectable one. In the case of underprivileged groups, this sometimes means developing cultural forms that shun social mobility. In other cases, people are not able to meet their needs for dignity and respect and live their lives through damaged identities and low self-esteem; their expressive needs are blocked, they have internalized negative self-images, and their chances for personal growth are extremely limited.

The researcher must note how and whether her subjects meet social-psychological needs. After getting answers, the researcher should consider the location of her group within society generally through examining the members' access to economic, political, and cultural resources. This will help to explain why they seek dignity in the ways they do and why they may fail to meet human needs for self-respect.

A ground-breaking study centered on related issues is Phil Wexler's *Becoming Somebody* (1992). Wexler sought to display an economy of symbolic forms through which identities are created and exchanged. The driving force behind this "economy" is what I am calling social-psychological needs (and, elsewhere in this book, recognition needs): it is the drive to become somebody, to have a valid identity recognized by other people. The "economies" Wexler described are related to what I am calling "social-psychological interests." Wexler found different symbolic economies constructed in three high schools that serviced three different socioeconomic classes. Within each high school were different identity-discourses employed by different groups of students—what traditional sociologists call subcultures.

Wexler's study took on a stage five sort of quality through partially explaining the symbolic economies he found in terms of social class (Wexler himself is highly suspicious of tight methodological theories and "stages" like the one I have developed in this book). His work is innovative and highly recommended reading. He believes that the identities constructed by the students studied were truncated, cut off from real needs for caring and authentic self-expression. Why? Because of institutional organization tied to system relations: relations between social classes. Wexler's study also has the merit of examining historical periods and their effects on cultural milieu and institutional structure. For me it is a wonderful example of subtle stage five analysis.

In general, the concept of interests intersects with macrosociological theory (for interests reflect the position of a group economically, politically, and culturally within society) and with microsociological empirical data to which the researcher has direct access. This is why the concept of interests is particularly helpful for stage five. The basic strategy, in summary, is to ask yourself how your subjects meet their material and social-psychological needs in order to characterize their interests. Get them to tell you, then "investigate" instead of "explain" why they must meet needs in these particular ways by examining their access to economic, political, and cultural resources. It may be that their gender is what most explains their interests, or it may be that their race or ethnicity does; it may be that their lack of wealth, and the way work is organized at the jobs they are able to get, best explain their situation. A combination of these is most likely; they all intersect on every social site.

Once your subjects have been located in a category theorized in the literature, you may use this literature to help explain the routines and culture you discovered during stages one through three. Additional interviews ought to be employed to help validate your arguments of match.

Stage Five and the TRUST Study

I never pushed the TRUST study very far with respect to stage five as it was an evaluation study, contracted for and with set deadlines. My first ethnography, *Community Schooling and the Nature of Power* (1991), exemplifies stage five analysis extensively, as do the studies of Willis (1977), McLaren (1993), Wexler (1992), and many others. With respect to Project TRUST, however, many things do stand out for stage five analysis.

Recall my description of the community surrounding West Forest in chapter two. These neighborhoods were clearly impoverished. People lived in crowded apartment complexes that were badly in need of repair. The physical environment was rife with violence, prostitution, and drug dealing. Parents were constantly struggling to get money in any way that they could. Children returned home from school to empty apartments because parents were at work. They often saw adults intoxicated and fighting. Murders were committed in the community park.

Corresponding to these conditions were cultural themes crafted as coping mechanisms. Children had to grow up fast, had to defend themselves physically. School was a place you had to go to but not a place around which your plans could revolve. School was dominated by racial and class others who sought to impose authority relations on children. Children were both used to harsh forms of discipline at home and to seeing their parents actively resist any efforts of others to dominate. Thus these children negotiated for harsh authority relations at school (the only form of authority they respected) while simultaneously resisting vigorously any form of authority. The culture of the neighborhood was not conducive to success at school. School work was rarely supported in the home, and few adults known by these children owed anything to past schooling for whatever life successes they displayed.

In the school, teachers like Alfred strived hard to help these children but found their hands tied in many ways. State-mandated testing was probably the biggest constraint on these teachers. Standardized test scores were used by the school district to compare schools and measure the worth of teachers. But children from the West Forest area lacked the home support necessary for achieving well on these tests. Alternative pedagogies and curriculums that may have better reached these children were impossible in a situation that required preparation for such tests.

Why do communities like West Forest exist? Why are standardized tests imposed on such schools? Answers lie in the economic system of the United States, the economic circumstances of Houston, the conjuncture of race and class categories within our society, and the political power of the middle and upper-middle classes to establish educational policies in their interests.

During a period of economic decline, lower-class people lose jobs in large numbers. When the economy picks up, the unemployed are reabsorbed into the most menial of positions. The economic system of the United States creates groups like the West Forest residents. The school system, which formally tries to give a chance to all children for decent jobs, is hindered by state laws controlling curriculum and pedagogy. Such laws are the result of political lobbies and interest groups, few of them representing the lower classes. Schools end up keeping children like those in the TRUST study off the streets, but the students ill prepared to do anything but unskilled labor. The schools are "baby-sitting institutions," in the words of some West Forest teachers. This is the result of complex system relations: the difficulty of teaching kids from communities like West Forest, and the constraints imposed by standardized tests.

CHAPTER SUMMARY

Stages four and five are what give critical qualitative research its specifically critical bite. Studies can be conducted using only stages one through three of the methodological scheme I advocate; many of my doctoral students, for example, find it practical only to use the first three stages. But without the last two stages, four and five, only part of the whole picture emerges. System relations penetrate all social sites and all group cultures.

Stage four uses empirical and reconstructive techniques to discover system relations between specific sites. Stage five examines the significance of a study in terms of macrolevel social theory. A number of core concepts help the researcher in stage five to build a systems analysis from the experiences and cultural terms of her participants. Ideally, use of these concepts in dialogue with your subjects will result in a fusion of horizons: the researcher attaining an insider's view of the cultural group, and group members attaining an insider's view of researcher culture. Practically, this goal of doing fully democratic research can only be striven for, not fully reached. But it is both morally and epistemologically important to aim for it. Remember that epistemologically, models of the social system must be built from a third-person insider perspective. The question to ask is "Inside to what group?" Ideally, such models will be inside to a newly formed cultural horizon, encompassing both the researcher's and subjects' cultures. Such models must aim to be intelligible and consented to by as broad a cultural audience as possible. Remember that, morally, social research will either hurt or help people: it rarely has purely neutral effects with respect to human welfare. Making your research project as democratic as possible, from start to finish, is the best way to help rather than harm.

Bibliography

Agar, M.H. (1986). *Speaking of Ethnography*. Newbury Park, CA: Sage.

Althusser, L. (1969). *For Marx*. London: Allen Lane.

Althusser, L., and Balibar, E. (1970). *Reading Capital*. London: New Left Books.

Anderson, G. (1989). "Critical Ethnography in Education: Origins, Current Status, and New Directions." *Review of Educational Research* 59 (3); 249–70.

Anyon, J. (1980). "Social Class and the Hidden Curriculum of Work." *Journal of Education* 162: 67–92.

——— (1988). "Schools as Agencies of Social Legitimation." In *Contemporary Curriculum Discourses*, (edited by W. F. Pinal 175–200). Scottsdale, AZ: Gorsuch Scarisbrick.

Apple, M. (1979). *Ideology and Curriculum*. London: Routledge and Kegan Paul.

——— (1983). *Education and Power*. London: Routledge and Kegan Paul.

——— (1986). *Teachers and Texts: A Political Economy of Class and Gender Relations in Education*. New York and London: Routledge.

———— (1993). *Official Knowledge: Democratic Education in a Conservative Age*. New York and London: Routledge.

Barker, R. G., ed. (1963). *The Stream of Behavior*. New York: Appleton-Century-Crofts.

———— (1968). *Ecological Psychology: Concepts and Methods for Studying the Environment of Human Behavior*. Stanford, CA: Stanford University Press.

Bernard, H. R. (1988). *Research Methods in Cultural Anthropology*. Newbury Park, CA: Sage.

Bernstein, R. (1971). *Praxis and Action*. Philadelphia: University of Pennsylvania Press.

Brown, G., and Yule, G. (1983). *Discourse Analysis*. Cambridge: Cambridge University Press.

Caputo, J. (1987). *Radical Hermeneutics, Repetition, Deconstruction, and the Hermeneutic Project*. Bloomington: Indiana University Press.

Carspecken, P. (1987). *The Campaign to Save Croxteth Comprehensive: An Ethnographic Study of a Protest Movement*. Ph. D. diss., Aston University, UK.

———— (1991). *Community Schooling and the Nature of Power: The Battle for Croxteth Comprehensive*. London and New York: Routledge.

———— (1992). "Pragmatic Binary Oppositions and Intersubjectivity in an Illegally Occupied School," *International Journal of Qualitative Research in Education* V.5 (1) (January–March 1992).

———— (1993a). "Afterword." In P. McLaren, *Schooling as a Ritual Performance*, 292–298. New York and London: Routledge.

———— (1993b). *The Phenomenology of Meaningful Action: Form, Feeling-Body, and Intersubjectivity in the Theory of Meaning*. University of Houston: CUSTodian Manuscript Series.

———— (1993c). *Four Scenes for Posing the Question of Meaning: Flux, Intersubjectivity and the Phenomenological Body*. University of Houston: CUSTodian Academic Papers.

———— (1993d). *Pragmatic Horizons*. University of Houston: CUSTodian Manuscript Series.

Carspecken, P., and Apple, M. (1992). "Critical Qualitative Research, Theory, Method, and Practice," in *Handbook of Qualitative Research in Education*, edited by M. LeComte, W. Millroy, and J. Preissley, 507–554. San Diego, CA: Academic.

Carspecken, P. and Cordeiro, P. (1995). "Being, Doing, and Becoming: Textual Interpretations of Social Identity and a Case Study." *Qualitative Inquiry*, vol 1, issue 1; pp. 87–109.

Dale, R. (1982). "Education and the Capitalist State: Contributions and Contradictions." *Cultural and Economic Reproduction in Education*, edited by M. Apple. London: Routledge and Kegan Paul.

Denzin, N. (1989). *Interpretive Interactionism*. Newbury Park, CA: Sage.

————(1992). *Symbolic Interactionism and Cultural Studies*. Cambridge, UK: Basil Blackwell.

————(1994). "The Art and Politics of Interpretation." In *Handbook of Qualitative Research*, edited by N. Denzin and Y. Lincoln, 500–515. Thousand Oaks, CA: Sage.

Denzin, N., and Lincoln, Y., ed. (1994). *Handbook of Qualitative Research*. Thousand Oaks, CA: Sage.

Derrida, J. (1962). *Edmund Husserl's Origin of Geometry: An Introduction*. Translated by John Leavey, Jr. Lincoln: University of Nebraska Press.

————(1973). *Speech and Phenomena: And Other Essays on Husserl's Theory of Signs*. Translated by David Allison. Evanston, IL: Northwestern University Press.

Eder, D. (1981). "Ability Grouping as a Self-Fulfilling Prophecy: A Micro-Analysis of Teacher-Student Interaction," *Sociology of Education*, 54: 151–62.

Eisner, E. W., and Peshkin, A. (1990): *Qualitative Inquiry in Education: The Continuing Debate*. New York: Teacher's College Press.

Everhart, R. (1983). *Reading, Writing, and Resistance: Adolescence and Labor in a Junior High School.* London: Routledge and Kegan Paul.

Flew, A. (1979). *A Dictionary of Philosophy.* 2d ed. New York: St. Martin's.

Foucault, M. (1970). *The Order of Things: An Archaeology of the Human Sciences.* New York: Vintage Books.

———(1979). "The Subject and Power," *Critical Inquiry,* 8(4), 777-95.

———(1979). *Discipline and Punish: The Birth of the Prison.* Translated by Alan Sheridan. New York: Vintage/Random House.

———(1980). *The History of Sexuality; Volume I: An Introduction.* Translated by Robert Hurley. New York: Vintage/Random House.

Georgiou, D. (1994). "An Expansion of R. Barker's Behavior Setting Survey for an Ethno-Ecological Approach to the Educational Environment." University of Houston: CUSTodian Academic Papers.

Giddens, A. (1979). *Central Problems in Social Theory.* London: Macmillan.

———(1984). *The Constitution of Society.* Cambridge, UK: Polity.

Goetz, J., and LeCompte, M. (1984). *Ethnography and Qualitative Design in Educational Research.* San Diego: Academic.

Goffman, E. (1974). *Frame Analysis: An Essay on the Organization of Experience.* Cambridge, MA: Harvard University Press.

———(1981). *Forms of Talk.* Philadelphia: University of Pennsylvania Press.

Guba, E.. ed.(1990). *The Paradigm Dialog.* Newbury Park, CA: Sage.

Guba E., and Lincoln Y., (1994). "Competing Paradigms in Qualitative Research." In *Handbook of Qualitative Research,* edited by N. Denzin, and Y. Lincoln, 105–117. Thousand Oaks, CA: Sage.

Gumperz, J. (1982). *Discourse Strategies.* Cambridge: Cambridge University Press.

Habermas, J. (1981). *The Theory of Communicative Action, Volume One: Reason and the Rationalization of Society.* Boston: Beacon.

———(1987a). *The Philosophical Discourse of Modernity: Twelve Lectures.* Cambridge: MIT Press.

———(1987b). *The Theory of Communicative Action, Volume Two: Lifeworld and System, A Critique of Functionalist Reason.* Boston: Beacon.

———(1988). *The Logic of the Social Sciences, Methodology Philosophy, and Social Theory.* Cambridge,: MIT Press.

Hammersley, M. (1989). *The Dilemma of Qualitative Method: Herbert Blumer and the Chicago Tradition.* London and New York: Routledge.

Husserl, E. (1962). *Ideas: General Introduction to Pure Phenomenology.* Translated by Boyce Gibson. New York: Collier.

———(1970). *The Crisis of European Sciences and Transcendental Phenomenology.* Translated by David Carr. Evanston, IL: Northwestern University Press.

Joas, H. (1993). *Pragmatism and Social Theory.* Chicago: University of Chicago Press.

Johnson, M. (1987). *The Body in the Mind: The Bodily Basis of Meaning, Imagination, and Reason.* Chicago: University of Chicago Press.

Johnson, R. (1983). *What is Cultural Studies, Anyway?* Occasional paper, SP No. 74, Centre for Contemporary Cultural Studies, University of Birmingham, UK.

Kagan, N. (1980). *Interpersonal Process Recall: A Method of Influencing Human Interaction.* Houston: University of Houston, IPR Institute.

———(1984). "Interpersonal Process Recall: Basic Methods and Recent Research." In *Teaching Psychological Skills,* edited by D.Larsen. Monterey, CA: Brooks Cole.

Kagan, N., and Kagan, H. (1991). "Interpersonal Process Recall." In *Using Video in the Behavioral Sciences,* edited by P. Dorwick. (221–30). New York: Wiley.

Kagan, N., and Schneider, J. (1987). "Toward the Measurement of Affective Sensitivity." *Journal of Counselling and Development,* 65: (May 1987).

Kamuf, P. (1991). *A Derrida Reader: Between the Blinds.* New York: Columbia University Press.

Kaye, H. (1984). *The British Marxist Historians: An Introductory Analysis.* Cambridge, UK: Polity Press.

Kinchloe, J. and McLaren, P. (1994). *You Can't Get to the Yellow Brick Road from Here.*

Lancy, D. (1993). *Qualitative Research in Education: An Introduction to the Major Traditions.* New York: Longman.

Lather, P. (1986). "Research as Praxis." *Harvard Educational Review* 56 (3); 257–77.

———(1991). *Getting Smart: Feminist Research and Pedagogy with/in the Postmodern.* New York and London: Routledge.

LeCompte, M. (1990). "Emergent Paradigms: How New? How Necessary?" In *The Paradigm Dialog,* edited by E. Guba, 246–55. Newbury: Sage.

LeCompte, M. and Preissle, J. (1993). *Ethnography and Qualitative Design in Educational Research.* 2d ed. San Diego: Academic.

LeCompte, M.; Millroy, W.; and Preissle, J., ed. (1992). *The Handbook of Qualitative Research in Education.* San Diego: Academic.

LeGuin, U.K. (1974). *The Dispossessed.* New York: Harper and Row.

Lévi-Strauss, C. (1967). *Structural Anthropology.* Translated by C. Jacobson and B. G. Schoepf. Garden City, NY: Anchor.

Lincoln, E. (1990). "The Making of a Constructivist: A Remembrance of Transformations Past." In *The Paradigm Dialog,* edited by E. Guba, 67–87. Newbury Park, CA: Sage.

Lincoln, E., and Guba, E. (1985). *Naturalistic Inquiry.* Beverly Hills, CA: Sage.

Marx, K. (1970). *A Contribution to the Critique of Political Economy.* ed. Maurice Dobb. New York.

———(1977). *Early Writings.* Harmondsworth: Penguin Books.

Marx, K., and Engels, F. (1976). *Complete Works.* London: Lawrence and Wishart.

Maybury-Lewis, D., and Almagor, U., ed. (1989). *The Attraction of Opposites: Thought and Society in the Dualistic Mode.* Ann Arbor: University of Michigan Press.

McCarthy, T. (1978). *The Critical Theory of Jurgen Habermas.* Cambridge: MIT Press.

McDermott, R.P. (1977). "Social Relations as Context for Learning." *Harvard Educational Review,* 47: 198–213.

McLaren, P. (1992). "Collisions with Otherness: 'Traveling' Theory, Post-Colonial Criticism, and the Politics of Ethnographic Practice—The Mission of the Wounded Ethnographer." *The International Journal of Qualitative Studies in Education,* 5(1), 77–92.

———(1993). *Schooling as a Ritual Performance: Towards a Political Economy of Educational Symbols and Gestures.* 2d ed. New York and London: Routledge.

McNeill, D. (1992). *Hand and Mind: What Gestures Reveal about Thought.* Chicago: The University of Chicago Press.

McRobbie, A. (1978). "Working Class Girls and the Culture of Feminity," in CCCS (ed) *Women Take Issue*. London: Hutchinson.

Mead, G. H. (1934). *Mind, Self, and Society*. Chicago: Chicago University Press.

Metz, M. 1978. *Classrooms and Corridors, The Crisis of Authority in Desegrated Secondary Schools*. Berkley, CA: University of California Press

Miles, M., and Huberman, M. (1994). *An Expanded Sourcebook: Qualitative Data Analysis*. Newbury Park, CA: Sage.

Mouzelis, N. (1991). *Back to Sociological Theory*. Basingstroke, UK: Macmillan.

Offe, C. (1974). "Structural Problems of the Capitalist State," in Beyme, K. *German Political Studies*. Thousand Oaks: Sage.

———(1984). *Contradictions of the Welfare State*. Edited by J. Keane. London: Hutchinson.

Ogbu, J. (1979). "Social Stratification and the Socialization of Competence." *Anthropology and Education Quarterly* 10:1.

Palmer, R. (1969). *Hermeneutics: Interpretation Theory in Schliermacher, Dilthey, Heidegger, and Gadamer*. Evanston IL: Northwestern University Press.

Quantz. R. (1992). "On Critical Ethnography (with Some Postmodern Considerations)." In *The Handbook of Qualitative Research in Education*, edited by M. LeCompte, W. Millroy, and J. Preissle, 447–506. San Diego: Academic.

Sartre, Jean-Paul (1956). *Being and Nothingness*. Philosophical Library.

Saussure, F. (1960). *Course in General Linguistics*. London: Peter Owen.

Schoggen, P. (1989). *Behavior Settings: A Revision and Extension of Roger G. Barker's Ecological Psychology*. Stanford, CA: Stanford University Press.

Schutz, A. (1967). *Collected Papers*. The Hague: Mouton.

Seung, T.K. (1982a). *Semiotics and Thematics in Hermeneutics*. New York: Columbia University Press.

———(1982b). *Structuralism and Hermeneutics*. New York: Columbia University Press.

Shapiro, S. (1990). *Between Capitalism and Democracy: Educational Policy and the Crisis of the Welfare State*. New York: Bergin and Garvey.

Silverman, D. (1985). *Qualitative Methodology and Sociology*. Aldershot, UK: Gower.

———(1993) *Interpreting Qualitative Data: Methods for Analyzing Talk, Text, and Interaction*. London: Sage.

Spradley, J. (1979). *The Ethnographic Interview*. New York: Holt Rinehart and Winston.

———(1980). Participant Observation. New York: Holt Rinehart and Winston.

Taylor, C. (1979). *Hegel and Modern Society*. Cambridge: Cambridge University Press.

Thompson, E. P. (1963). *The Making of the English Working Class*. London: Victor Gollancz.

———(1978). *The Poverty of Theory and Other Essays*. London: Merlin.

Vidich, A., and Lyman, S. (1994). "Qualitative Methods: Their History in Sociology and Anthropology." In *Handbook of Qualitative Research*, edited by N. Denzin and Y. Lincoln, 23–59. Thousand Oaks, CA: Sage.

Weber, M. (1978). *Economy and Society. Vol. 1*. Edited by G. Roth and C. Wittich, Berkeley: University of California Press.

Werner, O., and Schoepfle, G. M. (1987). *Systematic Fieldwork: Foundations of Ethnography and Interviewing*. Newbury Park, CA: Sage Publications.

Wexler, P. (1992). *Becoming Somebody: Toward a Social Psychology of School*. London: Falmer.

Willis, P. (1975). "How Working Class Kids Get Working Class Jobs." Occasional Paper, Centre for Contemporary Cultural Studies; University of Birmingham, UK.

———(1976). "The Main Reality." University of Birmingham Occassional Paper, Centre for Contemporary Cultural Studies; Birmingham, U.K.

———(1977). *Learning to Labor: How Working Class Kids Get Working Class Jobs.* London: Gower.

———(1981). "Cultural Production Is Different from Cultural Reproduction Is Different from Social Reproduction is Different from Reproduction." *Interchange* (12) 2/3.

Index